Grecians Seventies Style

Exeter City's Promotion in 1977

Mike Blackstone

Rel8 Media

2014

Published by Rel8 Media

Unit 7, Woodend Business Centre, Cowdenbeath, KY4 8HG

British Library in Publication Data.

A catalogue record for this volume is available from the British Library.

ISBN 978-0-9574645-4-4

Contents

Page 9	June-August 1976
Page 21	September-October 1976
Page 32	November-December 1976
Page 42	January-February 1977
Page 50	March-April 1977
Page 65	May-August 1977
Page 84	September-October 1977
Page 97	November-December 1977
Page 109	January-February 1978
Page 120	March-April 1978
Page 132	Who's Who Section
Page 146	Statistical Section

ABOUT THE AUTHOR

A Devon "boy", Mike Blackstone has lived the greater part of his life in Exmouth. However, since December 2002, he has resided "up north" in a far flung corner of North West Lancashire, in Heysham, Morecambe.

Some 300 miles from his beloved St James' Park - home of Exeter City Football Club - where he spent countless hours watching the Grecians, he still retains the same passion for recording the history of the Club as he did when first setting foot inside the "Park" during the 1959-60 season. An Exeter City statistician and programme collector, Mike started to contribute articles to the club's match programme in 1969 and then became the editor of the publication during the 1992-93 season.

Having won a string of awards for the programme, several years in succession, including best programme in the country on more than one occasion, he stepped aside for the 2011-12 season, having written hundreds of thousands of words about the City.

He has also contributed to numerous books, magazines, newspapers and programmes (as well as editing them), of many other clubs, and he is also the author of several books, prior to this one, as listed below.

Mike undertook a massive project compiling a complete A to Z biography of players who had played for Exeter City between the formation of the club in 1904 and 2011. This work is now in the care of the Exeter City Supporters' Trust and forms a valuable historical resource.

His enthusiasm for the game at the lower levels, together with his love of reading and writing about it, as well as sampling real ales and enjoying photography in the North West, shows no sign of diminishing. Mike has his own photographic Blog which is updated daily and can be found at:-

http://www.northwestimages.blogspot.co.uk

Now semi-retired, Mike continues to follow from afar the fortunes (or lack of them) of Exeter City F.C. Once a Grecian, always a Grecian!

ALSO BY MIKE BLACKSTONE

*Exeter City: A File Of Fascinating Football Facts. ISBN 0-946-65153-1. Obelisk Publications. 1992.
* Plymouth Argyle. A File of Fascinating Football Facts. ISBN 0-94665165-5. Obelisk Publications. 1993.
* The Brown Sauce Is off: A North West Non-League Odyssey. ISBN 0-954-82010-X. Mike Blackstone 2004.
* Exeter City F.C.: A Grecian Anthology. ISBN 978-0-9548201-1-4. Mike Blackstone. 2008
* Exeter City Down The Years. ISBN 978-09555307-9-1. Rel8 Media. 2012
* Grecians Going Up - A Journal of Exeter City F.C. Season 1963/4. ISBN 978-0-09574645-1-3. Rel8 Media 2013.

DEDICATION

To the management and players of Exeter City F.C. who represented the Club during the 1976/77 and 1977/78 seasons.

To Lynda for her usual support and encouragement throughout the writing of this book.

ACKNOWLEDGEMENTS

I would like to thank everyone who has assisted in the writing of this book. None more so than my late father, Jim. Together we kept records of the Club in a diary format stretching back to 1904.

Thank you to Lynda for the scanning of the photographs.

Finally huge thanks to Andy McGregor of Rel8 Media Publishing for his support, suggestions and having faith in the project from day one.

SOURCES

Other than those already acknowledged elsewhere in the book, I have constantly referred to the written history of the Grecians which has appeared in various publications over the years.

Apart from my own comprehensive records of the club, I would like to mention the following publications etc., all which have been of tremendous value in writing this book:-

Express and Echo Newspaper, Exeter.
Western Morning News newspaper, Plymouth.
The P.F.A. Premier & Football League Players' Records 1946-2005. Barry Hugman. Queen Anne Press.
Exeter City: A Complete Record 1904-1990 - Breedon Books
Match programmes from games played by Exeter City throughout the 1976/7 and 1977/78 season.

INTRODUCTION

The word "success" applying to Exeter City Football Club is a hard won accolade, for, apart from recent seasons, there has been little of it in their long history stretching back to 1904. Having won promotion for the first time in 1964, the Grecians were back in the Fourth Division after just a couple of seasons, and they had wait until 1977 before they climbed back up the footballing ladder.

The team had steadily improved under manager John Newman, but ironically he never stayed long enough to see his efforts rewarded by winning promotion. Newman left midway through the 1976/77 season to become manager of Grimsby Town, to be replaced by player-manager Bobby Saxton, a defender whom he had played alongside at Plymouth Argyle, and then signed for the Grecians.

Saxton continued to build on the excellent foundations laid by Newman, with a very small playing squad, and also made some astute loan signings to help the promotion push.

The final third of the 1976/77 season proved to be the turning point as the City hit a superb run of form, which included a memorable 4-3 win at Barnsley after trailing 3-0 at half-time. It was that haul of points that took Exeter City back into the promotion frame and eventually back into the Third Division.

The team were blessed with two outstanding goalscorers, Alan Beer and Tony Kellow, whilst the rest of the squad were hard working and determined. It was the perfect combination, even overcoming the loss of regular goalkeeper Richard Key who sustained a broken ankle in a match at Crewe.

This book charts, in diary format, and match by match, how the Grecians achieved promotion, and then follows on into their first season back in the Third Division which proved to be a lot harder.

Unfortunately matters were not helped with the loss of Alan Beer,, who was sidelined with a knee injury, that was to ultimately end his playing career. Not only does the book chart the progress of the team, but it also includes statistics relating to the team and the players. League tables are included as the 1976/77 and 1977/78 seasons unfold.

To give a flavour of the time, advertisements have also been reproduced which appeared in the Exeter City programmes.

The previous book covering Exeter City's first ever promotion season of 1963-64 is still available from publishers, Rel8 Media, and I hope that this latest volume proves to be as enjoyable to read as it has been compiling it.

Mike Blackstone

THURSDAY 1st JULY 1976

CITY CHAIRMAN RETURNS TO BOARD
Gerald Vallance has returned to the Board of Directors of Exeter City Football Club as chairman, and at last night's meeting he had a message for supporters.

"Forget the squabbles of the past and let us concentrate on getting a promotion side together for next season."

Following the meeting the Exeter City Board of Directors issued the following statement:-

"Certain outstanding problems have been resolved. The directors of Exeter City unanimously decided to request Gerald Vallance to rejoin the board and resume his chairmanship of the club, which he was pleased to accept."

Vallance added that he still wanted to add to the club's Board of Directors, but this will not lead to the dispute which resulted in his shock resignation.

The two men that Vallance had in mind then for the boardroom are no longer interested. Former City goalkeeper and Cockwood publican, Bert Hoyle, no longer wishes to be considered, whilst Exeter Speedway co-promoter, John Richards, has moved to live in Taunton.

"I went off the Board of Directors as a matter of principle," added Vallance. "But these problems have now been sorted out."

"With regard to the two men in question over directorships, one has left the area, and the other is no longer interested."

"We would still like to increase the board, but at this stage we have no one definitely in mind."

ROWAN SEEKS A LEAGUE CLUB
Former Exeter City winger Barry Rowan is halfway through a two-year contract with Tooting and Mitcham, where he also coaches the team. He is only part-time with the non-league club, combining that with a job as a computer programmer at Kingston-upon-Thames. Rowan, however, still hopes to return to a Football League club at some stage, and said he would welcome a chance to work as a full-time coach with the right club.

THURSDAY 8th JULY 1976

GRECIANS ENTER THE SOUTH WEST HOLIDAY TROPHY
Exeter City are one of four clubs who will be involved in a mini tournament as part of their pre-season build up for the coming season. They are being joined by Plymouth Argyle, Torquay United and A.F.C. Bournemouth, the tournament being played on a league basis with three points for a win, one for a draw and one for every goal scored.

The clubs will be playing for the South West Holiday Trophy and there will be individual mementoes for the winners and runners-up which have been sponsored by Joe Varley Trophies, who are based in Plymouth.

LADBROKES RATE THE CITY
Exeter City will win promotion next season according to bookmakers, Ladbrokes. They have made the Grecians second favourites to win the Fourth Division championship at odds of 8-1, behind Huddersfield Town. The City are also 2-1 to win promotion to the Third Division.

FRIDAY 9th JULY 1976

KELLOW TO SIGN FOR CITY
Falmouth Town striker Tony Kellow will sign for Exeter City this evening. Everything has been agreed between the player and both clubs, and City manager John Newman will complete the signing at a Plymouth

rendezvous. It will end two months of negotiations for the player by Newman.

"Kellow certainly knows how to find the net," said Newman. "He is a strong, aggressive player and has the ability to do well in the Fourth Division."

Earlier this year Kellow turned down an offer from Torquay United and also a trial period with Manchester City. Kellow started his footballing career with the Falmouth Docks reserve team in the Falmouth and Helston League. At the age of 15 he made his debut for the Docks first team in the Cornwall Combination League. Twelve months later Kellow joined Penzance of the South Western League and went straight into their first team. He played five times for the Cornwall County side and also won a Cornwall Senior Cup medal.

Kellow moved to Falmouth Town in the summer of 1973, who were then playing in the South Western League. That season he netted 62 goals and won a league championship medal as well as another Cornwall Senior Cup winners medal.

Kellow moved back to Penzance in 1974-75 where he played in their South Western League championship side.

In the 1975 close season, Kellow was back at Falmouth Town once more, who by then had joined the Western League. he had no problem in adapting to the higher level scoring over 50 goals.

SATURDAY 17th JULY 1976

RESERVE TEAM MANAGER APPOINTED
Former Exeter City goalkeeper, Bob Wilson, has been appointed manager of the club's reserve team in the Western League. Wilson will succeed Tony Long who had charge of the side after the departure of Keith Parsons to Exmouth Town as their manager last year.

There were four or five applicants for the post of reserve team manager, but City's first team boss, John Newman, recommended Wilson for the job.

"With two young goalkeepers in Richard Key and Phil Howe, I will be signing Bob Wilson on non contract forms to keep me covered in that position" said Newman.

"In that way he will have the occasional game in the reserve side to keep himself fit in case he is needed. His main job will be to take over the coaching of the reserves and the training of the amateur players."

"With fewer professionals on the staff this year it will make Wilson's job more difficult. I do not expect miracles of the Western League side, but I expect it to maintain its status in the Premier Division."

SATURDAY 24th JULY 1976

JULY FESTIVAL AT THE RACECOURSE
Today marks the start of a two-day 'July Festival' held jointly with Torquay United Football Club, featuring amongst other things a steam engine and vintage car rally. Staged at Newton Abbot Racecourse, today and tomorrow, it is hoped that this could be the first of such joint ventures between the clubs, to boost commercial income.

The event could not have gone ahead without the input of the following organisations:- Devon Traction Engine Club; Crash Box Club of Devon; Institute of Advanced Motorists; Plus all the owners of traction engines, and cars, and traders who have taken stands.

A souvenir programme has been produced, price 15p, where traction engine and vintage car entrants are listed, together with details of events throughout today and tomorrow.

Displays will be given by the Exeter and District Radio Control Club and the Stardust Free Fall Parachute team.

SATURDAY 31st JULY 1976

KELLOW WASTES NO TIME
South West Holiday Trophy
Exeter City 3 A.F.C. Bournemouth 0
Scorers: Exeter: Kellow, Jordan (2).
Attendance: 968
A scrambled goal by new signing Tony Kellow after just two minutes set the tone for Exeter City's win against Bournemouth. Kellow was an instant hit, playing with the kind of assurance one expects from a seasoned campaigner.

City's other two goals were scored by Mike Jordan, who spent most of last season in the reserves. His first came after 12 minutes from a Graham Weeks right wing cross, and two minutes later, a cross from Peter Hatch from the left found him to make 3-0.

Bournemouth had three reasonably good chances, but they were let down by their forwards who seemed to be clueless in front of goal. They got very little change out of a well organised City defence. All things considered it was a very useful display by Exeter who have every reason to feel optimistic about their prospects for the coming season.

Whether or not the result was a flash in the pan, or an augury of much better things to come, will no doubt become apparent on Tuesday night away to Torquay United.

RUNNING TRACK
Exeter City have completed laying a new "running track" around the St James' Park pitch. The 'track' which is at the same level as the playing surface, has been sponsored by E.C.C. Quarries.

TUESDAY 3rd AUGUST 1976

TOO MUCH LIKE LAST SEASON
South West Holiday Trophy
Torquay United 2 Exeter City 1
Scorers: Torquay: Brown, Hickman. Exeter: Hore.
Attendance: 1,800
The facts are plain and simple. Exeter had their chances but did not take them. City reverted to their old tentative pussy footing ways of last season with players seemingly scared to take the initiative in the opposition half of the field. Instead of pressing forward with determination, most seemed to be almost ludicrously anxious to get rid of the ball in any direction. As a result, promising moves broke down in disarray with passes being intercepted and players dispossessed.

City did have a good spell in the second half and took the lead in the 59th minute when John Hore came through the Torquay United defence unnoticed to score past Terry Lee.

After 75 minutes though it was all square again as Ian Hickman equalised. Then five minutes from the end Torquay gained a hotly disputed goal. A throw in from Ian Sandercock came to Willie Brown on the dead ball line. He gave an overhead flick and the ball hit the upright with Richard Key motionless and went into the net. The linesman raised his flag, but the referee overruled him and the goal, the winner, stood.

THURSDAY 5th AUGUST

GOOD WORK OUT FOR THE GRECIANS
Weymouth 0 Exeter City 2
Friendly
Scorers: Exeter: Kellow (2).

Exeter City scored twice and sent in two other shots that smacked against the woodwork, but they would probably be the first to admit that the Southern Premier League club gave them a good workout.

City took the lead after 20 minutes when Tony Kellow accepted a through pass from Alan Hooker, held off a defender and confidently slotted a goal just inside the post. Exeter's second goal was a mystery penalty in the 30th minute, taken successfully by Kellow, although the Weymouth keeper did get a hand to the ball.

The hosts looked lively in attack with Tom Henderson looking particularly useful and only a good Richard Key save late in the second half stopped him from scoring a consolation goal.

MARKET AT ST. JAMES' PARK MAY NOT BE LEGAL

Hundreds of people flocked to St James' Park as Exeter City Football Club staged a market consisting of around 50 traders, in direct competition with another group who have taken over a Thursday market at the Exeter Cattle Market.

Shopkeepers in the city are reported to be unhappy against what they argue is unfair competition that they are meeting from the markets. The Exeter City Council are also being criticised for encouraging the markets, whist the football club are being criticised for allowing its ground to be used. Talks were held last evening between the Council and Exeter City Football Club in a bid to have the market at St. James' Park stopped.

The club were warned by the Council that they may be prosecuted for breaking the Exeter Market Act of 1840, which makes it an offence to sell commodities in places other than the Higher and Lower Markets in the city, with the exception of people selling from shops and similar premises.

Exeter City Football Club Commercial Manager, Ray Ellis said that the club had no alternative but to let the market go ahead. He added that when the operators of the market were displaced from Marsh Barton, they asked if they could use the area of land behind the Big Bank terracing at St. James' Park. Advice was obtained that the market was legal and that it was possible to stage a market for fourteen weeks without planning permission being obtained. It was pointed out that the club earned extra revenue from the market which was greatly needed.

The Exeter City Council solicitor has, however, not agreed that such market was a legal venture. He warned that the Council would be taking another look at how much the Football Club paid in rates. This would possibly be increased to take into account land being used for a market.

SATURDAY 7th AUGUST 1976

LATE WINNER DEFEATS CITY

Friendly

Yeovil Town 1 Exeter City 0

Scorer: Yeovil: McMahon.

Exeter City manager John Newman said that he was not unduly worried by what on paper might seem a morale damaging defeat. City were without four first team players, out through injury.

Southern League Yeovil Town, who had been getting more and more on top in the last 15 minutes of the game, were awarded a penalty in the 89th minute. Bobby Saxton, shielding a ball chased by former Grecian Dick Plumb, brought it under control by using his arm and Frank McMahon netted from the spot.

MONDAY 9th AUGUST 1976

THE CORNISHMAN MEANS BUSINESS!

Friendly

Exeter City 1 Charlton Athletic 0

Scorer: Kellow

Attendance: 934

Fourth Division defences beware! Cornishman Tony Kellow means business. He is going to be a mighty menace during the next nine months if he continues to reproduce the kind of pre-season form that has brought him three goals in five matches.

Kellow oozes with confidence and is a glutton for work. He was outstanding against a Charlton Athletic side that included former City defender Jimmy Giles, who had the job of trying to stop Kellow.

True, Richard Key had to make an excellent second half save, but Exeter were full value for their win. They might have had a couple of goals in the first half through Bobby Hodge and Mike Jordan, but they had to wait until the 60th minute before going in front. From a corner, Kellow powered a header home. This was not just a one- man show though, for City produced fluent approach work with players expressing themselves and their Division Two opponents never had the opportunity to take a grip on the game.

WEDNESDAY 11th AUGUST 1976

BEER BACK ON THE GOAL TRAIL
Friendly
Ottery St. Mary 0 Exeter City 3
Scorers: Saxton, Hore, Beer.
With the new Fourth Division season just three days away, this friendly fixture at Ottery St. Mary proved to be a good work out for the City.

Exeter's scorers were Bobby Saxton, John Hore and last seasons leading goalscorer Alan Beer, the latter with his first of this season. One pleasing aspect of the game was that Harry Holman, who has been out with injury all pre-season, returned to the side and came through the game very well.

FRIDAY 10th AUGUST 1976

CITY APPEAL FOR MORE SUPPORT
Exeter City secretary Pat Wakeham has called for more support of the club, as it prepares to make the short trip to Plymouth Argyle tomorrow for the first round of The Football League Cup.

"The primary business of any business is to keep in business," said Wakeham. "To do that you have got to get and keep customers. That is to say you sell what you have. This does not necessarily mean players, but to sell the product of football to the public. Football is facing financial problems," he added. "I hope that the people of Exeter and the surrounding district acknowledge the need for a professional football club."

"The 1976-77 season will be hard and difficult. With your support the road ahead can be travelled and the destination of success reached safely."

SATURDAY 14th AUGUST 1976

KELLOW TO THE FORE
Football League Cup Round One First Leg
Plymouth Argyle 0 Exeter City 1
Plymouth Argyle: Barron, Darke (Johnson), Horswill, Randell, Sutton, Green, Hall, Harrison, Mariner, Collins, McAuley.
Exeter City: Key, Templeman, Hooker, Hore, Saxton, Hatch, Hodge, Kellow, Morrin, Beer, Jennings.
Scorer: Exeter: Kellow.
Attendance: 8,688.

What better way to kick off the season than an away win over local rivals Plymouth Argyle? The Home Park side were in the Second Division at the time and, on paper, it looked a tough tie for Fourth Division City. However, a fine team performance produced a shock result that was fully merited on the day. Newly signed striker Tony Kellow was the man who scored the vital goal on 21 minutes. However, his overall performance did much to please the travelling Exeter fans - as well as his finishing he looked to have plenty of skill and an ability to hold the ball up. The victory was oh so sweet for the three former Plymouth players in the City ranks - Bobby Saxton, Nicky Jennings and John Hore all did well against their previous employer.

TUESDAY 17th AUGUST 1976

CITY TO BEAT DROUGHT
The bath water used by the players after tomorrow's Football League Cup tie between Exeter City and Plymouth Argyle will be used to water the St. James' Park pitch.

This summer has had the longest period without rain for 80 years, and it is feared some reservoirs - already depleted by last year's dry weather - will be only 15% full by early November. Parts of Devon have not seen any rain fall for the whole of July, nor have they so far for the month of August, with temperatures hitting 80 degrees for several days running.

City manager John Newman explained: "Due to the ongoing severe drought, we shall find some way of syphoning the water out and then use it on the pitch, on areas like the goalmouths or corners. It is our way of beating the drought."

WEDNESDAY 18th AUGUST 1976

JORDAN GOAL SEALS PROGRESS
Football League Cup Round One Second Leg
Exeter City 1 Plymouth Argyle 0
Exeter City: Key, Templeman, Hooker, Hore, Saxton, Hatch, Hodge, Kellow, Clapham, Beer, Jordan
Plymouth Argyle: Ramsbottom, Darke, Horswill, Randell, Sutton, Green, Hall, Johnson, Mariner, Collins, McAuley.
Scorer: Exeter: Jordan
Attendance: 8,859

City completed the job they started on Saturday with a 1-0 second leg win over Argyle at the Park. The 2-0 aggregate win over a team from two Leagues above them was a fine achievement. A first half goal by Mike Jordan put City in command and they never really looked like losing the tie after that. The start of the second half was delayed for a few minutes as police dealt with rival fans fighting in the ground. The victory secured a place in the potentially lucrative Second Round stage when the "big guns" enter the competition. City fans heading home afterwards were talking confidently about the season ahead. Argyle fans, on the other hand, knew they were in for a tough season which would ultimately end in relegation.

NEWMAN: "DON'T SPOIL IT IN THE COOKING."
Exeter City manager John Newman is optimistic for a good season and has been impresssed by the team performances so far.

"The atmosphere at the club, as we enter the long season, is electric," he said. "The entire attitude at St James' Park has to be positive and progressive. I trust the enthusiasm will rub off on the supporters, for I am overwhelmed by your desire to be connected with a professional football club."

"The players have worked hard in pre-season training and I have been encouraged by the performances, especially the team performance at Plymouth Argyle on Saturday last, but the job now has to be finished. The ingredients have been prepared, the cake is looking good, but we must not spoil it in the cooking. The attitude of my players and myself is that we will not talk about losing throughout the season. Success is winning matches and I want the supporters to feel the same way."

"We are on the road. The race is on. Together we must drive to reach the chequered flag."

CITY MATCH PROGRAMME: NEW DESIGN
The Exeter City match programme has been given a new look. The first issue was for today's Football League Cup tie against Plymouth Argyle.

Grecians' Commercial Manager, Ray Ellis said: "We hope everyone will enjoy the programme and we would like to hear your comments. The increased price to 12p is unavoidable owing to increased printing costs. I would like to thank Wilf Denning of Exeter, who designed the cover and so wins two tickets in our recently run programme cover competition."

THURSDAY 19th AUGUST 1976

FOOTBALL HOOLIGANISM AT ITS WORST
Pressure for tougher action against football mob rule came in Exeter today, after what Police called the worst exhibition of football hooliganism the city has seen. Plymouth Argyle supporters were on the rampage last night after their club had been defeated by Exeter City in The Football League Cup. A total of 29 arrests were made by the Police.

A train was wrecked, and 150 Plymouth Argyle supporters were locked in Northernhay Gardens behind the park gates as Police tried to control their forays through the streets.

Both Exeter City and Plymouth Argyle club secretaries condemned the fans behaviour and called for a much tougher line in terms of sentences for those arrested.

Trouble began early in the afternoon with the arrival of the Argyle supporters. There were several minor incidents in the Exeter city centre. Police managed to segregate City and Argyle supporters at the ground, but at half-time fighting broke out. Plans to bring show cars onto the pitch during the interval - the game being sponsored by Dunns Motors - were scrapped as Police tried to restore order.

At the end of the game, Argyle fans went on the rampage, breaking several shop windows and scattering rubbish from dustbins. They smashed light fittings and slashed seats on the train taking them back to Plymouth causing hundreds of pounds of damage.

SATURDAY 21st AUGUST 1976

KELLOW GOALS EARN CITY A POINT
Fourth Division
Hartlepool United 2 Exeter City 2
Hartlepool United: Richardson, Goad, Maggiore, Veitch, Scott, O'Donnell, Elliott, Spelman, Endean, Scaife, Bielby
Exeter City: Key, Templeman, Hooker, Hore, Saxton, Hatch, Hodge, Kellow, Clapham, Beer, Jordan.
Scorers: Hartlepool: Endean, Elliott. Exeter City: Kellow (2).
Attendance: 1,602

Tony Kellow came to Exeter City's rescue at Hartlepool with two goals that brought home a point. But it was not a result that City really deserved. Exeter were ragged and untidy, and in the second half in particular, gave away the ball far too often.

Right from the start City found themselves up against it conceding three corners in the first six minutes, and Richard Key had to make a desperate dash off his line to thwart Scaife. The City attack were rarely in the picture up until the 23rd minute when they shocked Hartlepool by taking the lead through a freak goal.

A Hartlepool clearance struck Kellow who was only three-yards out and the ball rebounded into the net. This sparked off a renewed challenge from the home side who deservedly equalised in the 40th minute, Endean nodding home a cross from the ever dangerous Bielby.

It was no surprise when Hartlepool went ahead after 70 minutes. Bielby put in a strong cross drive and whilst Key got a hand to it, the ball rebounded off the foot of the post into the net.

Less than a minute later Exeter were back on terms. Bobby Hodge found space on the left and as he sent the ball across, Kellow was there to head home.

TUESDAY 24th AUGUST 1976

LAMMIE TO REJOIN CITY
Exeter City midfielder Lammie Robertson will be back at St. James'Park by the end of the week. He has spent the summer playing for Chicago Stings in the North American League, and jets into London some time tomorrow. He will report for training back at Exeter City on Thursday or Friday.

WEDNESDAY 25th AUGUST 1976

NORWICH CITY TICKET RUSH
It is a sell out already. In just over six hours Exeter City have filled their grandstand for next Tuesday night's Football League Cup second round tie against Norwich City at St. James' Park.

City secretary Pat Wakeham said: "There has been a fantastic response for tickets. The ground tickets went on sale for the first time this morning and there was a big queue of supporters waiting outside the Near Post selling point. There are 14,000 tickets available at various selling points in and around the city."

"The ground will be segregated with each entrance having a different colour ticket and this means supporters must use the entrances stipulated on the tickets. They will not be allowed to transfer from one area to another once inside the ground."

SATURDAY 28th AUGUST 1976

CITY START THE SEASON ALL SQUARE
Fourth Division
Exeter City 1 Cambridge United 1
City team: Key, Templeman, Hooker, Hore, Saxton, Hatch, Hodge, Kellow, Morrin, Beer, Jordan.
Cambridge United team: Webster, Lyon, Baldry, Batson, Fallon, Howard, Horsfall, Spriggs, Biley, Finney (Tuddenham), Watson.
Scorers: City: Kellow. Cambridge United: Biley.
Attendance: 3,606

Exeter City made a disappointing start with a draw their first home game in the Fourth Division this season. Although Cambridge United looked as though they are going to be a force this season, City should have won, because overall they had more of the game, especially in the second half.

Despite this territorial advantage however, they rarely looked like scoring as they failed to create chances. The Grecians lacked creative imagination to set up openings from the midfield area, and their game was too similar, too predictable.

Alan Biley had put Cambridge United ahead as early as the 8th minute with a superbly taken shot, and from then on Exeter knew they had a real fight on their hands. They gradually came back into the game and equalised nine minutes later, to deliver a perfect response.

Tony Kellow seized onto a defensive mistake, took the ball around the goalkeeper and pushed it into an empty net.

Exeter missed a great chance just before half-time when they were awarded a penalty, but Peter Hatch rather telegraphed his intentions with the spot kick and it was saved by Webster.

SUPPORTER OF THE YEAR AWARD

Exeter City's Commercial manager, Ray Ellis, has invited fans to start their bid to become the Supporter of the Year for 1976-77.

"I feel this is an ideal time for fans to consider competing for the Supporter of the Year award", said Ellis. "Already many supporters have commenced work, by raising funds during the close season."

"These include Graham Sparks of Branscombe, who has held several very successful Discos, and Mike Brady of Bradninch, who is continuing his "Mike's Marathon" by attempting to visit every Football League ground in the country."

MONDAY 30th AUGUST 1976

LOOKING FORWARD TO THE CHALLENGE

Exeter City manager John Newman and his players are looking forward to tomorrow night's Football League Cup tie at St. James' Park against First Division, Norwich City.

"I am sure everyone is looking forward to the game," said Newman. "Norwich City have many fine players of international reputation and a fine manager in John Bond. Cup football has a very special flavour of its own and much can be gained from the League Cup competition for a club such as ours. We look forward to the challenge and Norwich can be sure that we will give everything to ensure our entry into the third round. The test is to show that we can live in this sort of company. I think we can, and we will do ourselves justice."

TUESDAY 31st AUGUST 1976

EXETER SHOW GREAT SPIRIT

Football League Cup Round Two

Exeter City 1 Norwich City 3

City team: Key, Templeman, Hooker, Hore, Saxton (Clapham), Hatch, Hodge, Kellow, Morrin, Beer, Jordan.

Norwich City team: Keelan, Ryan, Sullivan,Powell, Forbes, Steele, Grapes, MacDougall, Boyer, Suggett, Peters.

Scorers: City: Kellow. Norwich City: Boyer, Grapes, MacDougall.

Attendance: 9,449

Despite conceding a penalty, losing Bobby Saxton with a pulled muscle, and then having Bobby Hodge injured, but continuing to play, Exeter City showed a healthy disregard for Norwich City's position and reputation and gave them a game to remember.

City found themselves with a mountain to climb when they were two goals down after 34 minutes, but they pulled one back before the interval. Then through sheer persistence and spirit the Grecians took the second half honours by forcing the Canaries mainly into a secondary role. Perhaps had the run of the ball been kinder, then Exeter may have earned a replay.

Norwich obviously showed their stature in flashes of fluent, faultless football, particularly in the first half, but equally they showed weaknesses which has given them a disappointing start to the season in the First Division. While Exeter played well, it must be said that they also missed a couple of chances that might have changed the course of the cup tie.

Norwich took the lead after just six minutes from the penalty spot through Ted MacDougall, after Alan Hooker had handled a shot from Steele, with Richard Key well beaten. City went 2-0 down after 34 minutes. A corner was not cleared properly by the Exeter defence, and Steve Grapes took advantage to hammer the ball into the net.

A minute before the half-time break Tony Kellow gave City some hope, scoring after receiving a pass from Peter Hatch. Despite City's valiant efforts the tie was all over three minutes from the end when Phil Boyer raced away to score the third goal for Norwich.

GET SMOKING FOR CITY

Rothmans are once again backing Exeter City in a form of sponsorship that involves smokers of their products. By saving any of the following brands of packet top, supporters can help the Grecians by 1p or 2p dependent upon the brand. Smokers should save tops from Rothmans King Size, Piccadilly No7, Consulate Menthol,, Black Cat filter, Piccadilly Filter and Black Cat No.9.

"Sponsorship in football is a relatively new idea," said City Commercial Manager, Ray Ellis. "I am sure in years to come we will only survive by forms of sponsorship, so please support all of our sponsors whenever possible."

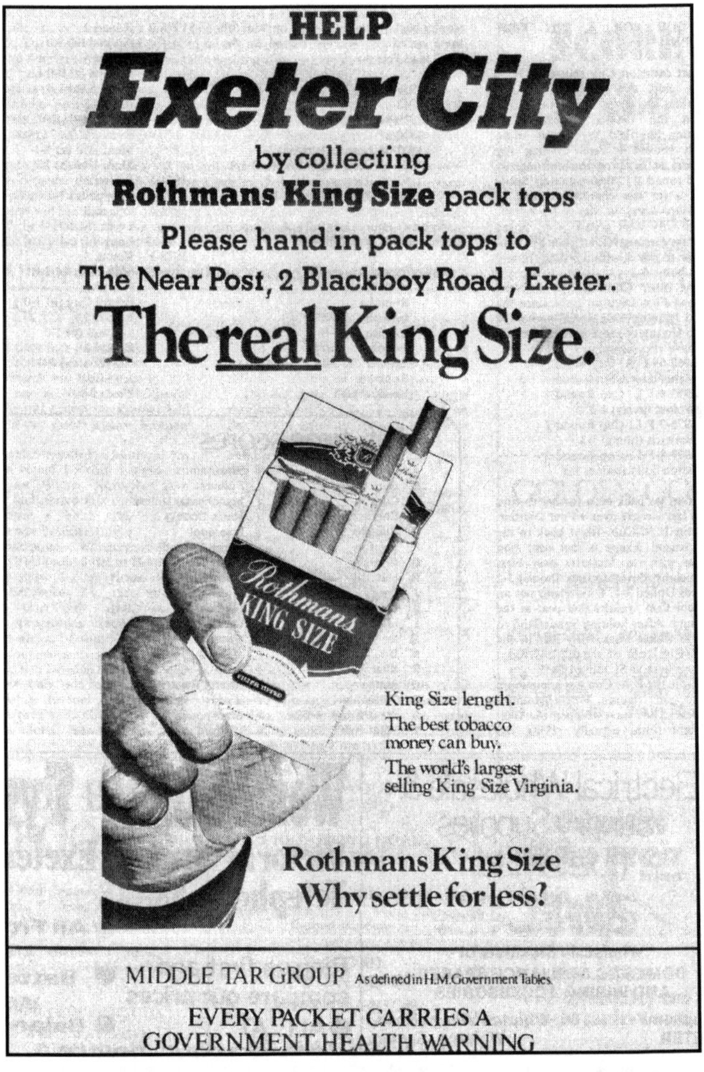

NB - Vintage advert from the 1970s - do not respond!

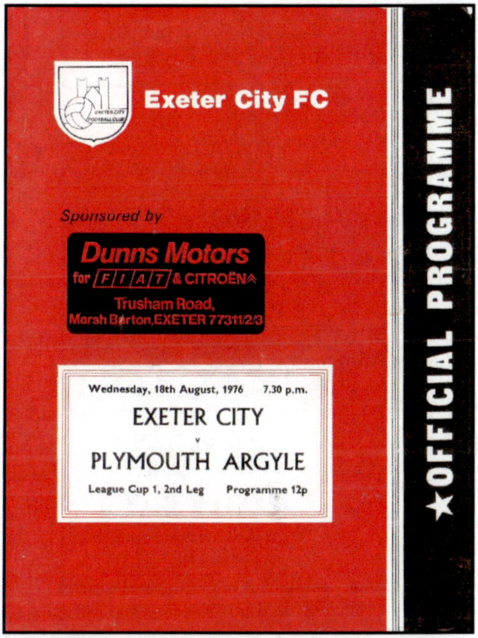

BACK ROW (L-R) Harry Holman, Tony Morrin, Mike Jordan, Nicky Jennings, Tony Kellow. MIDDLE ROW John Hore, John Templeman, Mike Green, Phil Howe, Richard Key, Graham Weeks, Keith Clapham, Alan Hooker. FRONT ROW Lammie Robertson, Alan Beer, Bobby Saxton, Bobby Hodge, Peter Hatch

NB - Vintage advert from the 1970s - do not respond!

FRIDAY 3rd SEPTEMBER 1976

NO PROBLEMS AT THE PARK
Exeter City were delighted with their supporters for their Football League Cup tie against Norwich City, the attendance being 9,469.

There was no trouble reported, no arrests and everyone left the match having enjoyed themselves.

It was pleasing that, in this age of trouble on the terraces, City supporters led the field in common sense and good behaviour.

SATURDAY 4th SEPTEMBER 1976

FIVE MINUTE SPELL DECIDES MATCH
Fourth Division
Colchester United 3 Exeter City 1
Colchester United team: Walker, Dyer, Williams, Bunkell, Smith, Packer, Garwood, Gough, Froggatt, Allinson, Cook
City team: Key, Templeman, Hooker, Hore, Clapham, Hatch, Jordan (Weeks), Kellow, Morrin, Beer, Jennings.
Scorers: Colchester: Froggatt, Garwood, Cook. City: Smith (o.g.).
Attendance: 2,516

Two goals in a five minute spell in the second half changed the course of Exeter City's match at Colchester United.

At half-time City seemed to be heading for a good result, but then United struck and Exeter were beaten for the first time in a Division Four fixture this season. City looked a very lively side before the interval, with Tony Kellow looking particularly dangerous. It was Colchester, however, who took a 25th minute lead when John Templeman miskicked. Froggatt raced on to the ball, and despite the attentions of Peter Hatch, he had little trouble in stroking the ball into the net.

Six minutes later City were on terms. Nicky Jennings hit a hard, low cross, which was diverted into his own net by Smith, with goalkeeper Walker having come out of his goal. The game continued to be entertaining with both sides producing good football and at that stage the final result could have gone either way.

Exeter went behind in the 54th minute, Gough crossing to Cook to move in with a fine header. Five minutes later City were in more trouble, when Garwood netted with a superbly struck shot.

Exeter's defence, for the first time in the game, were under pressure as Colchester threatened again, but they held out until the final whistle.

SATURDAY 11th SEPTEMBER 1976

VICTORY FOR CITY DESPITE INJURIES
Fourth Division
Exeter City 2 Rochdale 1
City team: Key, Templeman, Hooker, hore, Saxton (Clapham), Hatch, Robertson, Kellow, Morrin, Beer, Jennings.
Rochdale team: Poole, Hallows, Lacey, Hanvey, Summerscales, O'Laughlin, Melledew, Mullington, Whelan, Cooper (Mountford), Tarbuck
Scorers: City: Beer, Kellow. Rochdale: Hanvey.
Attendance: 2,829.

It was a day of firsts for Exeter City. They won their first Fourth Division match of the season and Alan Beer scored his first goal, as City defeated Rochdale 2-1.

Beer struck with a superb goal in the 9th minute, and Tony Kellow hit the second, his sixth of the season in the 27th minute. Exeter lost Bobby Saxton with an aggravated muscle injury after only four minutes, and then goalkeeper Richard Key turned his ankle and was heavily strapped for the rest of the match.

Exeter went ahead with the best goal seen at St. James' Park this season. Peter Hatch broke down the left and put over a cross for Beer who timed his run perfectly to head firmly into the net. Kellow's goal came from a pass by Lammie Robertson, the City striker shaking off a tackle and tucking a low shot into the net.

Rochdale scored a shock goal after the interval. Cooper was brought down by Key and Hanvey stepped up to score from the penalty spot. After that both sides became careless with their passing, but they were creating chances. Key twice had to rush off his line to punch away crosses, whilst at the other end Kellow had a great opportunity in the 80th minute, but hit his shot well over the top.

CITY BOSS DISAPPOINTED WITH MENU
Exeter City manager John Newman admits he has been bitterly disappointed with his teams performances in the League so far, especially when they have shown character and the measure of their ability against opposition such as Plymouth Argyle and Norwich City.

"I have always maintained that the most important competition for us is the League," said Newman.

"It is the bread and butter of our existence. We tasted spaghetti bolognaise, followed with a little camembert, washed down with vin rose and thoroughly enjoyed the feast of football provided in the Football League Cup. Bread and butter may not be as tasty, but the flavour can be improved and made more palatable if we care to add a little sweetener."

"Galloping Gourmets make good television entertainment, but such fixtures are not always available and sometimes only lead to indigestion. The simple "bangers and mash" that mother used to make can also be enjoyed and the theme of our talking this week has been to do the simple things well and the difficult will become easier."

TUESDAY 14th SEPTEMBER 1976
7-A-SIDE SUCCESS FOR CITY
Exeter City won the Minehead Football Club 7-a-side tournament last night, defeating the local club 1-0 in the final to take the Conoco-Jet Cup. Four teams took part in the competition, Exeter City, Bristol City, Torquay United and Minehead. Peter Hatch scored the winning goal for the Grecians after the Final had gone into a period of extra-time.

SATURDAY 18th SEPTEMBER 1976
KELLOW BACK ON THE GOAL TRAIL
Fourth Division
Halifax Town 1 Exeter City 2
Halifax Town team: Gennoe, Flavell, Hunt, Johnston (Bullock), Rylands, Phelan, McGill, Trainer, Jones, Lawson, Bell.
City team: Key, Templeman, Hore, Morrin, Clapham, Hatch, Weeks, Kellow, Robertson, Beer, Jennings.
Scorers: Halifax: Lawson. Exeter: Kellow, Beer.
Attendance: 1,424

Tony Kellow struck again to give Exeter City victory over Halifax Town at The Shay before a very small crowd. Graham Weeks was included in the City side for his first full Legaue match.

There is no stopping the 24-year-old Cornishman and once again he was City's most dangerous player. Exeter had chances in the first half, but had to come from behind after Halifax had taken the lead after 54 minutes. There was some scrappy football from both sides in the first half against background of little or no atmosphere. Halifax made the first aggressive move after the interval, when Richard Key saved Flavell's free-kick after John Hore had handled.

The home side went ahead from the penalty spot following a foul on Johnston by Weeks. Lawson took the spot kick to beat easily beat Key. Exeter equalised eleven minutes later when they were awarded a free-kick midway inside the Halifax half. Tony Morrin knocked the ball forward to Alan Beer, who hit a cross shot that Gennoe failed to hold, and as usual Kellow was on the spot, to net with the easiest of chances.

With the game having gone into injury time, City grabbed the points when Alan Beer scored the winner, leaving Halifax no time to do anything about it.

SATURDAY 25th SEPTEMBER 1976

CITY CRASH TO HEAVY BUT UNJUST DEFEAT
Fourth Division
Watford 4 Exeter City 1
Watford team: Rankin, How, Walsh, Craker, Eades, Garner, Bond, Joslyn, Poole (Coffill), Mercer, Hayes.
City team: Key, Templeman, Hore, Morrin, Saxton (Jordan), Hatch, Jennings, Kellow, Robertson, Beer.
Scorers: Watford: Poole, Bond, Mayes, Joslyn. Eexter: Beer.

Attendance: 5,079

Exeter City suffered their biggest defeat of the season because they played attacking football. Such is the fate of a side that persists in going forward. City conceded two goals in the closing minutes as they threw everything into attack looking for an equaliser. Thus the final score was a heavy defeat for Exeter, yet they were in the Watford half for a good two thirds of the match.

Bobby Saxton once again had to leave the field through injury, this time with a hamstring problem in the first half. Watford's opening goal came after 21 minutes when Poole netted his first goal for the club.

Alan Beer equalised for City five minutes later when Graham Weeks headed the ball down to him, and he made no mistake. John Templeman, who had been playing an excellent game, blotted his copybook in the 34th minute when fouling Mayes. Bond gave Watford the lead once again from the resultant penalty.

After the interval Beer went extremely close to equalising with two shots that were brilliantly saved by Rankin. With all their efforts concentrated on attack in an effort to save a point, Exeter left gaps at the back which Watford exploited to the full in the last eight minutes. Mayes made it 3-1 to Watford in the 82nd minute and with two minutes remaining Joslyn added a fourth.

MONDAY 27th SEPTEMBER 1976

CITY TO SIGN A DEFENDER
Exeter City manager John Newman was involved in a race against time today in a bid to sign a central defender on loan in order for the player to make his debut in Wednesday's match against Scunthorpe United.

The transfer deadline is 12 noon today. Yesterday he tried to take Hereford United's Billy Tucker, but they would not release the player. Then Newman made a move to sign Oxford United's Nick Lowe, but once again the club did not want the player to leave.

The injury to Bobby Saxton is likely to keep him out of the game for at least a month, and Newman is anxious to plug the gap in his absence on a temporary basis.

DIVISION FOUR TABLE	P	W	D	L	F	A	Pts
Stockport County	7	5	1	1	13	6	11
Bradford City	7	4	2	1	20	9	10
Cambridge United	7	4	2	1	13	4	10
Aldershot	7	4	2	1	10	7	10
Rochdale	7	3	3	1	9	8	9
Bournemouth	7	3	3	1	9	7	9
Watford	7	4	0	3	14	12	8
Huddersfield Town	7	3	2	2	7	6	8
Southend United	7	2	4	1	8	7	8
Coclhester United	7	3	1	3	10	8	7
Doncaster Rovers	7	2	3	2	11	11	7
Swanse City	7	2	3	2	10	14	7
Scunthorpe United	6	2	2	1	1	7	6
Barnsley	6	2	2	2	8	7	6
Crewe Alexandra	7	2	2	3	8	11	6
EXETER CITY	6	2	2	2	9	12	6
Torquay United	5	2	1	2	6	5	5
Newport County	7	2	1	4	4	7	5
Halifax Town	7	1	3	3	6	10	5
Workington	7	1	3	3	5	10	5
Darlington	7	2	1	4	6	12	5
Brentford	6	1	2	3	6	7	4
Hartlepool	7	0	3	4	5	13	3
Southport	7	0	2	5	3	13	2

TUESDAY 28th SEPTEMBER 1976

A SAINT BECOMES A GRECIAN
Exeter City have signed 20-year-old central defender Forbes Phillipson-Masters from Southampton.

City manager John Newman cleared the deal with just 90 minutes to spare last night, following a car dash to Southampton, and then onto London, to get the necessary transfer forms to The Football League. This will enable Phillipson-Masters to make his debut against Scunthorpe United at St. James' Park tomorrow night.

The player was due to link up with his new City teammates today and join in a training session, in preparation for tomorrow's game.

WEDNESDAY 29th SEPTEMBER 1976

BEER JUST LOVES PLAYING AGAINST SCUNTHORPE
Fourth Division
Exeter City 2 Scunthorpe United 0
City team: Key, Templeman, Hore, Morrin, Phillipson-Masters, Hatch, Hodge, Kellow, Robertson, Beer, Jennings.
Scunthorpe United team: Letheran, Markham, Peacock, Oates (Pilling), Wiggington, Money, Davidson, Collier, Keeley, Green, O'Connor.
Scorers: City: Beer (2).
Attendance: 2,934

Alan Beer has a happy habit of scoring against Scunthorpe United. He netted a hat-trick against them last April, and he has now added a further two goals that gave Exeter City a well deserved victory.

It had been a question of patience for City. They knew Scunthorpe were not going to be an easy outfit to beat. The Grecians had to keep running and working and this is what they did. Had it not been for the visitors keeper, Glan Letheren, they would have won more comfortably.

The all important breakthrough came in the 17th minute. A cross from Bobby Hodge went through the Scunthorpe defence to Nicky Jennings out on the left. He knocked the ball back in and Beer beat Letheren with a fine glancing, but powerful, header that gave the keeper no chance. Exeter made the game safe in the 75th minute when Tony Kellow flicked the ball on. Clive Wiggington made a defensive mistake as he tried a back header, and Beer immediately pounced for a well taken chance.

SPONSORED WALK
Last year's winner of the Exeter City Supporter of the Year award, Stafford Spurway of Willand, is once again walking from Willand to Exeter on a sponsored walk.

Spurway is hoping that he can exceed the £125 he raised last year and will be making the walk on Saturday, 16th October, arriving just prior to Exeter City's match against Workington.

FRIDAY 1st OCTOBER 1976

CITY OUT AND ABOUT IN THE COMMUNITY
This past week the Exeter City manager and players spent an enjoyable afternoon at Clark's shoe factory in Exmouth. This was the first of what is hoped of many such visits to different organisations within the area and is viewed by manager John Newman as an exercise to meet the public.

The team will shortly be visiting Exeter-based printers, Wheatons, and will follow that with a visit to the Tiverton Labour Club. City are welcoming invitations from other parliamentary groups within the community, and indeed from any organisation, institution or school.

"When people give of their time and energy to come and see us, we feel that it is correct to pay them a visit in their own environment, to talk to them and to listen to them" explained Newman.

"We enjoy being talked about, for as Oscar Wilde once said: There is only one thing in the world worse than being talked about, and that is not being talked about."

"I feel a lot of good can come from such meetings and I have always maintained that if this is not always the case, then it may not have done any harm either."

SATURDAY 2nd OCTOBER 1976

CITY WIN IN STYLE
Fourth Division
Exeter City 3 Crewe Alexandra 0
Exeter City team: Key, Templeman, Hore, Morrin, Phillipson-Masters, Hatch, Hodge, Kellow, Robertson, Beer, Jennings.
Crewe Alexandra team: Crudginton, Lowry, Evans, Lugg, Nicholls, Purdie, D. Davies, Abbott, W. Davies, Mayman, Tully (Bowles).
Scorers: Exeter: Beer (2), Hatch.

Attendance: 3,337

Exeter City are well on their way now. Two successive home wins have lifted them into fifth place in Division Four.

Three good goals crippled Crewe Alexandra and there was never really any doubt as to the outcome, as Exeter were by far the better side throughout the 90 minutes. Crewe were a spoiling team - a hard outfit. City did lose their way a little in the second half when the game became scrappy, but they soon recaptured their drive to completely trounce the visitors.

Exeter went ahead in the 26th minute. John Templeman hit a superb 30-yard pass to catch Crewe completely flat footed, and Alan Beer did the rest with his swift reaction to lob the ball over Geoff Crudginton.

The second goal came in the 75th minute. A Lammie Robertson free-kick was blocked, but Tony Kellow drove the rebound against the post, only for it to rebound to Peter Hatch who crashed the ball into the net with a left foot shot.

From then on there was never any real doubt as to who was going to win. Exeter scored again in the 80th minute with a superbly executed goal. Once again it was Templeman who started the move. He passed the ball down the right for Robertson to sweep a perfect cross for Beer to side foot into the net.

SATURDAY 9th OCTOBER 1976

YO-YO GRECIANS
Fourth Division
A.F.C. Bournemouth 2 Exeter City 0
A.F.C. Bournemouth team: Baker, Butler, Miller, Benson, Impey, Barton, Johnson, Rudge, Riley, Buttle.
Exeter City team: Key, Templeman, Hore, Morrin, Phillipson-Masters, Hatch, Hodge, Kellow, Robertson, Beer (Weeks), Jennings.
A.F.C. Bournemouth scorers: Rudge, Barton.
Attendance: 4,621.

Exeter City are up and down the Fourth Division table like a yo-yo. One game they play classic football, the next, it is so mediocre. They simply have to show more consistency if they are to figure in this season's promotion race.

City lacked the killer punch in front of goal, and their cause was not helped by the injury to seven-goal Alan Beer, who limped off with a twisted knee. Bournemouth took an early lead in the 14th minute following a 40-yard pass over the top of the City defence. Exeter were caught flat at the back and John Rudge netted with a low shot into the far corner .

Bournemouth's second came in the 64th minute from the penalty spot. Bobby Hodge had nudged Rudge in the penalty area and Frank Barton scored from the spot.

THURSDAY 14th OCTOBER

AWAY FORM NOT GOOD ENOUGH
Exeter City manager John Newman is well aware at the concerns over his team's form on the road this season.

"You can't win them all, I realise this only too well, but I am extremely concerned about our performances away from home," said Newman.

"We seem to be able to do the job required of us at St. James' Park, but when we travel away and need to keep the impetus going, we tend to become far too lethargic and even polite. We must learn to treat the opposition away from home as the other party, and whilst having respect for their principles and ideals, we must be in the mood to destroy them with the venom of a deadly poisonous snake."

"They must be punished into submission, so that when the points are tallied, they are the losers. When I speak of punishing the oppositon, I do not mean by physical abuse, but by skills and determination, by the sheer artistry of a performance. We must become a team unit and attack the opposition with the skill and daring of a regiment of soldiers, so that in the end, attack becomes the best form of defence."

"The defeat at Bournemouth last Saturday was a setback. We must now get back on the victory path and not play follow the leader. The only leader to follow is the bottom side in the Third Division. By achieving that at least a start will have been made."

SATURDAY 16th OCTOBER 1976

ANOTHER INJURY BLOW FOR CITY
Fourth Division.
Exeter City 0 Workington 0
Exeter City team: Key, Templeman (Weeks), Hore, Morrin, Phillipson-Masters, Hatch, Hodge, Hooker, Robertson, Holman, Jennings.
Workington team: Rogan, Kisby, Ellison, Kavanagh, Ashworth, Leng, Honour, Lowrey, Moore, Donaghy, Goodwin.
Attendance: 2,958

Exeter City suffered another injury blow in this game as full-back John Templeman became the latest victim. He could be out of action for at least six weeks after sustaining a cracked rib and a fractured cheekbone in the last minute of the goalless draw with Workington.

City are now down to just 13 fit professionals and are without Alan Beer, Tony Kellow and Mike Jordan, as well as Templeman. It was always going to be a struggle up front for the Grecians, and so it proved. Exeter though, did not play well in what was a poor match. Workington did not help matters, for it was blatantly obvious that they had travelled to Devon for a point by playing several back passes to their keeper.

What little football that was played, and there was not much of it, came from City, but they missed out in front of goal where Lammie Robertson, Harry Holman and Nick Jennings might have scored.

Workington were so unimpressive, yet they so nearly won the game. They were awarded a penalty in the 46th minute, but Ray Ellison put his kick way over the bar. It would have been a grave injustice had the Cumbrians bagged the points, but more worrying for the Grecians is the current injury situation.

BILLY MUSTARD
Well known former Exeter City player after the War, Billy Mustard, has died suddenly at the age of 55. Mustard, who lived at Countess Wear in Exeter, played for City in the 1940s, and was an all round sportsman having also played cricket, golf, hockey and table tennis.

THURSDAY 21st OCTOBER 1976

TWO PLAYERS TURN DOWN CITY
Exeter City's efforts to bring in a new loan striker to help them through their crippling injury crisis looks to have fallen through.

Reading turned down manager John Newman's approach to take Mick Hollis on loan, and then worse was to follow for the City boss.

Newman was let down by former Chelsea, Ipswich Town, Coventry City and Queen's Park Rangers striker John O'Rourke.

The player first agreed to sign for the Grecians after having returned from a spell playing in South Africa, but then had a change of mind and telephoned Newman to tell him that he would be signing for Weymouth instead.

FRIDAY 22nd OCTOBER 1976

LEY CONTRACT OFFER
Exeter City have made a short term contract offer to former Grecians' defender George Ley, who has been training with the club. Ley has also been offered an option of a longer contract after he has completed his trial period with City. Ley is expected to give his answer on Monday.

LOAN PERIOD EXTENSION?
Exeter City manager John Newman has contacted his opposite number at Southampton, Laurie McMenemy, with a view to extending the loan period of defender, Forbes Phillipson-Masters for a further month.

SATURDAY 23rd OCTOBER 1976

CITY GOAL DROUGHT CONTINUES
Fourth Division
Southend United 2 Exeter City 0
Southend United team: Freeman, Moody, Ford, Nicholl, Townsend, Young, Pountney,, Clark (Parker), Denny, Cunningham, Goodwin.
Exeter City team: Key, Hore, Hooker, Morrin, Phillipson-Masters, Hatch, Hodge (Green), Weeks, Robertson, Holman, Jennings.
Scorers: Southend: Denny, Parker.
Attendance: 4,605

Exeter City's defeat at Southend United was the third successive match in which they have failed to score. The current injury problems at the club are obviously not helping matters. City though, in truth, never looked like scoring, and the Southend keeper, Neil Freeman, did not have a direct attempt to save all game.

Exeter produced some promising build up work, but it never led to anything against a home side that seemed to be well contained in the first half. The opening goal for Southend came in the 27th minute, at a time when the Grecians were concentrating on possession football. It was Southend's first real attempt at goal, as Paul Denny scored.

City were still in the match at half-time and it became pretty clear that they were not going to get a goal. Southend wrapped the game up with a second goal in the 70th minute from Stuart Parker, and it was all over for the Grecians after that.

MONDAY 25th OCTOBER 1976

BLANK WEEKEND FOR CITY
Fourth Division
Stockport County 0 Exeter City 0
Stockport County team: Holbrook, Loadwick, Rutter, Thompson, Lennard, Fogarty, McBeth, McNeill, Daniels, Johnson (Sutcliffe), Massey.
Exeter City team: Key, Hore, Hooker, Morrin, Phillipson-Masters, Hatch, Weeks, Kellow, Robertson, Holman, Jennings.
Attendance: 5,490

Although the Grecians did pick up a point at Stockport, they once again failed to hit the back of the net, following on from their 2-0 defeat at Southend United 48-hours earlier. City shocked their hosts as early as the second minute when Lammie Robertson headed into the net, but the referee, after consulting a linesman, disallowed the goal. Tony Morrin, returning to the team after injury, also had a goal disallowed against his former club.

Exeter then survived a hectic ten-minute spell when Richard Key made a magnificent flying save and the City goal post was also struck as Stockport piled forward. By half-time City were holding their own and even took the initiative after the interval when Stockport lost the sparkle of their opening burst.

Tony Kellow, also back in the side after injury, sent in a shot on the half turn which grazed the post with the goalkeeper unable to get to the ball. Morrin worked tirelessly to inspire Exeter's attacks and there was a good chance when Robertson and Harry Holman cut open the Stockport defence only to fail to get in a finishing shot.

Stockport grew desperate to avoid failing to score for the first time at home in League matches so far this season, and the referee turned down their appeal for a penalty when Massey thought he had been fouled by Key.

THURSDAY 28th OCTOBER 1976

ARGYLE DEFENDER SIGNS FOR CITY
Injury hit Exeter City have signed central defender Peter Darke on loan from rivals Plymouth Argyle, initially on a one month deal.

The signing was completed today, and while the Exeter-born player trained with his new team mates, the registration forms were being taken to London by chief scout Tony Long before tonight's 48-hour transfer deadline. Darke will be a straight replacement for Forbes Phillipson-Masters who has been recalled by his parent club, Southampton.

City boss John Newman tried to sign another player before clinching the Darke deal. He originally made moves to sign Cambridge United centre-half Terry Eades, but the move fell through.

Plymouth Argyle manager Tony Waiters was able to help Newman out and provide a replacement for Phillipson-Masters by loaning Darke.

KEITH CLAPHAM TRANSFER-LISTED
City defender Keith Clapham has been placed on the transfer list by mutual agreement, following talks with City boss John Newman.

The player was upset when he was overlooked for a first team spot, with another loan player being brought into the club. Newman, however, told Clapham that his game had not been decisive as it should be and he was prepared to let him go to another club on a free transfer.

"I feel it might be a good thing for Clapham if he could have a fresh start somewhere else," said Newman.

FRIDAY 29th OCTOBER

DIVISION FOUR TABLE	P	W	D	L	F	A	Pts
Bradford City	11	7	2	2	29	17	16
Stockport County	10	6	2	2	17	11	14
Cambridge United	10	5	3	2	18	9	13
Rochdale	10	4	5	1	11	6	13
AFC Bournemouth	10	4	5	1	12	8	13
Swanse City	11	5	3	3	20	20	13
Colchester United	10	5	2	3	19	11	12
Huddersfield Town	10	5	2	3	13	9	12
Aldershot	10	5	2	3	13	10	12
Southend United	10	3	6	1	11	9	12
Barnsley	11	4	3	4	14	13	11
EXETER CITY	10	4	3	3	14	14	11
Crewe Alexandra	11	4	3	4	15	17	11
Scunthorpe United	10	4	2	4	14	10	10
Watford	10	4	2	4	15	15	10
Darlington	10	4	2	4	10	14	10
Torquay United	9	3	3	3	10	9	9
Doncaster Rovers	11	3	3	5	17	19	9
Newport County	11	2	3	6	6	13	7
Brentford	10	1	4	5	13	17	6
Halifax Town	10	1	4	5	7	14	6
Workington	10	1	4	5	6	15	6
Southport	11	1	4	6	7	17	6
Hartlepool United	10	0	4	6	9	23	4

SATURDAY 30th OCTOBER 1976

LAMMIE ENDS GOAL DROUGHT WITH THREE OF HIS OWN
Fourth Division
Exeter City 3 Southport 1
Exeter City team: Key, Hore, Hooker, Morrin, Darke, Hatch, Weeks, Kellow, Robertson, Holman, Jennings.
Southport team: Coates, Sibbald, O'Brien, O'Neil, Higham, Taylor, Dewsnip, Lyon, Galley, (Snookes), Wilson, Blair.
Scorers: Exeter: Robertson (3). Southport: Wilson.

It was the first time that Lammie Robertson had scored a hat-trick in his ten-year career, and it also ended a four match goalless run for Exeter City. It was a match that had plenty of excitement, incident and entertainment. Yet for just over an hour you wondered if the Grecians were ever going to score again.

City dominated the match from the word go, but a combination of missed chances and a superb display from Southport goalkeeper John Coates, simply held them up. Southport went ahead completely against the run of play in the 27th minute when Alan Wilson netted with a fine near post header.

City had to wait until the 62nd minute before breaking their recent goal drought and equalising from the penalty spot. Tony Kellow was brought down in the area and Robertson stroked home the resultant spot kick. Six minutes later Robertson rose superbly to head a goal from Nicky Jennings corner. They then made victory certain in the 82nd minute when Harry Holman was brought down on one of his many direct and impressive runs into the box. Robertson again netted with the penalty to complete his hat-trick.

LEY NOT FOR CITY
Former Exeter City full-back George Ley will not be signing for the club for a second spell at St. James' Park. City manager John Newman said that he had a long talk with Ley yesterday, but could not agree terms. There were too many complications.

ADVERTISIING REVENUE VITAL FOR THE GRECIANS
The field of advertising is vital to the finances of any football club, and linked with sponsorship provides a very important section of any commercial department. Exeter City are very fortunate in as much as their match programme advertising has grown season by season, and whether they are a large national company, or a small local firm, the club appreciate the support given to them.

The advertising boards around St. James' Park are slowly increasing in number and the club will shortly be launching a campaign to fill the empty spaces that remain.

Advertising is of course a means by which companies can improve their businesses and it is up to all City fans to support the advertisers, and when their services are required to state that they are an Exeter City supporter.

NB - Vintage advert from the 1970s - do not respond!

AFC BOURNEMOUTH
THE OFFICIAL JOURNAL OF AFC BOURNEMOUTH
season 1976/77
A F C B
AFC BOURNEMOUTH
v
EXETER CITY
SATURDAY, 9th OCTOBER, 1976
Football League Division Four
12p

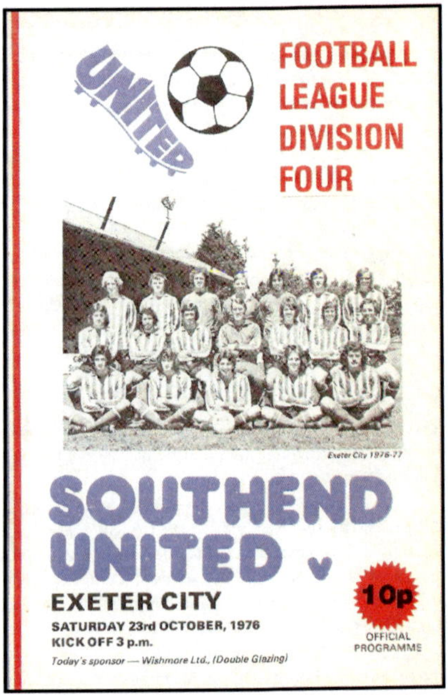
UNITED
FOOTBALL LEAGUE DIVISION FOUR
Exeter City 1976-77
SOUTHEND UNITED v
EXETER CITY
SATURDAY 23rd OCTOBER, 1976
KICK OFF 3 p.m.
Today's sponsor — Wishmore Ltd., (Double Glazing)
10p
OFFICIAL PROGRAMME

FOOTBALL LEAGUE DIVISION IV — SEASON 1976/77
STOCKPORT COUNTY
versus
EXETER CITY
EDGELEY PARK
MONDAY, OCTOBER 25th, 1976
Kick-off 7-30 p.m.
OFFICIAL PROGRAMME:
10p

Exeter City FC
Saturday, 30th October 1976
3.00 p.m.
EXETER CITY
v
SOUTHPORT
Fourth Division
Programme 12p
★ OFFICIAL PROGRAMME

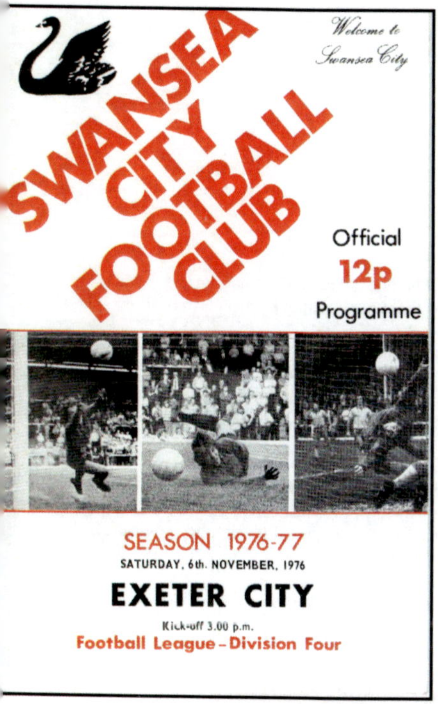
Welcome to Swansea City
SWANSEA CITY FOOTBALL CLUB
Official
12p
Programme
SEASON 1976-77
SATURDAY, 6th. NOVEMBER, 1976
EXETER CITY
Kick-off 3.00 p.m.
Football League – Division Four

Exeter City FC
Friday 12th November 1976
7.30 p.m.
EXETER CITY
v
HUDDERSFIELD
Fourth Division
Programme 12p
★ OFFICIAL PROGRAMME

EXETER CITY F.C.
Official Programme
EXETER CITY v NEWPORT COUNTY
F.A. Cup Replay 1st Round
Wednesday 30th November 1977
Kick-off 7.30 p.m.
Price 15p

WEDNESDAY 3rd NOVEMBER 1976

FIVE GOAL THRILLER AT THE PARK
Fourth Division
Exeter City 3 Brentford 2
Exeter City team: Key, Hore, Hooker, Morrin, Darke, Hatch, Weeks, Kellow, Robertson, Holman, Jennings.
Brentford team: Priddy, Fraser, Allen, Riddick, Goldthorpe, Carlton, Graham, Glover, Cross, McCulloch, Johnson (French).
Scorers: Exeter: Kellow (2), Robertson. Brentford: McCulloch, Graham.
Attendance: 2,779

Tony Kellow hit the goal trail again having gone six matches without finding the back of the net. He took his tally for the season to nine, as his two goals helped Exeter City to victory and lift them to ninth spot in the Fourth Division table.

City had to keep battling and working hard throughout the match against a Brentford side who never gave up, and as a result, it was an absorbing game to watch. City took the lead in the 25th minute. Nicky Jennings struck a deep corner and Lammie Robertson out jumped goalkeeper Paul Priddy to score with a header. Brentford's 51st minute equaliser followed an off the line clearance by Alan Hooker, who kept out Bob Goldthorpe's header, but the ball was knocked back and Andy McCulloch made no mistake with a far post header.

Graham Weeks, who had yet another impressive match, set up City's 57th minute goal. He fed Hooker, who chipped the ball to Jennings, and in went the cross for Kellow to score with a remarkably powerful header. Brentford paid the penalty for a hesitative defence in the 80th minute. A long ball from the right caught out the visitor's defence who were in a dither, and Kellow nipped in for his second goal of the game.

Brentford though didn't give up and were rewarded for their efforts in the 89th minute when Jackie Graham showed superb ball control before tucking away his shot.

PARKER FOR EXMOUTH TOWN
Former Exeter City midfielder, Graham Parker, has been appointed player-coach at Western League, Exmouth Town. Parker was originally signed by the Grecians from Lincoln City, and subsequently had a short spell at Torquay United.

THURSDAY 4th NOVEMBER 1976

SOUTHEND TOLD: NOT FOR SALE
Exeter City have confirmed today that they have received inquiries from Southend United for two of their players. They are believed to be Lammie Robertson and Harry Holman. The Southend manager Dave Smith has been in attendance at St. James' Park for the last two matches. Grecians boss John Newman said that he did not want to sell players who he felt could do a good job for Exeter City.

FRIDAY 5th NOVEMBER 1976

SWANS NEED NO REMINDING
With Exeter City due to visit Swansea City tomorrow afternoon, the Vetch Field club have been quick to remind their supporters all about the Grecians' and last season.

They write: "No one needs telling less than Swansea's players about the dangers that Exeter City can present. The Devon club were the only side to win a League game at the Vetch last season, and the only club to take four points out of four against the Swans. It was three goals each time and no one played a more signifcant role than former Swansea winger Alan Beer in gaining the victory at the Vetch last February. He scored two of the three goals on his way to becoming Exeter's top scorer, and he is still the number one target man for Exeter."

SATURDAY 6th NOVEMBER 1976

KEY MAN FOR CITY
Fourth Division
Swansea City 0 Exeter City 0
Swansea City team: Brown, Evans, Bartley, Harris, May, Bruton, Lally, James, Curtis, Charles, Coppell.
Exeter City team: Key, Hore, Hooker, Morrin, Darke, Hatch, Weeks, Kellow, Robertson, Holman, Jennings.
Attendance: 3,856

Exeter City's promising young goalkeeper Richard Key saved a point for his promotion chasing side with a defiant display in the Swansea mud. He threw himself around every inch of the mud splattered goalmouth with a show of stubborn resistance which frustrated the Swans talented front runners.

Each time the Swansea unlocked the Grecians defence, Key was seemingly always on hand to stop them, with good positioning and equally good saves. The match was in jeopardy until two hours before kick off following torrential rain that had fallen on the Vetch Field playing surface.

The result extended Exeter's unbeaten run to four league matches and kept them well in touch with the top teams. Exeter relied largely on their rigid defensive ploys making the occasional breakaway which almost brought them a goal when a 20-yard sizzler from Lammie Robertson was saved by Brown at the second attempt. Graham Weeks set up a chance for Tony Kellow, but just as he was about to shoot when well placed, the ball was whipped away from him by Bruton.

The rest of the stage was left to Swansea's promising forwards and Exeter's defiant defenders. The sticky conditions, particularly in the centre of the field, made it difficult for both sides at times.

TUESDAY 9th NOVEMBER 1976

SPONSORSHIP BOOST FOR CITY
Another incentive for Exeter City to achieve success in the Fourth Division this season has come in the form of a sponsorship deal that involves pounds for points. Renwicks Travel of Exeter are to sponsor City for £10 for every away point, and £5 for every home point.

The scheme has been backdated to the start of the season and so City have so far earned £100 through sponsorship. B Supporters will be able to follow the scheme by means of a "pointsometer" which will appear in each of the home match programmes.

THURSDAY 11th NOVEMBER 1976

SPECIALIST VISIT FOR BEER
Exeter City striker Alan Beer, who has scored 7 goals this season, is to consult a specialist about his knee injury. Beer is also to have further x-rays, which it is hoped will reveal the full extent of the injury. He has not played for a month since hobbling off in the match at AFC Bournemouth. His general fitness is good, but once he tries to kick a ball, the injury flares up again. It is a frustrating time for Beer, whose excellent early season form was attracting attention from the Welsh international manager.

FRIDAY 12th NOVEMBER 1976

BEST START IN TEN
Fourth Division
Exeter City 2 Huddersfield Town 0
Exeter City team: Key, Hore, Hooker, Morrin, Darke, Hatch, Weeks, Kellow, Robertson, Holman, Jennings.
Huddersfield Town team: Poole, Hart, Oliver, Walker, Barnes, Hague, Gray, Campbell (Goldthorpe), Sidebottom, Fowler, Johnson.
Scorers: Exeter: Kellow, Robertson.
Attendance. 3,637.

Exeter City's best start to the season in 10 years has put them just two points away from the top spot in the Fourth Division, as the promotion momentum grows. It was another enjoyable and entertaining game between two sides that bookmakers had made pre-season favourites for promotion.

It was a good, efficient Exeter team performance. Huddersfield, though, made it hard for City, playing some good determined football, but they never really clicked in front of goal. Exeter took the lead in the 35th minute following a hard cross from Alan Hooker, and Tony Kellow struck a fine shot into the net for his 10th goal of the season.

The second City goal in the 55th minute developed from a quickly taken free-kick by the impressive Graham Weeks. He fed Nicky Jennings who hit an early cross for Lammie Robertson to rifle in another well struck goal. Exeter had run and battled for each other, and thoroughly deserved their win. A performance that, if reproduced throughout the season, will surely bring them a great deal of success.

THURSDAY 18th NOVEMBER 1976

CITY BOSS LINKED WITH GRIMSBY TOWN JOB
There was some speculation today that Exeter City manager John Newman has been linked with the vacant post at Grimsby Town. Newman said that he did not wish to comment on speculation. However, whilst the Grimsby club chairman, Paddy Hamilton, refused to comment, another club official did say that Newman's name had been mentioned. The Grimsby Town board of directors were due to meet today to discuss a possible appointment.

FRIDAY 19th NOVEMBER 1976

GRECIANS BEGIN THEIR CUP TRAIL
The first steps on the road to Wembley begin tomorrow as Exeter City entertain Southend United in the first round of the F.A. Cup.

"It is always pleasing to be drawn at home," said City boss John Newman. "I am especially pleased for the supporters. A good home draw against such a competitive side as Southend will, I am sure, provide good entertainment. It is a tough draw, but an exciting one and we must prepare ourselves, then adapt ourselves to the job in hand and make sure that our number goes into the bag for the next round."

"The Football League is our business, but a good cup run becomes so important to a club like ours at this stage of the season. Financially we need a good cup run, for as we progress the revenue increases and some of the pressures of football ease."

DIVISION FOUR TABLE

	P	W	D	L	F	A	Pts
Bradford City	15	9	3	3	33	18	21
Cambridge United	16	7	6	2	25	11	20
Rochdale	15	6	7	2	17	11	19
Stockport County	15	7	4	4	22	17	18
Huddersfield Town	15	7	4	4	19	14	18
AFC Bournemouth	15	6	6	3	19	16	18
Crewe Alexandra	16	7	4	5	21	24	18
Barnsley	15	7	3	5	23	16	17
EXETER CITY	15	6	5	4	20	19	17
Colchester United	14	7	2	5	27	17	16
Southend United	14	4	8	2	15	13	16
Watford	15	6	4	5	21	21	16
Darlington	15	6	4	5	19	19	16
Aldershot	15	6	4	5	16	17	16
Scunthorpe United	14	6	3	5	21	16	15
Swanse City	13	5	4	4	21	23	14
Torquay United	14	5	3	6	20	20	13
Doncaster Rovers	15	5	3	7	22	29	13
Halifax Town	15	3	5	7	15	20	11
Brentford	13	3	4	8	24	27	10
Newport County	14	2	5	7	8	16	9
Southport	15	1	7	7	10	22	9
Hartlepool United	15	1	6	8	14	28	8
Workington	15	1	4	10	7	25	6

SATURDAY 20th NOVEMBER 1976

CUP REPLAY BECKONS FOR CITY
F.A. CUP FIRST ROUND
Exeter City 1 Southend United 1
Exeter City team: Key, Hore, Hooker, Morrin, Saxton, Hatch, Weeks, Kellow, Robertson, Holman, Jennings.
Southend United team: Freeman, Banks, Ford, Laverick, Townsend (Cunningham), Moody, Pountney, Goodwin, Parker, Hadwin, Little.
Scorers: Exeter: Hatch. Southend; Pountney.
Attendance: 4,434

Southend United have now become the favourites to reach the second round of the FA Cup following this draw at St. James' Park. The Grecians are going to have to play a lot better in Monday evening's replay if they are to progress, for at one stage they looked a beaten side.

When Southend went ahead early in the second half it looked as though that might be the deciding goal, but Exeter gave themselves another chance with an equaliser ten minutes later. Exeter never really struck up a rhythm in their game. They did not put much together and City surely know they can play a good deal better. Southend even overcame losing Neil Townsend after just five minutes, when he sustained a fractured cheekbone.

Ron Pountney put Southend ahead after 52 minutes, and 10 minutes later Peter Hatch headed the equaliser from a Tony Morrin free-kick.

"WE MUST NOT LET IT SLIP" SAYS NEWMAN
A quarter of the way through the season, Exeter City manager John Newman has been speaking about his team's progress so far.

"The last five league games have been most satisfying and has seen us edge our way to be among the front runners," said the City boss.

"We must be aware though and not run away with any pre-conceived ideas that we are on cloud nine. The top twelve teams are only three points behind the leading club. We are a quarter of the way through the season. Every team is hungry for success, and we must make sure that by our own efficiency we continue to snap at the heels of the leaders. A quick look over our shoulder and the constant breathing on the back of the neck makes our task all the more difficult and serves as reminder that we have to stretch our ability to the limit."

"We have been on this position before, and we have to be positive enough not to let it slip. We must push on so that at the end of the long road, we successfully finish the race."

MONDAY 22nd NOVEMBER 1976

HEARTBREAK FOR CITY IN THE CUP
F.A. CUP FIRST ROUND REPLAY
Southend United 2 Exeter City 1 (after extra-time)
Southend United team: Freeman, Banks, Ford, Laverick, Moody, Young, Pountney, Goodwin, Parker, Hadley, Little.
Exeter City team: Key, Hore, Hooker, Morrin, Saxton, Hatch, Weeks, Kellow, Robertson, Holman (Hodge), Jennings.
Southend scorers: Parker, Hadley Exeter scorer: Kellow.
Attendance: 6,604

Exeter City have a dismal record in the FA Cup if recent seasons are taken into account. For this defeat at Southend now means they have gone five successive seasons without reaching round two. However, almost all the spectators inside Roots Hall, would probably agree that on this occasion the Grecians did not deserve to lose and another draw would have been a fairer result.

The Grecians fought and worked so hard throughout the game, and were holding out for a second replay when Southend snatched the winner five minutes from the end of extra-time through Hadley. Exeter had settled quickly and gave as good as they took. There was no let up in the game, and by half time it was still goalless. City worked and battled hard against a Southend side defending an unbeaten home record this season.

Their reward came in the 63rd minute when Harry Holman's 25-yard drive was only partially saved and Tony Kellow followed up to take an easy chance. Southend struck back almost immediately, equalising six minutes later. It was a disputed goal which was awarded by the linesman. Lammie Robertson claimed he had cleared Parker's header off the City goal line, but the linesman disagreed.

The game went into a period of extra-time, and in the 98th minute Hadley seemed to have put Southend ahead with a superb cross shot, but to City's relief the ball rebounded off the crossbar. However, Hadley then broke City's hearts when he netted the decisive and winning goal in the 115th minute of the tie.

TUESDAY 23rd NOVEMBER 1976

CUP DISAPPOINTMENT

There was a sense of disappointment at St James' Park this morning following Exeter City's FA Cup first round exit at Southend United in last night's replay.

"Our exit from the F.A. Cup disappoints me and I am sure did not bring much pleasure to any of us," said City manager John Newman.

"Whilst we did not play well enough to save the journey to Southend for the replay, our performance was far above that given at Exeter. The players fought and grafted for the entire 120 minutes, but again fortune was not ours. Whilst I do not wish to repeat what has already been written about luck being on our side, I am constantly reminded and very much aware that if we keep talking about our bad luck, people will start reminding us about our good luck, although there doesn't seem to have been too much of that lately."

"The players share the disappointment and are determined to drain themselves in an effort to establish a top position in the league and to maintain it."

SATURDAY 27th NOVEMBER 1976

UNBEATEN RUN COMES TO AN END

Fourth Division

Darlington 2 Exeter City 1

Darlington team: Ogley, Nattress, Cochrane, Stone, Craig, Noble, Lyons, Rowles, Ferguson, Holbrook, Wann.

Exeter City team: Key, Darke, Hooker, Hore, Saxton, Hatch, Weeks, Kellow, Robertson, Jordan, Jennings.

Scorers: Darlington: Winn, Noble. Exeter: Kellow.

Attendance: 2,997.

Darlington added to their sound home record when they ended Exeter City's recent good run of five unbeaten league matches. Both sides opened briskly and built up their attacking moves. Darlington steadily mounted pressure and this paid dividends when they took a 25th minute lead. A half hit clearance fell to Wann who crashed in a rising shot from the edge of the area.

The Grecians were now struggling as Darlington surged forward. Only the cool play of Bobby Saxton and Peter Hatch prevented a further setback. Exeter were constantly falling foul of the referee and at times the players showed their frustrations at some of his decisions. Peter Darke almost presented Darlington with a gift goal in the second half when he headed against his own goal post.

The tempo of the match had lifted with Exeter beginning to grit their teeth, but they found it hard work against an aggressive side that gave them very little chance to settle on the ball. Two quick Darlington corners were held by Richard Key, then with three minutes remaining, Noble increased his sides lead from the penalty spot. Exeter never gave up though and were rewarded for their efforts with a consolation goal in the 89th minute as Tony Kellow found the back of the net.

FRIDAY 3rd DECEMBER 1976

COMPETITION IS HEALTHY

Exeter City's recent injury problems seem to have taken a turn for the better according to Grecians' manager John Newman.

"Competition for places is healthy and no one player can expect an automatic place in the side," said Newman. "Selection has to be earned and I am happy to report that healthy competition and spirit is very apparent within the club."

SATURDAY 4th DECEMBER 1976

CITY WERE SIMPLY AWFUL!
Fourth Division
Exeter City 0 Doncaster Rovers 2
Exeter City team: Key, Templeman, Hooker, Hore, Clapham, Hatch, Weeks (Jordan), Kellow, Robertson, Beer, Jennings.
Doncaster Rovers team: Peacock, Brookes, Bailey, Robinson, Uzelac, Taylor, Miller, Murray, O'Callaghan, Kitchen, Laidlaw.
Scorers: Doncaster: O'Callaghan (2).
Attendance: 2,891.

It seems to have become an annual event with Exeter City. Just when it appears they are well placed and poised to make something happen, they flop. There can be no excuses, for Exeter were simply awful as they gave their worst display of the season.

The whole performance was devoid of ideas and their passing was simply atrocious. Doncaster probably couldn't have believed how bad a team they were facing. This was a truly shocking display by the Grecians, a team defending an unbeaten home record. It was Doncaster Rovers' first away victory for 16 games. They showed far more imagination than City.

The visitors scoring hero was Brendan O'Callaghan, with goals in the 30th and 62nd minutes. He was given room in the air to power in a header for his first goal, and then the City defence failed to stop him weave through two players for the second.

WEDNESDAY 8th DECEMBER 1976

FRIENDLY AT PLYMOUTH
A friendly between Plymouth Argyle and Exeter City was played behind closed doors at Home Park this afternoon The Grecians won 1-0, with the Bobby Hodge getting the goal.

SATURDAY 18th DECEMBER 1976

THE LIGHTS WENT OUT AT ALDERSHOT
Fourth Division
Aldershot 1 Exeter City 0 (Match abandoned - floodlight failure).
Aldershot team Johnson, Howitt, Wooler, Crosby, Mancini, Jopling, Walton, Morrisey, Howarth, McGregor, Brodie
Exeter City team: Key, Templeman, Hore, Morrin (Weeks), Saxton, Hatch, Hodge, Kellow, Robertson, Beer, Jennings.
Scorers: Aldershot: Howarth.

It all began on a wet, miserable December afternoon. While thousands of shoppers were making sure that the last Christmas presents had been snapped up, inside the Recreation Ground the traditional Saturday afternoon crowd were warming up for what was a crucial match in the Fourth Division.

Exeter were not playing well. They were a goal down with only three minutes to go, when all of a sudden the ground was in total darkness. Only the glow of the Christmas illuminations in the packed streets more than 200 yards away could be picked out.

The floodlights had failed. The match referee gave electricians 30 minutes to "resume normal service" but they failed to beat the deadline, so the match was abandoned.

The only goal of the game came from Aldershot's Jack Howarth in the 60th minute.

Exeter goalkeeper Richard Key had made a number of good saves in the first half to keep the Shots at bay. Unfortunately City lost Tony Morrin after just 18 minutes with a pulled thigh muscle and Peter Hatch was left to hobble through the game with damaged knee ligaments.

TUESDAY 21st DECEMBER 1976

WILL JOHN NEWMAN LEAVE EXETER CITY?

Is Exeter City manager John Newman poised to leave the club to take charge at Grimsby Town?
That was the major speculation today after a dramatic turn about that saw favourite for the post, Bob Stokoe, drop out of the running to become Grimsby's next manager. Newman's name has been linked with Grimsby for some weeks, and he is widely being tipped to take over within the next 48 hours. Grimsby Town chairman Paddy Hamilton has made an offer to a current Football League club manager, but he would not name the person concerned.

WEDNESDAY 22nd DECEMBER 1976

CHAIRMAN WARNS: IT WOULD BE THE END OF EXETER CITY F.C.
Exeter City Football Cub have announced that they made another big loss in the 1975-76 season of £22,451, compared to a loss of £30,909 the previous year. Club chairman Gerald Vallance issued a stern warning that the club could not bear another similar big loss.

"I do not think the club could stand another loss like that," he said. "It would be the end. Even so, I am confident that Exeter City will see out this season. In fact, things are a little brighter. We should come out even or with a small profit at the end of this season. It is the attendances at St. James' Park that are killing us. We just cannot exist on gates of under 4,000. If we were averaging that figure, we would be showing an annual profit."

Exeter City Football Club's overall debt at 31st May 1976 was £123,345.

Among the items on the latest balance sheet are as follows:-
* Home gate receipts - up from £19,591 to £25,345
* Share of gate receipts from away matches - £14,328 compared to £6,796.
* Share of Football League and Football Association pools - £34,306 as against £30,123.
* Fundraising - Increased from £18,576 to £26,560.
* Transfer fees received £10,000 compared to £5.000.
* Wages and signing on fees £101,901 as against £68,267, but included in this year's figures are a charge of £17,464 for service bonuses. Of this £7,889 relates to season 1974-75 and £9,565 to 1975-76.
* Transfer fees paid down by £3,500.
* Travelling and hotel expenses down by more than £2,000.
* Maintenance of the ground and premises increased by more than £1,000.
* Administration expenses were £10,008 compared with £6,784.

The Exeter City board of directors consider that the freehold property value shown in the accounts at £10,324 has market value of £50,000 at 31st May 1976.

THURSDAY 23rd DECEMBER 1976

CITY MANAGER JOHN NEWMAN TO LEAVE THE CLUB
Long serving Exeter City manager John Newman is to leave the club to take over in a similar capacity at Grimsby Town. Newman is City's longest serving boss since the War and met Exeter City's Board of Directors yesterday afternoon to tell them that he had been offered the job at Grimsby and wished to go.

"The board have accepted my resignation," said Newman. "There has been no animosity between the board and myself. They accepted that I had received a good offer from a club in a higher division. Iw ill follow Exeter City's results with a lot of interest. It was a hard decision to make. The Grimsby chairman rang me on Tuesday evening to offer me the job."

"I had already met the Grimsby Board of Directors last week, but it was a wrench to leave Exeter and the west country after 16 years. I would be absolutely delighted if Exeter City went on to gain promotion this season."

Jack Edwards, the man who led Exeter City to their first ever promotion in 1963-64 has been asked to act as a caretaker manager for the time being.

"We are extremely disappointed that John Newman is leaving," said Exeter City chairman Gerald Vallance. "However, he felt that it was such a good offer that he could not afford to turn it down. We wish him all the best for the future."

The general feeling among Exeter City supporters today seemed to be that Newman had done a good job for the club and they will be sorry to see him go.

Grecians' defender Bobby Saxton, like Newman, a former Plymouth Argyle player, is being strongly tipped by many to take over as player-manager at St. James' Park.

ANOTHER DEPARTURE

John Newman is not the only person to be leaving the club, for Graham Drew, the Commercial Assistant, is off to Bristol Rovers where he has been appointed Commercial Manager.

FRIDAY 24th DECEMBER 1976

CITY HOPE BALSON WILL RETURN TO THE CLUB

Exeter City were making an eleventh hour bid to beat a new transfer deadline and get international clearance for former defender Mike Balson, so that he can line up against Torquay United at St. James' Park on Boxing Day.

Balson, who has been playing in South Africa for the last three years, returned to Exeter earlier this week, and City still hold his registration. Exeter City secretary Pat Wakeham said efforts were being made to cable the South African Football Association requesting clearance on the Grecians' behalf. If successful, City will sign Balson on an initial one-month contract to overcome their current injury problems. Balson, along with his family, emigrated to South Africa in 1974, and lived in Johannesburg, where he has since been playing for the Highland Park club.

FRIDAY 24TH DECEMBER 1976

DIVISION FOUR TABLE

	P	W	D	L	F	A	Pts
Bradford City	19	10	5	4	36	23	25
Cambridge United	19	8	8	3	30	16	24
Stockport County	19	9	5	5	26	20	23
Colchester United	18	10	2	6	33	18	22
Barnsley	19	9	4	6	28	18	22
AFC Bournemouth	19	7	8	4	25	18	22
Southend United	18	5	11	2	20	15	21
Huddersfield Town	19	8	5	6	22	19	21
Rochdale	17	6	8	3	18	13	20
Aldershot	17	8	4	5	22	18	20
Swansea City	18	8	4	6	30	27	20
Watford	18	7	6	5	23	21	20
Crewe Alexandra	18	8	4	6	22	27	20
EXETER CITY	18	7	5	6	23	23	19
Darlington	18	7	5	6	21	24	19
Scunthorpe United	18	7	3	8	25	23	17
Torquay United	18	6	4	8	26	27	16
Halifax Town	18	4	7	7	17	21	15
Newport County	16	2	7	7	9	17	11
Southport	18	1	9	8	10	27	11
Brentford	17	3	4	10	24	31	10
Hartlepool United	18	2	6	10	16	34	10
Workington	17	1	4	12	9	33	6

MONDAY 27th DECEMBER 1976

THE PERFECT FESTIVE GIFTS

Fourth Division

Exeter City 3 Torquay United 0

Exeter City team: Key, Templeman, Hore, Weeks, Saxton, Clapham, Hodge, Kellow, Robertson, Beer, Jennings.

Torquay United team: Lee, Lynch, Sandercock, Bence, Kruse, Dunne, Provan (Twitchin), Rudge, Boulton, Brown,

Kennedy.
Scorers: Exeter: Saxton, Kellow, Jennings.
Attendance: 6,446.

Exeter City brought their own glad tidings and great joy to the start of the Christmas and New Year holiday period with a thoroughly deserved victory over Devon rivals Torquay United. It was the perfect send off for popular manager John Newman who takes over at Grimsby Town tomorrow.

Before the kick off Newman was given a tremendous reception as he received two gifts. City secretary Pat Wakeham presented him with a silver salver on behalf of the staff, whilst Derek Singleton handed over a bottle of whisky from the "Cowshed Choir."

Exeter never looked back after taking the lead in the first minute. John Templeman's right wing corner was flicked on by Alan Beer and Bobby Saxton, having moved up from defence, pushed the ball into the net. City were both purposeful and powerful as they continued to push Torquay back. It was high class, entertaining football, Man of the match was Lammie Robertson, who gave a performance that was sheer perfection. Although Torquay came into the game a little more in the second half, they never truly looked like upsetting Exeter. City went further ahead in the 35th minute. After a corner had been cleared, John Hore played the ball back into the danger area and Tony Kellow took his opportunity with perfect finishing.

Exeter struck again in the 75th minute. Robertson started the move near his own penalty area. Templeman pushed the ball out to Kellow who sent over a cross for Nicky Jennings to score with a strong shot.

THURSDAY 30th DECEMBER 1976

BALSON SIGNS FOR THE GRECIANS
Defender Mike Balson has been cleared by the South African Football Association to enable him to play for Exeter City. He has signed an initial one-month contract today and is expected to return to St James' Park this coming Saturday when he will line up for a reserve team fixture against Bideford.

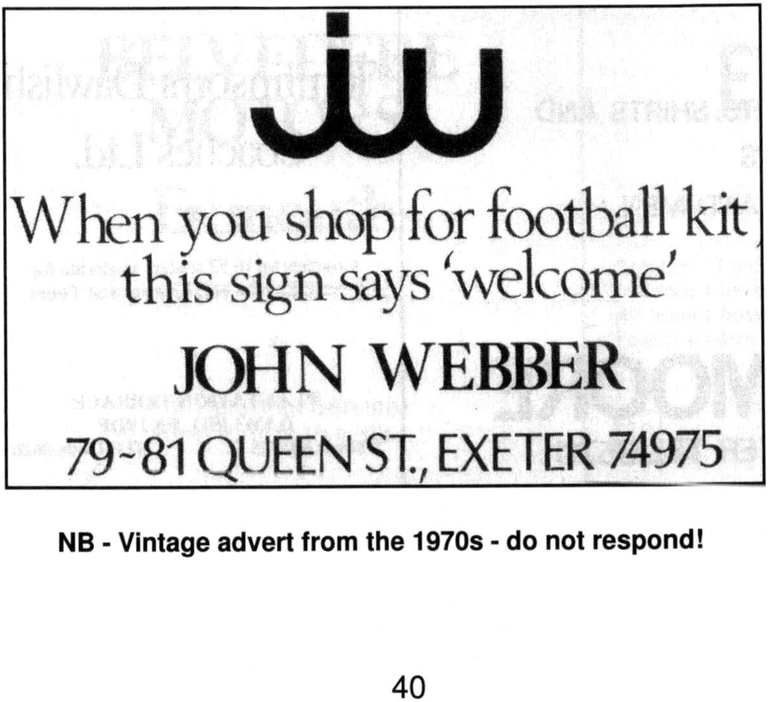

NB - Vintage advert from the 1970s - do not respond!

BRADFORD CITY
Association Football Club (1908) Limited
Registered Office : VALLEY PARADE GROUND, BRADFORD BD8 7DY
chairman: R. Martin
vice-chairman: J. Dunne
directors: W. T. Davidson, J. H. Garside, K. D. Morrison, W. Roper, D. Simmons R. Stead, J. C. Tordoff, D. W. Wilkinson
vice-Presidents: F. N. Curl, P. Goodall, K. C. Kelsall, H. A. Koch-Osborne, E. Sutcliffe, G. Sutcliffe, T. M. Walker
general manager and secretary: C. S. Thompson
hon. medical officer: Dr. A. D. Campbell
commercial manager: S. P. Smith
team manager: R. Kennedy
a.f.c.
Football League - Division Four
Saturday, 29th January 1977
versus
EXETER CITY
Kick-Off 3-00 p.m.
Official Programme 12p

Reproduced by courtesy of "The North Devon Journal Herald."
ROTHMAN'S WESTERN LEAGUE
EXETER CITY
Official Programme : Price 5p
SAT., 1st JANUARY, 1977
Issued by Bideford A.F. Supporters' Club

OFFICIAL MATCHDAY MAGAZINE
SOUTHPORT
FOOTBALL
CLUB
Champions
Division 4
1972-73
PRICE 10p
FC
Runners-Up
Division 4
1966-67
3 Jan SOUTHPORT K.O. 3 pm
v.
EXETER CITY

ALDERSHOT
OFFICIAL PROGRAMME 10p
SURRIDGE
COBBLER
FOOTBALL LEAGUE
Division Four
EXETER CITY
SATURDAY, 18th DECEMBER
Kick-off 3 p.m.
1976

SATURDAY 1st JANUARY 1977

ANOTHER HOLIDAY SUCCESS FOR CITY
Fourth Division
Exeter City 2 Swansea City 0
Exeter City team: Key, Templeman, Hore, Clapham, Saxton, Hodge, Weeks, Kellow, Robertson, Beer, Jennings.
Swansea City team: Potter, Evans, Bartley, Smith, May, Lally, Chappell. James, Curtis, Charles (Griffiths), Conway.
Scorers: Exeter: Kellow (2).
Attendance: 3,596

Exeter City had to work hard for their victory against a good Swansea City side. The visitors may have felt that they deserved something in the end. The game was a tighter affair than the scoreline suggests, but City had what Swansea did not possess, the finishing power. Overall though this was another very good Exeter team performance.

The game only went ahead after two pitch inspections in the hour before the kick off. There was still a lot of surface water and it continued to rain. Exeter scored two magnificent goals in the opening 13 minutes. In the 9th minute Tony Kellow executed a perfect shot, and then four minutes later he finished off a superb move involving Bobby Saxton and Alan Beer.

The Grecians were at their best in the first half when they produced some outstanding football. Swansea were a bigger side, but many teams would have crumbled after such a start. They never gave in, however, and had they been sharper in front of goal they might have hauled themselves back into this game.

MONDAY 3rd JANUARY 1977

DISAPPOINTING GRECIANS SHOULD HAVE DONE BETTER
Fourth Division
Southport 1 Exeter City 1
Southport team: Coates, Hughes, Snookes, O'Neil, Higham, Taylor, Sibbald, Wilkinson, Galley, Wilson, Dewsnip.
Exeter City team: Key, Templeman, Hore, Weeks, Saxton, Clapham, Hodge, Kellow, Robertson, Beer, Jennings.
Scorers: Southport: Sibbald. Exeter: Jennings.

Exeter City could and should have won this match at Haig Avenue, with Southport totally out of form. City slowly but surely took control of the match, only to waste their many chances of the second half when they were well on top.

Southport could thank their keeper, Coates, for a series of several fine saves which kept his side alive at time when City put them under a vast amount of pressure. Equally however, Exeter should have made more of their clear cut openings and not really have given Southport a chance of a point.

City survived a shaky opening which saw both sides struggling to keep their feet on a slippery pitch. Southport went ahead after 13 minutes when Wilson turned past a City defender and chipped the ball against the bar with Richard Key beaten. Sibbald pushed home the rebound.

Southport's lead lasted just three minutes. Alan Beer sent over a hard, low cross and Nicky Jennings ran in at the far post to touch the ball into the net. From then on it was really Exeter's game for the taking, especially in the second half when it was all one way traffic towards the Southport goal. The combination of Coates and the missed chances cost Exeter City dearly, and denied them what should have been another win for them.

THURSDAY 6th JANUARY 1977

GREAT INTEREST IN CITY MANAGER VACANCY
There has been a lot of interest shown for the vacant position of manager of Exeter City, and a replacement for John Newman, now with Grimsby Town. Exeter City chairman Gerald Vallance said they had received 20 applications for the post and that two of them had come from current members of staff. A meeting of the Board of Directors was due to be held very shortly and an appointment will be announced soon after that.

FRIDAY 7th JANUARY 1977

CARETAKER MANAGER VERY PLEASED
Exeter City's caretaker manager Jack Edwards has been very pleased with the progress of the team since stepping in to

take charge following John Newman's move to Grimsby Town.

"Nothing gave me more pleasure than our defeat of Torquay United, not because of my previous association with them, but it provided a fitting tribute to John Newman on his last day in charge at St. James' Park," said Edwards.

"Whatever our fortunes may now be, we should always remember that John laid a very sound foundation stone upon which to build. Now it is up to us to make sure that stone does not crumble.

I was very pleased with the way in which we continued the good work against Swansea last Saturday and even more delighted with our result at Southport on Monday. The holiday period therefore brought us 5 points out of a possible 6. Not a bad start to 1977! Following the Torquay game I left the ground sad at the departure of John, but realising that a job remained to be done, and it was up to all of us to see that the job was done."

SATURDAY 8th JANUARY 1977

CITY CHASE A PROMOTION PLACE.
Fourth Division
Exeter City 1 Barnsley 0
Exeter City team: Key, Templeman, Hore, Weeks, Saxton (Clapham), Hatch, Hodge, Kellow, Robertson, Beer, Jennings.
Barnsley team: Springett, Murphy, Collins, Pugh (price), Saunders, Pickering, Felton, Joicey, Peachey, Millar, Brown.
Scorer: Exeter: Kellow.
Attendance: 3,784

Exeter City are rapidly closing in the Division Four leaders. They are currently sixth in the league and just one point away from a top four place. Barnsley as expected, were a stubborn and well organised side at the back. Exeter had more of the game and the important point was that they kept working and plugging away to finally break down their opponents.

The vital breakthrough came in the 65th minute from top scorer Tony Kellow. Once City scored, they began to make more impression on the Barnsley defence. Bobby Hodge and Alan Beer were involved in the build up to the Exeter goal which ended with Kellow sweeping in an unstoppable rising shot from four-yards.

It might have been so different had Felton put away an easy chance or Barnsley in the first half and only a good save by Richard Key stopped him from opening the scoring. Nonetheless, Exeter deserved their victory and again it proved to be an excellent advert for what team effort is all about.

THURSDAY 13th JANUARY 1977

BOBBY SAXTON APPOINTED EXETER CITY MANAGER
Exeter City have appointed a new player-manager. He is 33-year-old defender Bobby Saxton. He was officially appointed today after being chosen from a total of 26 applications for the post left vacant by John Newman's departure for Grimsby Town.

"It has always been my ambition to go into management," said Saxton. "I am sure we have a chance of promotion and I am sure I can keep it going."

City chairman Gerald Vallance announced the appointment this morning to the playing staff.

"We had a short list of four people for the vacancy," explained Vallance. "We felt that Bobby Saxton has great determination and will do a good job for Exeter City." It is understood that City midfielder, Lammie Robertson was also on that short list for the manager's post at St. James' Park. With Saxton in the player-manager role, Jack Edwards, who had been caretaker boss since Newman left the club, will now revert to his post of trainer.

TUESDAY 18th JANUARY 1977

SHAREHOLDERS FAIL TO SHOW AT A.G.M.
Although Exeter City has more than 300 shareholders, only two, apart from the club directors and officials felt it was important enough to attend last night's Annual General Meeting. Chairman Gerald Vallance spoke of cautious optimism for the future. The meeting lasted for just 20 minutes.

"The club lost £22,451 last year," Vallance told those present. "It was essential, however, that a closer look is taken at the financial results."

"The loss was made during a period of severe inflation, coupled with falling gates. The average admissions at the turnstiles for the 1975-76 season was 2,637, of which 31% were juveniles or senior citizens at lower rates."

The chairman added that the results for the first six months of this financial year, compared favourably with the budget that had been drawn up by the directors, and that the club was looking towards the possibility of breaking even this year by discounting any dealings in the transfer market.

"Our recent performances have been encouraging and we are currently maintaining a favourable League position," added Vallance. "I therefore appeal to everyone to give support to the club to ensure that our ultimate aim of promotion is achieved. I therefore look forward to the future with cautious optimism."

WEDNESDAY 19th JANUARY 1977

CITY MIDFIELDER TRANSFER LISTED
Exeter City's skilful and talented midfielder, Lammie Robertson, has been placed on the transfer list at his own request. Exeter have circulated his name to other clubs, and although no fee has been disclosed, it is believed that the Grecians will be looking for around £10,000.

Robertson was recently a target for Southend United, but Exeter turned down their offer which was not high enough. Robertson was on the short list to become player-manager at St. James' Park, but the job went to Bobby Saxton instead. The midfielder stresses however, that the appointment of Saxton had no bearing on his wish to leave Exeter City.

WILSON LEAVES THE GRECIANS
Former first team goalkeeper Bob Wilson, who has been managing Exeter City's Western League side this season, is leaving the club.

He feels that because of increased business commitments he does not have the time to devote to the role. Wilson will, however, continue until an appointment is made for his replacement. The club are to advertise immediately for either a manager or a player-manager.

DIVISION FOUR TABLE

	P	W	D	L	F	A	Pts
Cambridge United	24	10	11	3	38	21	31
Bradford City	24	12	6	6	45	30	30
Southend United	22	9	11	2	31	16	29
Colchester United	22	13	2	7	44	21	28
AFC Bournemouth	23	9	9	5	30	21	27
EXETER CITY	22	10	6	6	30	24	26
Stockport County	23	10	6	7	28	26	26
Watford	22	9	7	6	30	23	25
Swansea City	23	10	5	8	36	32	25
Rochdale	22	8	9	5	20	16	25
Huddersfield Town	24	9	7	8	27	25	25
Crewe Alexandra	23	10	5	8	26	33	25
Barnsley	23	10	4	9	29	21	24
Aldershot	21	10	4	7	24	24	24
Darlington	21	9	6	6	26	27	24
Doncaster Rovers	24	8	7	9	31	35	23
Scunthorpe United	21	8	4	9	28	26	20
Torquay United	23	7	5	11	29	40	19
Hartlepool United	23	4	9	10	24	37	17
Halifax Town	20	4	8	8	17	22	18
Southport	22	1	13	8	15	32	15
Brentford	22	4	4	14	33	43	12
Newport County	20	2	7	11	10	28	11
Workington	22	2	5	15	17	45	9

THURSDAY 20th JANUARY

LAST POST FOR BILLY.
The death of William "Billy" Hillman at the age of 88 will recall to many old timers his playing days with the Exeter City Football Club Band before and after the Great War.

Hillman later became landlord at the Crown and Anchor in Newtown, Exeter, but the building was destroyed during the Exeter blitz. He then ran the Locomotive Inn, also in Exeter. Until a few years ago, he was a regular attender of matches at St. James' Park where he had many friends.

SATURDAY 22nd JANUARY 1977

HODGE SETS CITY ON THEIR WAY
Fourth Division
Exeter City 3 Hartlepool United 1
Exeter City team: Key, Templeman, Hore, Weeks, Saxton, Hatch, Hodge, Kellow, Robertson, Beer, Jennings.
Hartlepool United team: Richardson, Creamer, Wiggett, Scott, Simpkin, O'Donnell, Scaife (Bielby), McMordie, Goad, Poskett, Goldthorpe.
Scorers: Exeter: Hodge, Kellow, Robertson. Hartlepool: Goldthorpe.
Attendance: 3,285.

In heavy, difficult conditions, Exeter City again proved that if they can remain consistent they must have a good chance of getting out the Fourth Division this season. Exeter had much more possession overall, with every player playing his part by helping each other where and when it counted, as Hartlepool made a spirited comeback in the second half when they reduced the arrears and it must have caused some apprehension in the City camp.

Bobby Hodge put Exeter in front midway through the first half, after a brilliant run from the halfway line which was rounded off with a 25-yard shot that powered into the corner of the net. It was 2-0 after 47 minutes. From John Templeman's free-kick, Lammie Robertson deceived the Hartlepool defence and Tony Kellow was on the blind side for his 17th goal of the season.

Hartlepool hit back in the 63rd minute when Wayne Goldthorpe stabbed the ball in from close range following two consecutive corners.

Exeter clinched victory five minutes from the end. Hodge was brought down in the area after another positive run and up stepped Robertson to strike a perfectly taken penalty.

SATURDAY 29th JANUARY 1977

DISAPPOINTING OUTCOME IN BRADFORD
Fourth Division
Bradford City 1 Exeter City 1
Bradford City team: Downsborough, Hardcastle, Podd, Johnson, Middleton, Fretwell, McGinley (Ingram), Spark, Cooke, Dolan, Hutchins.
Exeter City team: Key, Templeman, Hore, Weeks, Saxton, Hatch, Hodge, Kellow, Robertson, Beer, Jennings.
Scorers: Bradford City: Ingram. Exeter: Hodge.
Attendance: 4,979.

Exeter City must have returned from Valley Parade, Bradford City, wondering what they have to do to secure two points. On a treacherous skating rink of a surface, they always looked more nimble and sure footed and were largely in command from start to finish.

On the face of it, an away point against their promotion rivals looks good, but for every clear cut chance created by Bradford City, at least half a dozen were created by the Grecians. City's overall team work, midfield composure, and lively raiding, made them so distinctly superior that they would have had no more than their due if they had been comfortable victors.

As it was they had cause for self reproach in some degree in squandering too many of their first class chances their slick raiding created. Exeter took a 14th minute lead when John Templeman's cross was laid into the path of Bobby Hodge who scored with a superb low shot just inside the Bradford City area.

The longer the game went on, the more likely a City victory seemed. But in injury time a long ball was pumped into the Exeter area. Richard Key tragically slipped on the frozen surface and Ingram pushed the ball in for an undeserved equaliser.

THURSDAY 3rd FEBRUARY 1977

SECOND CITY PLAYER TRANSFER LISTED
Exeter City midfield player, Tony Morrin, has been put on the transfer list at his own request. Morrin asked for a move

and this was granted by the City Board of Directors yesterday following a meeting with player-manager Bobby Saxton. Exeter will be seeking a small fee for the payer, who is unhappy that he cannot gain a regular place in the first team.

This is the second time that Morrin has been on the transfer list, having come off it last summer when he signed a new contract. There are currently three players on the Exeter City transfer list, namely, Morrin, Lammie Robertson and Keith Clapham.

SATURDAY 5th FEBRUARY 1977

CITY GAIN POINT AT THE LEADERS
Fourth Division
Cambridge United 1 Exeter City 1
Cambridge United team: Webster, Batson, Howard, Stringer, Fallon, Seddon, Watson, Spriggs, Hall, Finney,, Biley.
Exeter City team: Key, Templeman, Hore, Weeks, Saxton, Hatch, Hodge, Kellow, Robertson, Beer, Jennings.
Scorers: Cambridge United: Hall. Exeter City: Beer.
Attendance: 4,428.

It was cheers all round for Exeter City away at top of the table Cambridge United, as they maintained their push for promotion. It also ended Alan Beer's goalless run as the striker snatched City's equaliser 10 minutes after half-time in a red-blooded Fourth Division promotion battle.

Exeter, a goal down after 15 minutes, hit back strongly with the wind at their backs in the second half, and Beer's goal was superbly taken. He swivelled on a low Bobby Hodge cross 10-yards out and side footed a precise first time shot inches inside the near post for his first goal in seven matches.

Exeter started as if they had walked all the way from Devon. For the first 20 minutes they were all at sea and it was no surprise when Cambridge centre-forward Jim Hall pounced on an Alan Biley header to shoot the home side ahead. Bobby Saxton was a key figure as Exeter tackled and hustled fiercely in efforts to get into the game. Lammie Robertson ran the midfield for City as they came on strongly towards the end of the first half and took up the cudgels in a fluctuating second period.

TUESDAY 8th FEBRUARY 1977

FRIENDLY
Exeter City 1 Guernsey XI 3
(The match was played at the Royal Marine Camp, Exton).
Player-manager Bobby Saxton used the game to play people in new positions and try a few things out. As a fitness and training session, it was extremely good, however, as a football match it was a disappointment, for Exeter did not play well.

FRIDAY 11th FEBRUAY 1977

SAXTON URGES SUPPORTERS TO CHEER ON TEAM
Player-Manager Bobby Saxton has praised the support that his team received during the last home game against Hartlepool United, and now wants more of the same.

"It's nice to be back on our own territory tomorrow following our travels to the north and east. Both trips were made worthwhile by the fact that we returned from each game with something to show for our labours" said Saxton. "We are now in a position where we look to our supporters to give the vocal encouragement we received in our last home game against Hartlepool."

"It was without doubt the best encouragement we have had for a long time and I am sure that the game against Colchester tomorrow will result in our fans doing even better. Colchester are one of the most successful sides in Division Four, currently occupying the second spot. They also enjoyed success in the F.A. Cup being narrowly beaten by Derby County, having held them to a draw at Layer Road in the fourth round of the competition. They will surely be a difficult side to overcome, but after our last two results the lads are looking forward to the challenge and if the supporters can all get behind us we are confident that the battle can be won."

SATURDAY 12th FEBRUARY 1977

GRECIANS EXTEND UNBEATEN RUN
Fourth Division
Exeter City 1 Colchester United 0.
Exeter City team: Key, Templeman, Hore, Weeks, Saxton, Hatch, Hodge, Kellow, Robertson, Beer, Jennings.
Colchester United team: Walker, Williams, Cook, Leslie, Smith, Dowman, Garwood, Gough, Froggatt, Bunkell, Packer.
Scorer: Exeter: Hodge.
Attendance: 6,132

In past seasons jittery January and fumbling February have been Exeter City's downfall when the club has been well placed in the Fourth Division. Now it is a different story, for City are unbeaten in 8 league matches and the promotion pains are becoming a little more acute.

Exeter defeated Colchester United in what was a tense, absorbing and exciting match. It was like a cup-tie. The game was packed with the kind of incidents that supporters want to see. The match was evenly balanced at half-time, although the Grecians did have the luxury of a 6th minute goal when Bobby Hodge beat Walker with a left-foot shot.

In the second half Colchester did push City back more, but Richard Key was on top form equaling those saves that Walker had made before the interval. Despite this win, Exeter are still not in the top four, but with at least one game in hand on their rivals, they are certainly well placed.

TUESDAY 15th FEBRUARY 1977

SOMERTON PARK WATERLOGGED
Exeter City's match at Newport County this evening fell victim to the weather after the Somerton Park pitch was waterlogged. Newport wanted to try and play tomorrow evening, but City player-manager Bobby Saxton would not agree, for he felt that there was little prospect in his opinion of the pitch improving in time.

It was also a wasted journey for more than 100 Exeter City supporters who arrived at the ground to find that the game had been called off. The referee made his decision, an inevitable one it must be said, just 45 minutes before kick off.

Five hours before the game Newport Speedway Club were making repairs at the ground which they share with the Football Club, when a bulldozer severed an electricity cable connecting one of the floodlight pylons. Newport won the race against time to get the cable repaired, but then down came the torrential rain turning the pitch into a muddy morass.

THURSDAY 17th FEBRUARY 1977

CITY BID TURNED DOWN
Barnstaple Town have turned down a bid from Exeter City for their 20-year-old midfielder, Barrie Vassallo, who had previously cost £10,000 when he joined Plymouth Argyle from Arsenal. Vassallo dropped out of the Football League this season after playing a few matches for Aldershot, however, he is keen to return to the full-time game.

Exeter are not the only club interested in the player, with Torquay United and Sheffield United keeping tabs on the situation. City offered Barnstaple a small fee for Vassallo but were told no deal. It is understood that the North Devon club wanted £8,000 for the player. Exeter are unlikely to pursue their interest any further.

SATURDAY 19th FEBRUARY 1977

CITY MAINTAIN PROMOTION PUSH
Fourth Division
Rochdale 1 Exeter City 2
Rochdale team: Poole, Hallows, Lacey, Banton (Mullington), Summerscales, O'Laughlin, Helliwell, Cooper, Mountford, Melledew, Whelan.
Exeter City team: Key, Templeman, Hore, Weeks, Saxton, Hatch, Hodge, Kellow, Robertson, Beer, Jennings.
Scorers: Rochdale: Whelan. Exeter: Weeks, Beer.
Attendance: 1,523

Exeter City continued their promotion thrust with a deserved victory at Rochdale, where a poor crowd of just over 1,500 saw the Grecians at their penetrating best. After surviving a shaky opening, City never looked back, particularly after Graham Weeks had scored in the 35th minute. With better shooting they might have won more convincingly and saved themselves the anxiety of seeing Rochdale equalising from the penalty spot.

The Spotland pitch churned up badly and both sides had difficulty in keeping their feet. Perhaps against the run of play, Exeter went ahead. Tony Kellow beat a couple of defenders and chipped over a low centre for Weeks to drive the ball against the goalkeeper, but he made no mistake with the rebound. Having scored, Exeter now began to play with a huge amount of confidence and really had Rochdale on the run for the rest of the first half.

City continued to be well on top after the interval and had it not been for the goalkeeping of Poole they would have had the game sewn up. Exeter were shocked in the 72nd minute though when Mullington was brought down by Peter Hatch and Whelan equalised with the penalty. Within two minutes, however, justice was done when Alan Beer raced onto a through ball and rolled it into the net for the winning goal.

	P	W	D	L	F	A	Pts
Cambridge United	29	13	12	4	46	24	38
Bradford City	28	14	8	6	50	32	36
Colchester United	27	16	2	9	50	24	34
Southend United	27	10	14	3	38	22	34
Barnsley	29	15	4	10	41	27	34
EXETER CITY	27	13	8	6	38	28	34
AFC Bournemouth	29	11	11	7	39	28	33
Huddersfield Town	28	13	7	8	39	28	33
Watford	27	11	9	7	36	26	31
Stockport County	27	11	9	7	33	30	31
Doncaster Rovers	28	11	8	9	41	37	30
Aldershot	27	12	6	9	29	30	30
Swansea City	26	12	5	9	44	35	29
Rochdale	28	10	9	9	32	25	29
Crewe Alexandra	28	11	7	10	30	41	29
Darlington	27	10	8	9	31	40	28
Halifax Town	28	8	9	11	33	35	25
Scunthorpe United	28	9	7	12	32	36	25
Torquay United	29	10	5	14	35	46	25
Hartlepool United	29	6	9	14	33	50	21
Southport	27	1	13	13	18	44	15
Brentford	28	5	4	19	37	57	14
Newport County	23	2	8	13	11	33	12
Workington	28	2	8	18	21	59	12

SATURDAY 26th FEBRUARY 1977

REFEREE REPORTED TO THE FOOTBALL LEAGUE
Fourth Division
Exeter City 1 Halifax Town 0
Exeter City team: Key, Templeman, Hore, Weeks, Saxton, Hatch, Hodge, Kellow, Robertson, Beer, Jennings.
Halifax Town team: Leonard, Bradley, Trainer, Flavell, Dunleavy, Phelan, Hoy, Carroll, Bullock, Lawson, Johnson.
Scorer: Exeter: Beer.
Attendance: 5,995.

The Football League will be asked to hold an investigation into the handling of the match by Bristol-based referee, Don Biddle, by the Halifax Town manager, Alan Ball. He will be making an official complaint after Biddle sent off two of his players, booked another, and then ordered the Halifax trainer from the dug out.

This, it has to be said, would appear to be nothing more than sour grapes, for the antics of the Halifax team could well have seen the referee taking even sterner action by sending off another player. Halifax did no credit to the game of football with a display of what can only be described as crude and crunching tackles.

They contributed exactly nothing to the match with a string of physical challenges that was a shocking advertisement for the Yorkshire club. First to be sent off was Bobby Flavell in the 34th minute, He had been booked only moments earlier and then promptly fouled Nicky Jennings.

As Flavell walked off the pitch, Halifax manager Ball patted the player on the back and shook hands with him! Jimmy Lawson was the next to go in the 67th minute for aiming a kick at Bobby Hodge. The Halifax manager again upset the crowd and incensed them as he walked along the running track to commiserate with Lawson.

The outcome of the eventful 90 minutes for all the wrong reasons? A deserved 1-0 win for Exeter City. It could have been a lot more, for both Lammie Robertson and Bobby Saxton had efforts cleared off the line. The winning goal came in the 53rd minute when Chris Dunleavy's back pass was pounced on by Alan Beer, and the little striker kept calm to stroke the ball low into the net.

KEEP RIGHT ON TO THE END
Player-manager Bobby Saxton has warned that it will be hard road to follow if Exeter City are to go on to win promotion.

"In the words of Harry Lauder, "Keep right on to the end of the road." With 27 down and 19 to go, this is exactly what we have to do," explained Saxton. "We have come though a difficult patch against some formidable opposition in the league, and like that grand old man of variety we must ensure that though the way be long, our hearts will be strong to keep right on to the end."

"Let us make no mistake about it, for it is going to be a very hard road and promotion is a long way off. I am cautious, but full of optimism and promotion is my aim. It is marvellous to see the city buzzing and talking again of the football club, to see the crowds winding their way along Sidwell Street and all the approach roads to St. James'Park, because in the end, that is what it is all about."

CITY COMMERCIAL STAFF CHANGES
The Commercial Department at Exeter City has undergone a few changes in personnel during the past few weeks. Pat Le Leivre has left the Near Post shop to have an addition to her family, with Pat Wright taking over in her place. Another addition to the staff has been Stuart Brailey, who will be assisting Commercial Manager, Ray Ellis, with general commercial duties. This has brought the total commercial staff to four, with Bill Dimond also working in this important area of fundraising for the club.

MONDAY 28th FEBRUARY 1977

BIDDLE: DENIES CHARGES MADE BY HALIFAX MANAGER
Referee Don Biddle has denied that he used foul and abusive language to Halifax Town players during Saturday's eventful match at St. James' Park against Exeter City. The 44-year-old Bristol referee sent off two Halifax Town players, booked another and asked their trainer to leave the bench.

After the match Halifax Town manager Alan Ball delivered an astonishing verbal attack on Biddle.

"The referee used foul and abusive language to my players throughout the match. I shall be making an official complaint to The Football League," said Ball.

Biddle, a Detective Inspector and finger print expert with the Avon and Somerset Police denied the claims. "Mr Ball's opinion on my refereeing I can accept, because that is his opinion" said Biddle. "However, at no stage did I use foul and abusive language whatsoever. To say that I did is a deliberate lie. I did say on the field of play to several Halifax players that their performance was a disgrace."

JOHN BAUGH SIGNED BY GRECIANS
Exeter City player-manager Bobby Saxton has signed St. Lukes College goalkeeper, John Baugh. He is signed on non-contract forms as cover for regular keeper Richard Key. Baugh plays for the College Western League side.

NB - Vintage advert from the 1970s - do not respond!

WEDNESDAY 2nd MARCH 1977

LATE SHOW BY CITY
Fourth Division
Aldershot 2 Exeter City 2
Aldershot team: Johnson, Howitt, Wallace, Crosby, Earls, Jopling, Hibbs (Wooler), Morrisey, Bell, Brodie, McGregor.
Exeter City team: Key, Templeman, Hore, Weeks, Saxton, Hatch, Hodge, Kellow, Robertson, Beer, Jennings.
Scorers: Aldershot: Bell, Morrisey. Exeter City: Kellow, Templeman.
Attendance: 3,789

Exeter City managed to keep their promotion bid on course at the Recreation Ground, but it took an injury time goal to earn the Grecians a point. City had played the more constructive football, but it proved to be a nail biting night for them.

Twice they found themselves behind and twice they fought back. The point brought home from Aldershot mean that the Grecians have now stretched their unbeaten run to eleven games, putting them in fourth spot in the league table. Aldershot took the lead after 22 minutes. Pat Morrissey crossed and as Richard Key came for the ball it went over his head and Terry Bell stole in to score an easy goal.

Exeter equalised in the 38th minute when a cross from Alan Beer was headed home by the unmarked Tony Kellow, his 18th goal of the season.

Aldershot seemed to have got the goal that mattered in the 68th minute when after a goal kick the ball was held in the middle and Morrissey hit a 30-yard shot that streaked into the City net. Then just as it looked all over for City, Nicky Jennings took a corner kick and following a melee in front of goal, John Templeman hammered the ball home.

THURSDAY 3rd MARCH 1977

MORRIN TRANSFERRED TO COUNTY
Exeter City's transfer listed midfielder, Tony Morrin, has left the club on completing a move to Stockport County. Morrin completed the deal yesterday after travelling to Stockport for talks. A small fee will be paid by County to Exeter. This will be the second time that Morrin has played for Stockport, having appeared for them earlier in his career.

FRIDAY 4th MARCH 1977

AUSSIE BOUND
Defender Keith Clapham, who has been on the transfer list at Exeter City, has left St. James' Park for a new "life" down under. Clapham, unhappy at the lack of first team opportunities at City, has left for Australia where he hopes to resume his playing career.

SATURDAY 5th MARCH 1977

PROMOTION BATTLE ENDS ALL SQUARE
Fourth Division
Exeter City 2 Watford 2
Exeter City team: Key, Templeman, Hore, Weeks, Saxton, Hatch, Hodge, Kellow, Robertson, Beer, Jennings.
Watford team: Rankin, Geidmintis, Pritchett, Bond, Horsfield, Garner, Downes, Joslyn, Mercer, Hayes, Jenkins.
Scorers: Exeter: Beer, Kellow. Watford: Mercer, Mayes.
Attendance: 5,867.

Exeter City got off to a great start in this promotion battle. After just three minutes a long ball from John Templeman eluded the Watford defence and Alan Beer controlled it well before scoring from six-yards. Watford's tactics soon became obvious with a lot of high balls aimed at their tall striker Ross Jenkins, who laid it off to their effective forwards.

Watford equalised in the 15th minute through Keith Mercer. This followed a free-kick which had been headed on by Jenkins to Alan Mayes who crossed low into the area. Exeter were struggling at times to put their game together by the tight marking Watford side whose forwards were certainly testing the Grecians' defence.

Up front for City, Beer was having a superb game, and it was he who set up the 55th minute chance for Tony Kellow to make it 2-1. With 12 minutes left Watford equalised for a second time as the City defence seemed to freeze, the ball finding Mayes who shot wide of Richard Key into the net.

HUDDERSFIELD TOWN BID FOR LAMMIE
Exeter City have turned down a bid for transfer listed midfielder, Lammie Robertson, from Fourth Division promotion rivals, Huddersfield Town. Huddersfield's bid was not considered to be high enough and City player-manager Bobby Saxton had no hesitation in turning it down. It is believed that Exeter want around £10,000 for Robertson, who has been short listed for the player-manager vacancy at Torquay United, and is to be interviewed for the post later this week.

DOG EAT DOG STAGE OF THE SEASON
Exeter City manager Bobby Saxton has been commenting on his team's win over Halifax Town, as well as the promotion race. "I do not wish to enter into any controversy on the events surrounding our win over Halifax Town, and it is sufficient for me to say that I was very pleased with the manner in which the entire City team conducted themselves throughout the match," said Saxton.

"From the supporters point of view, it is understandable that they were not too enthusiastic about the style of football we were made to play. In circumstances like that, one has to be patient, wear the opposition down, and wait for the sort of opportunity which eventually presented itself and gave us the deciding goal."

With the Grecians very much in the promotion race, Saxton added: "We have reached the stage in the season when the dog eat dog situation will become more apparent. We have one heck of a chance of gaining promotion and in the end it will be the strength of character in teams which will be the deciding factor. You will have read in the Press that I am anxious to sign at least two players to provide the necessary cover for the important push to the end of the season, and this I shall be aiming to do with the full support of the Board of Directors."

MONDAY 7th MARCH 1977

CITY IN TALKS WITH A LOAN SIGNING
Exeter City are hoping to sign the experienced Portsmouth defender, Billy Wilson, on loan until the end of the season. Wilson is due in Exeter for talks later today, having made more than 300 appearances for Blackburn Rovers and Portsmouth.

TUESDAY 8th MARCH 1977

DEADLINE MOVES BY SAXTON
Exeter City player-manager Bobby Saxton was expecting to be involved in a hectic beat the transfer deadline talks with two players today. They are Geoff Gay, a young utility player from Bolton Wanderers, and Lee Roberts, a defender from Shrewsbury Town.

Gay was due to meet the City boss at St. James' Park this afternoon, whilst Roberts would be in talks with the City boss at an Exeter hotel this evening.

Saxton suffered a disappointment late yesterday when the experienced Portsmouth player, Billy Wilson, changed his mind about joining Exeter on loan until the end of the season. City are anxious to strengthen their playing squad by the Thursday transfer deadline to boost their hopes of promotion to the Third Division.

WEDNESDAY 9th MARCH 1977

LOAN DEALS COMPLETED
Exeter City have successfully completed two loan deals which run until the end of the season. Both Geoff Gay, from Bolton Wanderers, and Lee Roberts, from Shrewsbury Town, agreed to sign for the Grecians following talks yesterday with City player-,manager Bobby Saxton.

FRIDAY 11th MARCH 1977
GAY'S EVENTFUL DEBUT
Fourth Division
Crewe Alexandra 2 Exeter City 0
Crewe Alexandra team: Brand, Lowry, Roberts, Lugg, Bowles, Bevan (Rimmer), D.Davies, Mayman, W.Davies, Humphreys, Tully.
Exeter City team: Key (Roberts), Gay, Hore, Weeks, Saxton, Hatch, Hodge, Kellow, Robertson, Beer, Jennings.
Scorers: Crewe: Lugg, Humphreys.

Attendance: 2,500

Exeter City's new loan signing from Bolton Wanderers, Geoff Gay, will go into the record books as having one of the most remarkable Football League debuts for the club. He was booked in the 7th minute, and then played the last 33 minutes as a goalkeeper, after Richard Key had to be helped off the field with what seemed a serious right ankle injury.

With Gay taking over between the posts, City's other loan signing of the week, Lee Roberts, came on as a substitute. What a superb fight Exeter put up, and they were certainly unlucky to lose their 12-match unbeaten run. It was a tough, aggressive battle, which ended with Crewe's Kevin Tully being sent off in the closing minutes.

City produced some good build up play in the first half, and after the interval Crewe goalkeeper Drew Brand denied Exeter with some outstanding work. Crewe took the lead from the penalty spot in the 37th minute through Lugg, after Mayman had been bundled over in a ruck of City players. With Exeter going all out for the equaliser, it was Crewe who settled the issue late in the game when Humphreys netted with a shot that went in off a post.

If Exeter had taken the one or two chances that fell to them, they could well have come out of this game with at least a point.

SATURDAY 12th MARCH 1977

MASSIVE BLOW FOR CITY: KEY OUT FOR SEASON.
The promotion hopes of Exeter City received massive blow today with the news that goalkeeper Richard Key will not play again this season. After being helped off the field during the game at Crewe Alexandra, it has been revealed that Key sustained a broken right ankle.

With no other senior goalkeeper on the books, player-manager Bobby Saxton will now call on the services of student and non-contract player, John Baugh to make his debut in Tuesday night's fixture at Scunthorpe United. It will be huge step up for the St. Lukes College goalkeeper, who plays for their Western League team.

TUESDAY 15th MARCH 1977

FIRST HALF DISASTER FOR THE GRECIANS
Fourth Division
Scunthorpe United 4 Exeter City 1
Scunthorpe United team: O'Meara, Peacock, Pilling, Oates, Wiggington, Money, Czuczman, Kilmore, Keeley, Lumby, Lee.
Exeter City team: Baugh, Gay, Hore, Weeks, Saxton, Hatch, Hodge, Kellow, Robertson, Beer, Jennings.
Scorers: Scunthorpe: Lumby 2, Czuczman, Hore o.g.: Exeter: Jennings.
Attendance: 2,147.

Exeter were left in the cold in a disastrous first 30 minutes at The Old Showground as Scunthorpe United established a three-goal lead. The Grecians were at sixes and sevens, being pulled apart by the combined efforts of Kilmore and Lumby. City found themselves a goal down after just 6 minutes. Money's free-kick was chipped over John Baugh's head by Lumby.

St. Lukes College student and debutant Baugh was beaten again in the 21st minute when Czuczman's shot gave him no chance of saving. Two minutes later it got even worse. John Hore's back pass sailed over the head of Baugh who was yards off his line for an own goal.

Nicky Jennings was the one Exeter player to trouble Scunthorpe and he pulled a goal back with a cross shot in the 34th minute, as one wondered whether City would turn the game in the second half. It was the hosts turn to face the full force of a gale force wind and driving rain, but they never allowed the Grecians a chance of getting back into the game.

Certainly Exeter were far more in the game, but it was all over when Lumby scored his second goal, neatly deflecting a through pass from Czuczman. City's promotion prospects have now been dampened by two successive away defeats and much of their failure was due to their own schoolboy defensive shortcomings, and inability to control the middle of the field.

DIVISION FOUR TABLE	P	W	D	L	F	A	Pts
Cambridge United	32	16	12	4	52	25	44
Colchester United	32	20	2	10	59	29	42
Bradford City	32	16	9	7	56	40	41
Huddersfield Town	31	16	7	8	46	31	39
Barnsley	33	16	6	11	43	29	38
Doncaster Rovers	32	15	8	9	49	40	38
EXETER CITY	31	14	10	7	43	34	38
Southend United	31	11	15	5	39	24	37
Watford	31	12	12	7	43	31	36
AFC Bournemouth	33	11	13	9	41	32	35
Crewe Alexandra	31	14	7	10	34	41	35
Swansea City	30	14	5	11	54	43	33
Stockport County	31	12	9	10	36	35	33
Aldershot	31	13	7	11	38	38	33
Darlington	32	12	9	11	40	49	33
Rochdale	33	11	10	12	39	33	32
Scunthorpe United	32	10	7	15	35	45	27
Torquay United	32	11	5	16	40	52	27
Halifax Town	32	8	10	14	35	40	26
Hartlepool United	33	8	9	16	37	52	25
Brentford	32	9	4	19	49	62	22
Southport	31	1	13	17	21	55	15
Workington	32	3	9	20	26	68	15
Newport County	28	3	8	17	16	43	14

SATURDAY 19th MARCH 1977

CITY HELD BY BOURNEMOUTH
Fourth Division
Exeter City 1 AFC Bournemouth 1
Exeter City team: Baugh, Gay, Hore, Weeks, Saxton, Hatch, Hodge, Kellow, Robertson, Beer, Jennings.
AFC Bournemouth team: Baker, Butler (Rudge), Miller, Cunningham, Impey, Barton, Johnson, Cave, Howarth, Gritt, Stuckey.
Scorers: Exeter: Robertson: Bournemouth: Gritt.

Conditions at St. James' Park were atrocious, but nevertheless this was a disappointing performance by Exeter City. Had they shown the form they produced after the interval for the entire 90 minutes,
then it might well have been a different result.

The first half was as dull as the weather, but what a change in the second half as the Grecians stepped up a gear. After Bournemouth had taken the lead in the 46th minute, Exeter really came to life in the mud. It was virtually all one way traffic as they kept going forward with relentless pressure, but Bournemouth battled bravely in defence.

18-year-old debutant Steve Gritt put Bournemouth in front, but then it was all Exeter until the final whistle. They did everything but score with visiting goalkeeper Keiron Baker making some outstanding saves, in particular from Alan Beer and Bobby Hodge.

It took a piece of a sheer individual brilliance by midfielder Lammie Robertson to get that City equaliser. Showing superb skills and artistry he beat two players and then smashed a 25-yard cross shot into the far corner of the net.

FRIDAY 25th MARCH 1977

COMMERCIAL MANAGER ELECTED
Exeter City's 31-year-old Commercial Manager, Ray Ellis, who has been in that St. James' Park post for three years, has been elected as Treasurer of the Football League Commercial Manager's Association.

This is the first time that a representative from a Fourth Division club has been on their management committee, and Ellis was elected unanimously at this week's annual meeting held in Leicester.

SATURDAY 26th MARCH 1977

LONG JOURNEY NORTH IS REWARDED WITH A WIN
Fourth Division
Workington 1 Exeter City 3
Workington team: Monkhouse, Leng, Ashworth, Kavanagh, Brown, Blant, Honour, Kisby, Prudham, Coleman, Higgins (Donaghy).
Exeter City team: Baugh, Gay, Hore, Weeks, Saxton, Hatch, Hodge, Kellow, Robertson, Beer, Jennings.
Scorers: Workington: Kavanagh: Exeter: Jennings 2, Beer.
Attendance: 1,365.

Exeter City moved smoothly back into the promotion reckoning with and enthusiastic and skilful victory against re-election candidates, Workington. After the long trip up north, City dominated the play with the lively Alan Beer frequently in the picture, prompted by some clever work from Nicky Jennings.

Exeter went in front after 37 minutes. Bobby Hodge created the goal with some skilful play along the right wing and after beating a defender, he crossed low for Beer to turn the ball expertly into the net. Workington made a spirited comeback at the start of the second half, and City had to defend more than at any time in the match. Workington equalised on the hour mark when Kavanagh blasted home a superb free-kick.

Exeter regained the lead in the 67th minute when Tony Kellow centred for Jennings to side foot into the net. Kellow then had a "goal" disallowed for offside in the 81st minute, but there was no disputing Exeter's third.

Jennings lobbed the ball over a stranded Monkhouse in the 87th minute to cap a fine all round performance both from the team and himself.

SATURDAY 2nd APRIL 1977

CITY MOVE INTO FIFTH PLACE
Fourth Division
Exeter City 3 Southend United 1
Exeter City team: Baugh, Templeman, Hore, Weeks (Gay), Saxton, Hatch, Hodge, Kellow, Robertson, Beer, Jennings.
Southend United team: Freeman, Banks, Ford, Laverick, Moody, Townsend, Morris, Hadley, Parker, Clark, Goodwin.
Scorers: Exeter: Kellow, Beer, Saxton. Southend: Morris.
Attendance: 4,156.

Exeter City go into their three match Easter programme with confidence following this latest 3-1 victory, which lifted the Grecians into fifth place in the Fourth Division. Southend hardly had a chance to get into the match against an Exeter side that was by far the more determined, sharper and quicker.

The visitors can have no complaints about the outcome. A four minute spell just before half-time won the game for Exeter. Tony Kellow made the breakthrough in the 40th minute, lobbing his 20th goal of the season. The cheering had hardly stopped before Exeter struck again four minutes later, with Alan Beer calmly taking his chance for goal number 13 of his season.

City's third goal came in the 78th minute. Bobby Saxton moved up for a Nicky Jennings corner and timed his leap perfectly at the near post to score with a header. Southend, to their credit, did get a consolation for their efforts when they netted in injury time through Colin Morris.

NATIONAL SPONSORSHIP
Exeter City's commercial department has attracted sponsorship from international companies for the first time for the fixture against Southend United.

Commercial Manager Ray Ellis said: "This is the first time that Exeter City Football Club have received sponsorship from internationally known companies. It is very refreshing that we at Exeter are to the front in sponsorship, especially when we consider the importance that sponsorship will undoubtably have on football finance in the not too distant future."

"I am sure our supporters will join me in thanking Alliance, Kraft, Batchelors, Nestle and Whitworth's for their support and that they will endeavour to use their goods during the months ahead, thus making todays sponsorship beneficial to us all."

FRIDAY 8th APRIL 1977

GRECIANS START EASTER PROGRAMME IN FINE FORM
Fourth Division
Torquay United 0 Exeter City 1
Torquay United team: Robbins, Twitchin, Sandercock, Vassallo, Green, Boulton, Provan (Morrall), Lee, Rudge, Brown, Kennedy.
Exeter City team: Baugh, Templeman, Hore, Weeks, Saxton, Hatch, Hodge, Kellow, Robertson, Beer, Jennings.
Scorer: Exeter: Beer.
Attendance: 7,900

Cornish courage combined with Welsh wizardry got Exeter City the vital match winning goal at Plainmoor to give them a flying start to their Easter programme. The goal came in the 20th minute. John Baugh hit a long clearance, Tony Kellow, fearless as ever, headed on, and Alan Beer again showing his superb anticipation and speed off the mark took his chance with typical brilliance, with a close range shot when under pressure.

It was a wonderful result, if not a wonderful display by Exeter City, for they should have made the game more than safe by half-time. However, the Grecians then came under severe territorial pressure as Torquay chased an equaliser in the second half.

Torquay though, did not have enough shots at goal and now possibly face a battle against re-election. Exeter, to their credit, stuck to their task, to complete the double over their near neighbours and achieved their third successive win - two away - to make it a very Good Friday in both senses.

SATURDAY 9th APRIL 1977

HARD EARNED WIN FOR CITY
Fourth Division
Exeter City 1 Newport County 0
Exeter City team: Baugh, Templeman, Hore, Weeks, Saxton, Hatch, Hodge, Kellow, Robertson, Beer, Jennings.
Newport County team: Plumley, Derrett, Bell, Emanuel, Walker, Jones, Preece, Woods, Clark (White), Relish, Byrne.
Scorer: Exeter: Hodge.
Attendance: 5,249.

Exeter City kept their promotion hopes on track with there second victory during the Easter programme of fixtures. It was, however, tough going for the Grecians against a Newport County side who are far from as bad as their lowly position in the Fourth Division suggests.

It needed a piece of individual skill by Bobby Hodge to break the deadlock in the 65th minute, against a stubborn and hard working visiting team. Hodge raced on to a long clearance out of the City defence, and showing tremendous determination and application, scored with a strong, low shot.

EXETER CITY VICE PRESIDENTS' CLUB
Exeter City are proposing extensive alterations under the grandstand during the close season to enable them to form the first ever Exeter City Vice Presidents' Club.

"The plan involves combining the present boardroom and tea room to provide a much larger area to facilitate all the under the stand activities on a match day," explained City Commercial Manager, Ray Ellis.

"Present facilities are out of date and cramped. We anticipate that many of our supporters would like to become Vice Presidents and there will be a membership fee, probably in the region of £50, which will include a selected grandstand ticket. We have already received two applications to join and I would ask that if anyone is interested, please contact me at the *Near Post* shop."

TUESDAY 12th APRIL 1977

IT WASN'T SWEET(ZER) FOR CITY
Fourth Division
Brentford 1 Exeter City 0
Brentford team: Priddy, Fraser, Allen, Shrubb, Kruse, Graham (Bain), Johnson, Glover, McCulloch, Sweetzer, Carlton, Phillips.
Exeter City team: Baugh, Templeman, Hore, Gay, Saxton, Hatch, Hodge, Kellow, Robertson, Beer, Jordan (Roberts).
Scorers: Brentford: Sweetzer.
Attendance: 7,640.

It looked for a long time as if Exeter City were going to get a point until Brentford struck with the deciding goal 10 minutes from the end. City had battled and worked so hard, having gone into the match without two of their regular players and they probably felt they deserved something for their efforts.

Alan Beer was a lively first half raider for the Grecians, putting a 20-yard shot narrowly over the bar and having another effort smothered by Priddy. However, for the main part the first half was a battle in the midfield. Brentford tried to pressure John Baugh, but the St. Lukes College student was confident behind a defence that never gave an inch.

Brentford went at Exeter in the second half and McCulloch had the ball in the net, but the flag was already raised for offside. The killer goal was engineered by Johnson who crossed for leading scorer Sweetzer to beat the City defence with a header. It was a cruel blow for Exeter, but with a home game to come they can bounce back and continue their promotion claims.

FRIDAY 15th APRIL 1977

DIVISION FOUR TABLE (Leading Positions)							
	P	W	D	L	F	A	Pts
Cambridge United	38	21	12	5	68	31	54
Bradford City	39	21	10	8	68	45	52
Colchester United	39	20	8	11	66	37	48
Barnsley	39	20	8	11	52	31	48
EXETER CITY	38	18	11	9	53	42	47
Huddersfield Town	38	19	8	11	55	38	46
Swansea City	38	19	7	12	73	55	45
Doncaster Rovers	38	18	9	12	61	51	45
Southend United	38	14	15	9	47	33	43
Watford	39	15	13	11	57	43	43
Crewe Alexandra	39	17	9	13	42	51	43

SATURDAY 16th APRIL 1977

LATE WINNER KEEPS CITY ON TRACK
Fourth Division
Exeter City 2 Stockport County 1
Exeter City team: Baugh, Templeman, Hore, Weeks, Saxton, Hatch, Hodge, Kellow, Robertson, Beer, Jennings.
Stockport County team: Holbrook, Loadwick, Rutter, Thompson, Lennard, Fogarty, McBeth, Massey, Daniels, Morrin, Darling.
Scorers: Exeter: Robertson, Hodge: Stockport: Darling.
Attendance: 4,474.

It was not until the last ten minutes that Exeter City really got their game together, and it proved to be crucial. In that period they worried Stockport County and created two or three chances, whilst also scoring a memorable winner through Bobby Hodge.

Stockport equalised in the 77th minute, but Exeter did not let their heads drop and bounced back to score the winning goal and thus keep their promotion hopes alive. Lammie Robertson put City ahead after 37 minutes from the penalty spot, after former Grecian Tony Morrin was rather harshly adjudged to have handled the ball. Stockport equalised through Malcolm Darling, whose shot found the net despite the efforts of Bobby Saxton to clear after John Baugh had been beaten.

City's winner came in the 83rd minute. It was set up by Graham Weeks who pushed through a perfectly weighted pass to Hodge who finished it off with an explosive goal.

SAXTON: "WE HAVE IT ALL TO DO."
"With eight matches remaining including today's against Stockport County, we are well aware that we have it all to do in the League," said City player-manager Bobby Saxton.

"League positions are so tight that I do not believe anyone would be prepared to stake on the teams most likely to make the Third Division next term. I have said that we can do it - I still hold that belief. If anyone doubts that belief and suggests I will eat my words, I would remind them of an old Cornish saying – "There now, I've ate my words and I aren't no fuller."

CITY PLAYER OF THE YEAR VOTING
Today is the launch date for voting for the Exeter City Player of the Year. All supporters are eligible for one vote per person.

Members of the 'Centre Spot,' the Travelling Grecians, or season ticket holders are entitled to two votes each. Voting can be made by using the form in the match programme, or on a piece of paper and delivered to "The Near Post," 2 Blackboy Road, Exeter, to arrive no later than Saturday 21st May 1977.

The result and presentation will be made at Tiffany's on Monday 24th May at the Player of the Year Dance, which this year is being sponsored by Kentucky Fried Chicken. Dancing will be to Len Jackman - the popular radio and television star.

Tickets for the event cost £1.50p each which includes a chicken buffet and are available from "The Near Post" club shop.

TUESDAY 19th APRIL 1977

DIVISION FOUR TABLE

	P	W	D	L	F	A	Pts
Cambridge United	39	22	12	5	73	32	56
Bradford City	40	21	10	9	69	47	52
Colchester United	40	21	8	11	67	37	50
Barnsley	40	29	9	11	53	32	49
EXETER CITY	39	19	11	9	55	43	49
Swansea City	39	20	7	12	76	55	47
Huddersfield Town	39	19	8	12	55	40	46
Watford	40	16	13	11	59	43	45
Doncaster Rovers	40	18	9	13	61	52	45
Crewe Alexandra	40	8	9	13	44	52	45
Southend United	39	14	16	9	48	34	44
Darlington	40	16	11	13	52	60	43
Stockport County	40	13	14	13	48	49	40
AFC Bournemouth	40	12	15	13	46	42	39
Rochdale	40	13	11	16	44	45	37
Aldershot	39	14	9	16	43	51	37
Brentford	40	15	5	20	65	68	35
Halifax Town	40	11	10	19	43	52	32
Torquay United	40	12	8	20	48	64	32
Scunthorpe United	40	12	8	20	43	62	32
Hartlepool United	40	9	11	20	42	62	29
Newport County	37	8	9	20	29	53	25
Southport	40	3	17	20	28	66	23
Workington	39	4	10	25	34	84	18

WEDNESDAY 20th APRIL 1977

VALUABLE POINT AT THE PARK
Fourth Division
Exeter City 0 Bradford City 0
Exeter City team: Baugh, Templeman, Hore, Weeks, Saxton, Hatch, Hodge, Kellow, Robertson, Beer, Jennings.
Bradford City team: Downsborough, Middleton, Podd, Johnson, Nicholls, Fretwell, Watson, Dolan, McGinley (Raynor), Wright, Hutchins,
Attendance: 7,827.

Exeter City climbed back into the top four of the Fourth Division, a point clear of fifth placed Barnsley, and still with that game in hand on their rivals, as they continue to be involved in the tightest and toughest battle to win promotion for years. Their position would have been even stronger had they beaten Bradford City at St. James' Park, but in the end, Exeter had to settle for a goalless draw.

Somehow that crucial breakthrough eluded the Grecians, but at the final count it must be said that City wasted the chances they did have. They should have had a couple of goals at least after playing their best football for some weeks, but they failed in front of goal where both Tony Kellow and Alan Beer had good opportunities. Bradford City, for their part, would be happy with the result, for they survived almost incessant Exeter pressure in the second half.

SATURDAY 23rd APRIL 1977

TOP OF THE TABLE PERFORMANCE FROM CITY
Fourth Division.
Huddersfield Town 0 Exeter City 1
Huddersfield Town team: Starling, Sweeney, Oliver, Smith, Hart, Sidebottom, Gray, Fowler, Campbell, Johnson (McCaffery), Eccles.
Exeter City team: Baugh, Templeman, Hore, Weeks, Roberts, Hatch, Hodge, Kellow, Robertson, Beer, Jennings.
Scorer: Exeter: Hatch.
Attendance: 4,717.

Transfer-listed Lammie Robertson put Exeter City a step nearer to Division Three. He played one of the best games of his career and even received praise from the Huddersfield Town manager. However, the rest of the Exeter team were not that far behind as they turned in a top of the table performance. All that were missing were more goals to put the stamp of authority on City's richly merited win.

There were two occasions in the second half when the otherwise strong tackling defence were in trouble and Huddersfield might have snatched an undeserved equaliser.

The all important goal came on the half hour. Lee Roberts hit a long ball down the middle. Hart sliced his clearance which went straight to the unmarked Peter Hatch, who had run half the length of the field in support of his attack, and he made no mistake in firing past Starling.

After that Exeter's superior skills on and off the ball shone through. Robertson was shielding and holding the ball, and releasing time after time for the front runners to move on to, and this kept the Grecians in firm control. City's passing was a joy to watch with hardly a ball wasted all afternoon as confidence oozed throughout the team.

ATTENDANCES BOOST FOR THE GRECIANS
For the first time in several years Exeter City have been watched at home by more than 100,000 people this season, and there are still two Fourth Division fixtures left to play at St. James' Park this season.

In 21 league matches, City have attracted a total of 88,878 people, an average of 4,244 per game, and with 22,742 fans attending three Football League Cup and FA Cup ties, a total turnstile turnover has clicked up 111,620.

"At the start of the season the club stated that it need a minimum average of 4,000 attendances for home games to come out with a break even situation," said City secretary, Pat Wakeham. "At the moment we are ahead of that target and obviously that boosts our chances of coming out of the financial year with a profit. This will be a wonderful achievement after having lost more than £50,000 in the last two years" added Wakeham.

"The way we are going at the moment I think our final return will be even better than was anticipated. Figures from our monthly budget accounts show that we will be reporting an encouraging trading balance for the current financial year, whether or not we get promoted."

TUESDAY 26th APRIL 1977

CITY PROVE TOO GOOD FOR COUNTY
Fourth Division
Newport County 0 Exeter City 3
Newport County team: Plumley, Morgan, Bell, Emanuel, Walker, Murray, Preece, Woods, Clark, Relish (Williams), White.
Exeter City team: Baugh, Templeman, Hore, Weeks, Roberts, Hatch, Hodge, Kellow, Robertson, Beer, Jennings.
Scorers: Exeter: Jennings, Beer (2).
Attendance: 3,550.

With a gritty and grafting performance at Newport County, the Grecians are now poised for the final assault on the summit of promotion to the Third Division. They won this potentially and actually most difficult of matches against a side fighting for Fourth Division survival, by cool heads, constructive play and absolute application.

Exeter withstood the Newport pressure, calmly played their way out of trouble and into a position of command.

By the end City were, and deservedly so, the absolute victors. The first half though, had been a battle for control, with only a sprinkling of goalmouth action. Nicky Jennings harassed his way into getting a goal five minutes before the interval when the slow moving County defence failed to clear.

Another error in the home defence after 70 minutes was punished and led to Exeter's second goal, as Preece underhit a back pass and Alan Beer nipped in to intercept and score. Then three minutes from time the issue was put beyond doubt when a magnificent run by Bobby Hodge ended with Beer hooking a volley into the back of the net.

SATURDAY 30th APRIL 1977

PHEW! THAT WAS A BIT LATE.
Fourth Division
Exeter City 1 Darlington 0
Exeter City team: Baugh, Templeman, Hore, Weeks, Roberts, Hatch, Hodge, Kellow, Robertson, Beer, Jennings.
Darlington team: Owers. Crosson, Cochrane, Craig, Stone, Nattress, Lyons, Rowles,
Seal, Holbrook, Young.
Scorer: Exeter: Beer.
Attendance: 6,722.

Well that was close! Exeter City left it until just three minutes before the final whistle to score the only goal of the game. Alan Beer's header could prove to be the most crucial goal of the season as the Grecians edge a little closer towards the goal of promotion.

City played badly in the first half when Darlington were the better side. Exeter failed to put any meaningful moves together. They were not positive enough and so they missed out on any fluency as their passes went astray. In actual fact Darlington could have won this match, had it not been for two goal line clearances by Peter Hatch to deny them the points.

Although there was an improvement in the second half, it was not until the last 20 minutes that Exeter at last began to assert more authority. Keeper Phil Owers made a superb save from Nicky Jennings. Then with the minutes were ticking by, the third of successive corners saw Jennings float the ball across, and Alan Beer raced in to score with a superb header.

The relief was obvious to all concerned. Beer heeled away in delight and fell to his knees as he was mobbed by his colleagues. It could be the goal that takes Exeter City into Division Three.

HELP WANTED
Calling all Exeter City supporters. This summer Exeter City Football Club are embarking on two very exciting new projects. To do this they need the assistance of many supporters, both skilled and unskilled.

The projects involve the gutting of underneath the grandstand for the introduction of a Vice Presidents' Club and extensive alterations to The Centre Spot social club.

If you are a carpenter, electrician, plasterer, decorator or bricklayer - or indeed any other similar trade, and would like to help City during the summer, please contact Commercial Manager, Ray Ellis at the Near Post shop.

	£15 Boots	£10 Shirts	£5 Socks & Shorts
BOBBY SAXTON	Exeter Falcons Speedway	Exeter Falcons Speedway	Exeter Falcons Speedway
JOHN HORE	Stoneman & Bowker Ltd	Stoneman & Bowker Ltd	Stoneman & Bowker Ltd
JOHN TEMPLEMAN	Station Garage Crediton	Station Garage Crediton	Station Garage Crediton
ROY IRELAND	G.J. Bray Hongkong	G.J. Bray Hongkong	G.J. Bray Hongkong
PETER HATCH	Carrs Fish & Chips 191 Pinhoe Road Exeter 71547	Carrs Fish & Chips 191 Pinhoe Road Exeter 71547	Carrs Fish & Chips 191 Pinhoe Road Exeter 71547
PHIL HOWE	B. Lambell 10 Newhayes Close Exeter	B. Lambell 10 Newhayes Close Exeter	B. Lambell 10 Newhayes Close Exeter
KEITH FORD	Exe Vale Social Club, Exminster	Exe Vale Social Club, Exminster	Andrew Madge 9 School Rd, Exeter
GRAHAM WEEKS	Mr & Mrs E.F. Knight, 77 Water Lane, Exeter	Mr & Mrs E.F. Knight 77 Water Lane, Exeter	Mr & Mrs E.F. Knight 77 Water Lane, Exeter
BOBBY HODGE	Wheatons Staff	Wheatons Staff	Wheatons Staff
COLIN RANDELL	The International School	The International School	The International School
TONY KELLOW	B.R.S.A. South & Cornwall House Ladies University of Exeter	B.R.S.A. South & Cornwall House Ladies University of Exeter	B.R.S.A. South & Cornwall House Ladies University of Exeter
ALAN BEER	The Granville Hotel Ilfracombe	The Granville Hotel Ilfracombe	The Granville Hotel Ilfracombe
KEITH BOWKER	Forty Winks 24 Fore Street Cullompton	Forty Winks 24 Fore Street Cullompton	Forty Winks 24 Fore Street Cullompton
NICKY JENNINGS	Car Care 47-49 Albion Street Exmouth	Car Care 47-49 Albion Street Exmouth	Car Care 47-49 Albion Street Exmouth
HARRY HOLMAN	British Rail Staff Association (South)	Exeter Postmen	Gary, Mike & Andy Clyst St. Mary
PAUL SMYTHE	Dean Hunter The Tornadoes	Dean Hunter The Tornadoes	Dean Hunter The Tornadoes
LEE ROBERTS	Exmouth Round Table	Exmouth Round Table	Exmouth Round Table
JOHN BAUGH	Exeter Prison Officers	Exeter Prison Officers	Exeter Prison Officers
RICHARD KEY	Mr Rowe The Elms, Willand	Mr Rowe The Elms, Willand	Mr Rowe The Elms, Willand
JIM GILES	Graham Potbury Signs	Graham Potbury Signs	Graham Potbury Signs

NB - Vintage advert from the 1970s - do not respond!

Exeter City FC
SPONSORED BY
alliance
cash & carry
In conjunction with
KRAFT
NESTLÉ
BATCHELORS
WHITWORTHS
Saturday 2nd April 1977
3.00 p.m.
EXETER CITY
v
SOUTHEND
Fourth Division
Programme 12p
OFFICIAL PROGRAMME

Exeter City FC
Saturday 9th April 1977
3.00 p.m.
EXETER CITY
v
NEWPORT COUNTY
Fourth Division
Programme 12p

Exeter City FC
Wednesday 20th April 1977
7.30 p.m.
EXETER CITY
v
BRADFORD CITY
Fourth Division
Programme 12p
OFFICIAL PROGRAMME

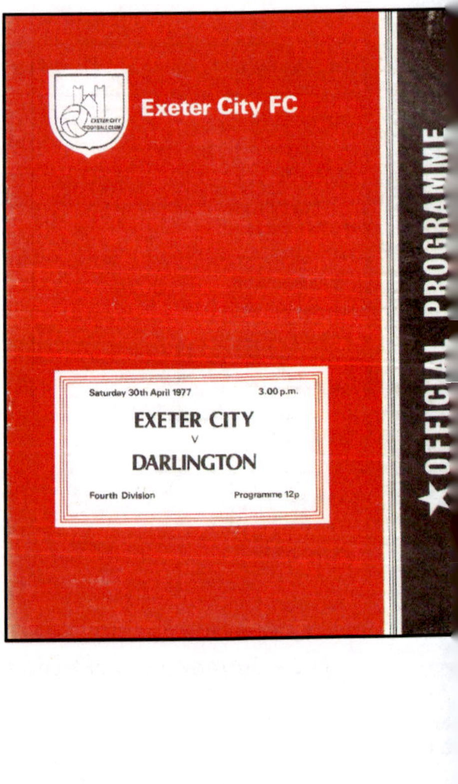
Exeter City FC
Saturday 30th April 1977
3.00 p.m.
EXETER CITY
v
DARLINGTON
Fourth Division
Programme 12p
OFFICIAL PROGRAMME

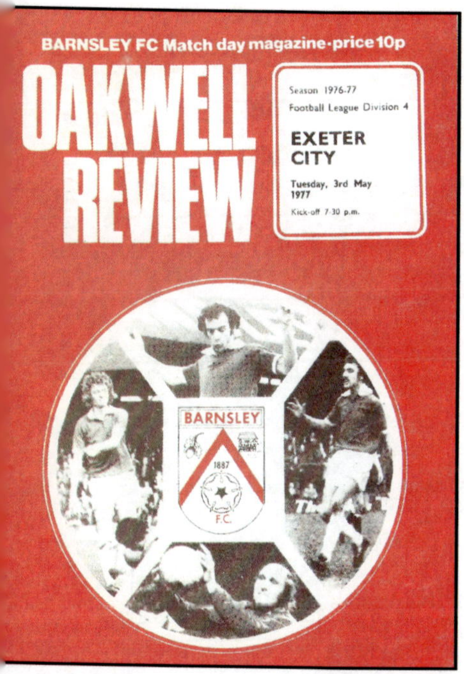
BARNSLEY FC Match day magazine-price 10p
OAKWELL REVIEW
Season 1976-77
Football League Division 4
EXETER CITY
Tuesday, 3rd May 1977
Kick-off 7-30 p.m.
BARNSLEY
1887
F.C.

DONCASTER ROVERS FC
official programme
FOOTBALL LEAGUE DIVISION 4
SEASON 1976-1977
10p
SATURDAY, 7th MAY, 1977
DONCASTER ROVERS
versus
EXETER CITY
KICK-OFF 3.00 p.m.

UDDERSFIELD TOWN
A.F.C. LTD
10p
OFFICIAL
PROGRAMME

TORQUAY UNITED A.F.C.
TORQUAY UNITED AFC
Plainmoor ground, Torquay
President: G. H. Gillin
Chairman: A. J. Boyce Vice-Chairman: M. C. Spedding
Directors: H. G. Licstone, C. W. S. Williams, J. H. Perry, Lt-Col. J. Elliott, MBE, FCIS
Secretary: D. Easton Manager: F. O'Farrell
Player-Coach: L. Chatterley Captain: C. Boulton
Commercial Manager: F. M. Easton
Pools Organiser: A. Jackson
Hon. Consultant Orthopaedic Surgeon: R. S. M. Ling
Club Physiotherapist: W. J. Wright
Hon. Medical Officers: J. C. Lindsay, MRCS, LRCP, C. D. W. Davies, MBBS, MRCS, LRCP
Programme team
Co-ordinator/Designer: N. F. Jope
Additional Material: E. Smith, G. Allman, A. Jackson, F. O'Farrell, J. Long.
Print: Torquay United F.C.
MAGAZINE 10P

City players celebrate after clinching promotion to Division Three

MONDAY 2nd MAY 1977

CITY BASE THEMSELVES IN THE DALES
A party of thirteen players left for the Derbyshire Dales today, for what is certainly going to be the most crucial week for the club for several years.

Exeter City have games at Barnsley tomorrow night and at Doncaster Rovers on Saturday afternoon.

Promotion to the Third Division hinges on the results that the City can achieve. If they win both, then promotion is a certainty.

The City party are basing themselves at the Lea Green Sports Centre, near the town of Matlock, where they will prepare for both matches.

"It is going to be a tough week," admitted player-manager Bobby Saxton. "But I am mighty confident we can do it and gain promotion."

GRECIANS RELEASE THREE PLAYERS
Despite the season still having a week to run, Exeter City have announced that they are to give free transfers to three players, and a fourth is to go on the transfer list.

Alan Hooker, Mike Jordan and Mike Green are all being "freed", whilst Lammie Robertson remains on the transfer list with City looking for a fee for the player, believed to be around £12,000.

Player-manager Bobby Saxton will therefore be left with 12 full professionals and one apprentice for next season. The City chief hopes to start the season with 18 professionals and perhaps a couple more apprentices.

Goalkeeper John Baugh who has done such an outstanding job as a stand in for the injured Richard Key, recovering from a broken ankle, has another year of studies at St Lukes College, and Saxton will be offering him terms to continue at Exeter City next season.

TUESDAY 3rd MAY 1977

YOU HAD TO BE THERE TO BELIEVE IT!
Fourth Division
Barnsley 3 Exeter City 4
Barnsley team: Springett, Murphy, Collins, Pugh, Saunders, Pickering, Felton, Joicey, Peachey, Millar, Brown.
Exeter City team: Baugh, Templeman, Hore, Weeks, Roberts, Hatch, Hodge, Kellow, Robertson, Beer, Jennings.
Scorers: Barnsley: Felton, Pickering, Joicey, Exeter: Beer (2), Kellow, Robertson.
Attendance: 5,141.

Have Exeter City ever played a game like this one? It had to be seen to be believed! For the Grecians staged one of the most remarkable comebacks ever staged in The Football League.

City were seemingly heading for a disastrous result in the first of their three match run for promotion, finding themselves 3-0 down at half-time and the odds stacked higher than a Barnsley slag heap. But no one could have forseen what would happen in the final 28 minutes of the game as Exeter staged a spectacular comeback to score four times and win the match.

Barnsley scored their first goal in the 32nd minute when Graham Felton's 20-yard shot appeared to take a deflection on its way into the net. Two minutes later Exeter conceded another goal. Pickering striking a first time shot past John Baugh. Worse was to follow, two minutes before the interval. While the linesman was flagging for offside, Baugh rolled the ball out assuming there was going to be a free-kick, but the referee did not agree, and Joicey promptly hammered the ball back into the net, much to the consternation of the City team.

The Grecians' transformation began in the 62nd minute with Alan Beer heading past Springett to make it 3-1. A corner in the 75th minute resulted in Lee Roberts putting in a header that bounced off the bar, and Tony Kellow was on the spot to nod it in. Two minutes later Exeter equalised from the penalty spot through Lammie Robertson after Bobby Hodge had been brought down.

Then with just six minutes remaining the unbelievable happened. Beer headed in the winner to make it a night to remember for all time.

THURSDAY 5th MAY 1977

GAY RETURNS TO BOLTON
Geoff Gay's loan period at Exeter City has ended, and he has now returned to Bolton Wanderers.

City's other loan player, Lee Roberts, is due to go back to Shrewsbury Town this coming Saturday, but player-manager Bobby Saxton is considering asking the Shrews if Roberts can stay and play in the final match of the season against Aldershot at St. James' Park.

FRIDAY 6th MAY 1977

NO FAVOURS FROM DONCASTER ROVERS
Doncaster Rovers manager Stan Anderson has said that he wants to see Exeter City going home pointless from their game at Belle Vue tomorrow.

"It now looks as if the promotion struggle rests with either Exeter or Swansea for the fourth spot," said Anderson. "In our last home match before the close of the season I hope we won't be doing Exeter any favours".

"It gives us the opportunity to achieve the double over them and I am confident that we can do it.
Whether Exeter achieve their goal this season will rest on tomorrow's result, one cannot be sure, but I want to see them going home pointless."

DIVISION FOUR TABLE (Leading Places)							
	P	W	D	L	F	A	Pts
Cambridge United	43	25	12	6	82	36	62
EXETER CITY	44	23	12	9	64	46	58
Colchester United	44	24	9	11	75	40	57
Swansea City	44	24	8	12	88	62	56
Bradford City	43	22	12	9	62	48	56
Barnsley	44	21	9	14	58	39	51

SATURDAY 7th MAY 1977

CITY WIN PROMOTION!
Fourth Division
Doncaster Rovers 0 Exeter City 3
Doncaster Rovers team: Peacock, Olney, Reed,
Robinson, Brookes, Taylor, Miller, Murray (Snodin), O'Callaghan, McConville, Laidlaw.
Exeter City team: Baugh, Templeman, Hore, Weeks, Roberts, Hatch, Hodge, Kellow, Robertson, Beer, Jennings.
Scorers: Exeter City: Beer 92), Kellow.
Attendance: 3,447.

EXETER CITY ARE PROMOTED! Without a doubt the Grecians' outstanding away form eventually tipped the scales in this truly memorable season. It was therefore perhaps appropriate that promotion to the Third Division as clinched with yet another away victory.

Exeter completely outplayed Doncaster, especially in the first half when their performance was outstanding. Although Doncaster came a little more into the game after the interval, Exeter had by then taken a 3-0 lead, and were never in any danger of missing out on their biggest occasion for 13 years.

City took a 13th minute lead when a long ball from John Hore exposed the Doncaster defence and Alan Beer moved in to take his chance well as he hooked a shot into the top corner of the net. It was 2-0 after 34 minutes and this time Beer was the architect as he brilliantly turned his marker and crossed for Tony Kellow to pounce at the far post with a header.

It was all over a minute later for Doncaster, when the ball was fed through for Beer to score with a perfectly placed shot.

The large contingent of Exeter City supporters couldn't wait for the final whistle as they chanted: "We are going up!" More than 500 of them swarmed onto the pitch at the end making their way towards the players' tunnel. Goalkeeper John Baugh was triumphantly chaired off the pitch.

The City team re-emerged from the dressing room and acknowledged the cheers of their supporters, as many of the players were lost for words in their finest hour. Before the coaches set off back to Devon, City director Wally Rice boarded each one to thank the supporters for being part of one of the most memorable days in the history of the club.

MONDAY 9th MAY 1977

CONGRATULATIONS POUR IN.
When Exeter City player-manager Bobby Saxton returned to his St James' Park desk this morning his first job was to open the telegrams and letters of congratulation from jubilant City supporters now that the club is back in the Third Division.

Saxton and his triumphant team were away all last week at the Lea Green Sports Centre in the Derbyshire Dales to prepare for games at Barnsley and Doncaster Rovers, and two outstanding wins that clinched promotion for the first time in thirteen years. It was ironic that Saxton should clinch promotion in his native Yorkshire. He was born at Balby, only a short goal kick from the Doncaster ground where Exeter won 3-0 on Saturday.

Saxton stood on the Belle Vue ground terraces as an 8-year-old. Now at 33 his childhood dreams have become reality, not only to be a player and a manager, but to be in charge of a promotion winning team. More than 500 Exeter supporters were at Saturday's match and when the team arrived back at St. James' Park in the early hours of yesterday morning about 1,000 fans were waiting to honour their heroes.

WEDNESDAY 11th MAY 1977

ALAN BEER IN WALES SQUAD
20-goal striker Alan Beer, whose goals have helped Exeter City into the Third Division for the first time in thirteen years, is on the verge of a full Welsh international cap. Beer has been picked as one one of the 24 Welsh strong squad for the coming Home International series of matches. Wales team manager Mike Smith has been charting the progress of the City player in recent weeks and has now called him into the full international squad.

THURSDAY 12th MAY 1977

IMPORTANT TO FINISH IN STYLE SAYS SAXTON
Although Exeter City have achieved their major aim of promotion, player-manager Bobby Saxton stressed the importance of finishing off the job in the final game of the season against Aldershot at St. James' Park on Saturday.

"Obviously most of the pressure is now off having clinched promotion," said Saxton. "Even so, we will be playing in front of our own crowd and we must show them that we have plenty to offer in the Third Division next season."

Exeter City's celebrations will start after the game. The players will pop the champagne corks in the dressing room, and there will also be champagne for the Aldershot team. Two hours later the Exeter City team will set off on their ride through the city centre in an open top bus, on their way to a reception at the Guildhall, hosted by the Mayor of Exeter. The bus will leave St James' Park at 6.50pm.

In addition, the City Board of Directors are to arrange a private celebration party for the players, their wives, and all the staff at St James' Park to honour promotion.

All the players will be presented with special silver commemorative medallions.

FRIDAY 13th MAY 1977

GRECIANS TO PLAY AT EXMOUTH TOWN
Exeter City's Division Four promotion side are to play Western League, Exmouth Town in a special benefit match. The

fixture will be staged next Friday with a 7pm kick off.

All the proceeds will be donated towards funds which are being raised to help the family of John "Paddy" Gibbons, the Exmouth betting office manager who was found dead at the bookmakers premises on 28th January.

"I want to thank the Exeter City player-manager Bobby Saxton for agreeing to send his full League side to Exmouth," said Exmouth town manager Terry Parsons. "Obviously we are delighted to have been able to arrange this game. We will make every effort to give the City side a good run and the event will also provide a special occasion for local people who have been unable to watch City play during their great run to the Third Division."

SATURDAY 14th MAY 1977

CITY ROUND SEASON OFF IN STYLE
Fourth Division
Exeter City 3 Aldershot 0
Exeter City team: Baugh, Templeman, Hore, Weeks, Saxton, Hatch, Hodge, Kellow, Robertson, Beer, Jennings.
Aldershot team: Rockett, Howitt, Wooler, Crosby, Youlden, Jopling, Hilton, Brodie, Bell, Earls, McGregor (Bainbridge).
Scorers: Exeter City: Hodge, Beer, Jennings.
Attendance: 10,751

Exeter City completed their programme of league matches by registering another win, this time against Aldershot. The game was almost an after thought as euphoria of promotion gripped the City supporters. The Aldershot players formed a guard of honour and sportingly clapped the Exeter team onto the pitch.

The Grecians turned on the style for the 90 minutes and it has to be said there really was only ever going to be one result as goals from Bobby Hodge, Alan Beer and Nicky Jennings gave them a 3-0 victory. On each occasion they scored the pitch was invaded by ecstatic Exeter fans. It was all good humoured stuff though and they quickly went back to their places. Prior to the final whistle hundreds of them lined the running track in front of the Cowshed terracing, and at the final whistle the pitch was once again invaded, this time by many more fans who vaulted over the fences.

Match referee Alex Lees had given the quietest peeps on his whistle to bring the game to an end and this allowed most of the players to quickly dash to the safety of the tunnel before they were enveloped by the fans.

Minutes later the players reappeared in the Directors Box to acknowledge the tributes from their supporters. Then it was back to the dressing room for the start of the champagne celebrations to mark one of the most successful moments in the history of the club.

Chairman Gerald Vallance summed things up by saying: "It has been a wonderful day. I hope we can repeat it next season."

CELEBRATION TIME IN THE CITY OF EXETER
One of the most moving and emotional days in the history of Exeter City Football Club ended in a colourful and carnival style. More than 2,000 supporters were outside the Exeter Guildhall in the High Street to greet the players before the reception by the Mayor of Exeter, John Landers.

Hundreds of them ran behind the open top bus that carried the players, their wives and club officials though the city centre. The noise was deafening as the cheering and chanting continued. When the players arrived they went onto the Guildhall balcony to wave to their supporters.

The cheers must have been heard all over Exeter as the chants rang out – "We want Saxton."

Many of the fans waited outside the Guildhall while the hour long reception continued. When the players reappeared the fans roared: "We will be playing Plymouth in the Third."

In the euphoria of the hour one important man behind Exeter City's success was not forgotten.

John Newman who built up what has turned out to be a promotion winning team before he departed for Grimsby Town earlier this year. He arrived in Exeter on Saturday evening after watching Grimsby lose at Reading, a defeat that ironically sent them crashing down to the Fourth Division.

WONDERFUL ACHIEVEMENT SAYS CITY CHAIRMAN
The Exeter City players will be sharing something in the region of £6,000 for winning promotion to the Third Division. That is the bonus earned by the players.

"It is the best money we have ever spent," said City chairman, Gerald Vallance. "I am absolutely delighted that we have won promotion. I have always said that we can afford it. I feel it is a wonderful achievement considering the small staff that we have had to work with."

"On behalf of the Board of Directors I would like to congratulate everyone who has been involved in this splendid effort. I have never been with a promotion team before and I must admit I feel a little shell shocked. This is a new era and a new challenge for the club and we must, and will face it. I would also like to place on record our thanks to John Newman for what he did for the club. he was well liked and admired at Exeter. All this of course in no way detracts from the marvelous impetus and drive that Bobby Saxton has given the team in the comparatively short time he has been in charge."

WHAT THE PLAYERS SAID
John Hore, Exeter City's 30-year-old captain said: "This is my second promotion season, having gone up with Plymouth Argyle. That was marvellous, but I rate the Exeter success as an even greater achievement considering the small squad we have. It is a fantastic achievement."

Winger Nicky Jennings added: "I thought we would achieve promotion, but this is better than I expected."

Alan Beer, whose goals have played a big part in the season said: "We have been magic. This is something I dreamed of."

Loan signing Lee Roberts said: "From playing in Shrewsbury Town's reserves and now being in a promotion side after playing so few games is unbelievable. Shrewsbury are retaining me as a player, but I would love to come back to Exeter City."

SUNDAY 15th MAY 1977

NO STOPPING THE CITY FANS
The South West belonged to Exeter City yesterday when their loyal band of supporters who had followed Bobby Saxton's team through thick and thin surged down to St. James' Park determined to have their day. Hours before the last match of the season that took Exeter City back to the Third Division for the first time in 13 years, bands of red-scarved fans chanted in the streets and waved banners.

The day was shared by the extra 6,000 people who discovered old loyalties and dusted off their rosettes to swell the crowd to 10,750 - the largest for a league game for quite some years. Throughout the match St. James' Park was alive with tingling electricity that craved the final whistle to signal the start of the celebrations.

Three times during the game the sea of red and white rehearsed their full-time pitch invasion by surging on to celebrate the three City goals. The referee was equal to them though. With a quiet peep of his whistle at the end of 90 minutes he rushed, along with the players, off the field before the crowd realised that the game was over.

Asking the fans not to invade the pitch would have been like trying to put a cork back in a champagne bottle. Bobby Saxton and his players, champagne and lager in their hands, received their tribute from the safety of the directors box. As the jubilant Exeter City fans claimed their own moment of glory, the team returned to the dressing room.

With the chants beginning to die away, City player-manager Bobby Saxton said: "Reaction from the fans and the people of Exeter have been marvellous. To be quite truthful I am not surprised that we have done it. When I took over I could see that we would have a chance of doing something this season, and I always thought we were good enough to go up. Even so, I cannot believe it. This is fairy tale that has meant a lot of hard work and dedication by everyone."

MONDAY 16th MAY 1977

REVIEW OF CITY'S SEASON
At the start of the 1976-77 season Exeter City were made one of the favourites by the bookmakers to win promotion from Division Four. City were always thereabouts from the time they started the season in temperatures that at one time reached the nineties. The heat was on but Exeter were always among the pack. As the season progressed, so it became clear that this was going to be one of the toughest fights for years to get out of the Fourth Division.

When the speculation that manager John Newman was off to Grimsby Town was confirmed, he left behind a team nicely poised in the table. Newman had maintained all along that this was going to be Exeter City's year and the players could not have given him a better send off than that 3-0 win over Torquay United on Boxing Day. There were presentations, handshakes and good luck messages, and for sure, a big lump in Newman's throat as he left the dressing room for the last time.

Bobby Saxton made a dream start with a home victory followed by draws at Bradford City and Cambridge United in successive weeks. The contest was becoming gripping. The tension was mounting and suddenly Exeter found themselves struck down with even more injury problems.

The outstanding Richard Key broke his ankle at Crewe Alexandra, and Saxton moved in to sign St Lukes College student, 20-year-old John Baugh. What an ordeal. Here was a side running for promotion without their first choice goalkeeper. It was asking a deal of courage and determination as the City squad was reduced to thirteen players, which included loan signings Lee Roberts and Geoff Gay.

Exeter though, never knew when they were beaten. Several times they struggled in front of their own supporters, but they looked an entirely different team when playing away. As the pressure and tension became even greater, Exeter gritted their teeth and buckled down to their job. They could not afford any slips as anyone of the eight clubs were in with a chance of promotion.

The win at Workington on 26th March proved to be a crucial milestone for Exeter City, because since then they have had an amazing run of ten wins and a draw, and only one defeat, in 12 games. That Tuesday night in Barnsley which saw the City stage a remarkable fightback to win meant that promotion crept even closer. Yet Exeter, if they were to make absolutely sure themselves, had to take three points from their last two games.

Swansea City were the big threat and of course there was Exeter's inferior goal difference. Then came the win at Doncaster, Swansea beaten at home and Colchester away, with Exeter completing their own task in style as they won away yet again.

EXETER FALCONS TO RECIPROCATE
Exeter City have been offered the freedom of the Exeter County Ground speedway facilities to fulfil a three year promise. Wally Mawdsley, the Exeter Falcons co-promoter said in 1974 that the football club invited his championship winning team to parade before one of the matches at St. James' Park, and at the time he said that if City achieved promotion they would return the compliment.

This they will do next Monday when the Falcons host King's Lynn at the County Ground, and all the City squad are looking forward to it.

TUESDAY 17th MAY 1977

CHAIRMAN DETERMINED TO STAY IN THE THIRD DIVISION
Exeter City chairman Gerald Vallance is determined that his newly promoted club will stay in the Third Division and that history will not repeat itself. The last occasion the Grecians were promoted to the Third Division, they only had two seasons at the higher level before being relegated again.

"I want to stay in the Third Division and to be battling away to reach the Second Division," said Vallance. "I think the club itself will benefit from being in Division Three providing we do not increase our costs too much. The Board of Directors will find the money for team strengthening if it is needed. I would have liked to have won the league, and I believe we would have done it had it not been for the injury problems."

BEER PLAYS FOR INTERNATIONAL XI
Exeter City striker Alan Beer will be playing in a special testimonial match at Wrexham next Tuesday as part of a dress rehearsal for Wales before the Home International series of matches.

He will line up for Mike Smith's International XI against a Micky Evans Testimonial XI, having already been included in the full Wales squad for the British Championships. Welsh team manager Mike Smith explained that the match would an ideal opportunity for Beer to get to know the international set up.

WEDNESDAY 18th MAY 1977

THREE FOR BEER
Ian Pope Benefit Match
Barnstaple Town 2 Exeter City 3
Exeter scorer: Beer (3).
Alan Beer celebrated his call up into the full Wales international squad with a fine hat-trick at Barnstaple Town in a Benefit match for the club's long serving player, Ian Pope.

Earlier in the day the Exeter City squad were guests of an Ilfracombe hotel where they had lunch. They then made a meet the public tour of the town.

THURSDAY 19th MAY 1977

DARKE TURNS DOWN CITY OFFER
Plymouth Argyle central defender, Peter Darke, has turned down a move to Exeter City. He had been released by Argyle on a free transfer. Darke had talks with City player-manager Bobby Saxton, but was unable to agree terms and is now tipped to be joining Torquay United. Darke was well known to Saxton, having spent a loan period with the Grecians during the season just ended.

FRIDAY 20th MAY 1977

GRECIANS WIN MEMORIAL MATCH
Paddy Gibbons Memorial Match
Exmouth Town 1 Exeter City 3
Exmouth Town team: Trump, Baulch, Hartnell, Thomas, Parson, M.Wilson, I.Wilson, Dunn, Hitchcock, Gibson, Morris.
Exeter City team; Key, Templeman, Hore, Hodge, Ford, Hooker, Weeks, Beer, Kellow, Hatch, Jennings. Sub also used: Green.
Est. Attendance: 1,000

Exeter City helped raise over £200 towards a memorial fund for the family of the late Exmouth betting shop manager, Paddy Gibbons. Exmouth took a first half lead with a 5th minute goal from guest player, and former Scottish international and City favourite, Dave Gibson. Gibson headed home a well placed cross from Joe Dunn. He had been joined in the Exmouth team by another former City player as a guest, Steve Morris.

Exeter had three efforts cleared off the line before half-time, but it was not until the 50th minute that a shot from Bobby Hodge was helped into his own net by Exmouth defender Billy Baulch. Alan Beer put City in front five minutes later when he ran onto a long ball from Peter Hatch. Substitute Mike Green sealed the match for Exeter in the 75th minute with a scorching shot that gave goalkeeper Allen Trump no chance.

ALLDER SAYS NO TO CITY
Orient winger Doug Allder has turned down the chance of a move to Exeter City because he does not want to leave the London area. Allder, available on a free transfer, had talks with City player-manager Bobby Saxton, but he prefers to try and get a club nearer home.

It is reported that Saxton is due to speak to another London-based player today. He is with a Second Division club and is described as a utility forward.

TUESDAY 24th MAY 1977

CITY PLAYER AWARDS
For the second successive season, Peter Hatch, has become Exeter City Player of the Year. He received his award at last night's Player of the Year dance held by the Exeter City Supporters Association. The trophy was presented to him by John Newman, who left Exeter to manage Grimsby Town at the end of December.

Newman had made a special trip back to the club for the presentations which were attended by around 500 people.

Amateur Player of the Year went to 20-year-old Keith Ford, who has had another outstanding season in Exeter City's Western League side, and it came after City player-manager Bobby Saxton announced that Ford had been offered a full professional contract for next season. Stafford Spurway from Willand, completed the double by being named Exeter City Supporter of the Season for the second successive year.

The Commercial Manager awards went to Bernard Lambell, Richard Knight and Dave Bright.

WEDNESDAY 25th MAY 1977

CITY KEEPER ASKS FOR TRANSFER
Exeter City have been shocked by a transfer request from goalkeeper Richard Key, who was first choice until sustaining a broken ankle in the match at Crewe Alexandra. Key who missed all the promotion run-in matches, is unhappy with the terms being offered to him for next season.

Since his injury his place between the posts has been taken by St. Lukes College student, John Baugh. Player-Manager Bobby Saxton said rather ominously: "There are no shortage of goalkeepers to sign."

THURSDAY 26th MAY 1977

KEY TRANSFER REQUEST GRANTED
The Exeter City Board of Directors have granted Richard Key's transfer request. It is no secret that several clubs were watching Key until his injury that forced him to miss the last few matches.

Those clubs believed to be interested include Cardiff City, Fulham, Tottenham Hotspur, West Bromwich Albion and West Ham United. It is reported that Exeter will be seeking a fee for Key, of between £15,000 and £20,000.

CITY MAKE OFFER TO ARGYLE MIDFIELDER
City player-manager Bobby Saxton had been hoping to sign Plymouth Argyle midfielder Colin Randell. However, with everything seemingly agreed, the player telephoned to say that he had now changed his mind and would not be coming to St. James' Park.

FRIDAY 27th May 1977

SCUNTHORPE BID FOR ROBERTSON
Exeter City have turned down a £5,000 bid from Scunthorpe United for transfer listed Lammie Robertson. The Grecians have told Scunthorpe that their offer is nowhere high enough. It is believed they are seeking at least £15,000 for the player. Rochdale have also made enquiries for the City midfielder, but no bid has been forthcoming as yet.

DORCHESTER TO SIGN TWO?
Two City players, Mike Green and Alan Hooker, who were released at the end of last season are considering an offer to join Southern League Dorchester Town.

THURSDAY 2nd JUNE 1977

TWO APPRENTICES SIGNED
Exeter City have signed two new apprentice professionals. Both are Exeter-born, Roy Ireland and Paul Smythe, who were two of the outstanding prospects in the Grecians' youth team last season.

WEDNESDAY 8th JUNE 1977

RANDELL DEAL BACK ON?
Negotiations have reopened between Exeter City and Plymouth Argyle for 24-year-old midfielder, Colon Randell. The player had originally agreed to join Exeter earlier this year, but then had a sudden change of mind. Two other clubs are interested in signing Randell, including Swansea City who have offered £5,000 for the player.

TUESDAY 28th JUNE 1977

PETERBOROUGH WANT LAMMIE
Exeter City's transfer listed midfielder, Lammie Robertson, is wanted by Peterborough United. There have been initial talks between the two clubs, although nothing can be finalised until Posh manager John Barnwell returns from holiday.

City player-manager Bobby Saxton said: "Peterborough United are very interested and we have had long talks about the transfer fee. If we agree terms, then Robertson is prepared to have talks with Peterborough to discuss a possible move."

TUESDAY 12th JULY 1977

CITY BID TURNED DOWN
Exeter City's bid to sign another Cornishman to play alongside Tony Kellow has fallen through. City had hoped to sign Falmouth Town striker Joe Scott, but the Western League club have turned down an offer made by the Grecians. Falmouth Town manager Richard Gray said he could not see his way clear to releasing Scott, who topped the Cornish club's goalscoring charts last season, because it would be a big blow to both the club and its supporters.

WEDNESDAY 12th JULY 1977

LEE ROBERTS: FEE TOO HIGH
As the Exeter City players reported back to St. James' Park today to begin pre-season training, player-manager Bobby Saxton said that he had failed in his bid to sign Lee Roberts from Shrewsbury Town. Roberts had a successful loan spell at the end of last season with City, when he played in the promotion run in. The fee wanted by Shrewsbury, who are reluctant to release the player, is too high and City are not increasing their offer

THURSDAY 14th JULY 1977

KEITH BOWKER COULD RETURN TO THE PARK
Exeter City are hoping to bring Keith Bowker back to St. James' Park. City player-manager Bobby Saxton has held talks with the player who is available on a free transfer from Cambridge United.

Saxton is hopeful of signing the player over the weekend, as Bowker is keen to move back to Exeter, having left the Grecians for Cambridge United in May 1976 for a fee of £8,000. Bowker has, however, failed to command a regular place in the Cambridge first team since he arrived at the Abbey Stadium. He originally joined Exeter from Birmingham City three season ago, when the Grecians paid £7,000 for his signature.

ANOTHER ATTEMPT TO SIGN SCOTT
The Grecians have been in contact again with Falmouth Town in another attempt to sign prolific goalscorer Joe Scott. Falmouth have quoted a fee of £5,000 for the player, but Exeter are not prepared to pay that much for someone who has not proved himself at Football League level.

NO GO GOLDTHORPE
Exeter City have enquired after centre-half Bob Goldthorpe, the former Crystal Palace and Charlton Athletic player. Goldthorpe though, has now taken a job outside of football and has turned down the chance to return to full time football with City.

TUESDAY 19th JULY 1972

HOW MUCH!!
Exeter City received a rude shock when they asked Colchester United they wanted for their central defender, Lindsay Smith. Colchester quoted a staggering £80,000 for the player. Needless to say that was the end of any possible deal!

WEDNESDAY 20th JULY 1977

SHREWS TURN DOWN CITY OFFER
Exeter City have had a £5,000 bid for central defender Lee Roberts turned down by Shrewsbury Town, who value the player at £8,000. It is the second time in a week that City player-manager Bobby Saxton has had an offer for the player turned down by Shrewsbury.

FRIDAY 22nd JULY 1977

SAFETY WORK AT ST. JAMES' PARK
Exeter City are not leaving anything to chance when it comes to crowd safety at St. James' Park as the club prepares for a new era of Third Division football. Four new crush barriers have been built in the Cowshed for crowd safety purposes.

"We have had talks with the Police about this section of the ground and we agreed that safety improvements were needed," said City secretary, Pat Wakeham. "We recognise that certain improvements had to be made and these will eventually become automatic following the Government's recommendations about safety policy at all grounds."

SATURDAY 30th July 1977

NORWICH CITY HIT FOR FIVE!
Pre-Season Friendly
Exeter City 5 Norwich City 0
Exeter City team: Baugh, Templeman, Hore, Weeks, Saxton , Hatch (Ford), Hodge, Kellow, Robertson, Beer, Jennings.
Norwich City team: Hansbury, Ryan, Sullivan, Fowler, Jones, Powell, Neighbour, Reeves, Busby, Suggett, Peters.
Scorers: Exeter: Weeks, Beer, Jennings, Kellow, Templeman.
Attendance: 1,912

Everything went right for Exeter City. They were three goals up in an hour against their First Division visitors and from then until the end dictated the game. The opening half was typical pre-season fare, until City went ahead through Graham Weeks after 23 minutes.

For Norwich the beginning of the end came in the 55th minute when Alan Beer slammed home a tap back from Lammie Robertson. City lifted their game and on the hour Nicky Jennings scored a third goal as the Grecians began to dominate the match. Tony Kellow had a rasping shot blocked by Roger Hansbury and the rebound fell to Beer. Hansbury again saved, but Jennings followed up to make no mistake. Worse was to follow for Norwich as Kellow made it 4-0 to Exeter after 70 minutes and John Templeman added a fifth five minutes later.

With time running out Jennings might have had his second, but his shot was saved by Hansbury. Nothing that Norwich did went right for them. At the back Exeter made no mistakes and the chances that came to the visitors were few and far between. Their best efforts fell to Viv Busby and John Ryan, but John Baugh, the City keeper, saved from both.

There was no doubt that Exeter were the superior team. Even in the first half, when things were fairly slack, they showed slightly more enterprising play and could have been a goal up through Weeks after just three minutes. Norwich too, had their chances early on. Two openings fell to Martin Peters, while Martin Fowler had a chance just before the interval, but his low bouncing shot lacked power and went wide.

SUNDAY 31st JULY 1977

ADMISSION PRICES ANNOUNCED
Admission prices for the forthcoming 1977-78 Third Division season at St. James' Park have been announced. They will be as follows:- Grandstand £1.50p; Ground 80p; Senior citizens and juveniles ground price will be 50p.

For reserve team Western League fixtures, the grandstand admission price will be 25p, with senior citizens and juveniles paying 15p.

TUESDAY 2nd AUGUST 1977

CITY DEFENCE LEFT IN TATTERS
Friendly
Exeter City 1 Sheffield United 4
Exeter City team: Key, Templeman, Hore, Weeks, Ford, Hatch, Hodge, Kellow, Bowker, Holman, Jennings.
Sheffield United team: Not known.
Scorers`; Exeter: Holman; Sheffield United: Campbell (2), Edwards, Hamilton.
Attendance: 1,498

Exeter City were given a sharp lesson of what it will be like to face teams at the top end of the Third Division. The Grecians contributed to their own downfall, in complete contrast to their performance against Norwich City.

At times their passing was slap happy and careless. On the other hand chances were created to have at least given them a more favourable look to the scoreline, but the reflexes up front need more fine tuning. Bobby Campbell gave Sheffield United the lead in the 8th minute with a simple goal from an unmarked position on the edge of the six-yard area, following a cross from Hamilton.

The same two players gave United a virtual carbon copy repeat for their sides' final goal of the match three minutes from time. City equalised in the 15th minute when a cross by John Templeman to Tony Kellow as headed down to Graham Weeks, whose shot was parried by the keeper, but Harry Holman was on hand to crash the ball home from 15-

yards. Edwards put United back in front after 37 minutes and Hamilton made it 3-1 in the 43rd minute, when intercepting bad pass from Weeks.

FRIDAY 5th AUGUST 1977

THIS WAS EMBARRASSING!
Friendly
Exeter City 1 Minehead 4
Exeter City team: Baugh (Key), Templeman, Hore, Hatch, Ford, Hodge, Robertson, Weeks, Holman, Beer, Jennings.
Minehead team: Not known.
Scorers: Exeter: Beer. Minehead: Jenkins (2), Bryant, Leitch.
Attendance: Not known.

Exeter City foundered then sank against the Southern League part-timers from Minehead. It was a complete night of misery for City. To make matters worse, if they could be, City had Lammie Robertson sent off after an incident with Brian Durbin, after being tackled in the 75th minute.

Quite frankly, Exeter were a shambles. They were outplayed at times by Minehead and found themselves embarrassingly 4-1 down after 62 minutes. The game itself tended to be over physical at times, but City obviously decided that all they had to do was to stroll through the match and they would be sure to win. How wrong that proved to be.

Minehead adopted a completely different approach to Exeter, for they had the will to win, with striker Jim Jenkins proving to be a real handful for the Exeter defence. He scored in the 16th minute, beating John Hore for speed, and firing home from 20-yards to give his side the lead.

Seven minutes later Jenkins made no mistake again with an opportunist goal to put Minehead in the driving seat.

City did pull a goal back in the 25th minute when Alan Beer scored, but Minehead went onto net in the 55th minute through Derek Bryant. Andy Leitch wrapped things up for the visitors in the 62nd minute, after Richard Key, not for the first time in the match, fumbled the ball.

SUNDAY 7th AUGUST 1977

A TESTING SEASON FOR THE GRECIANS
Exeter City's "best in the west" claim will be put to the test this season. Even they were saddened when neighbours Plymouth Argyle dropped down from the Second Division last season. Yet inwardly they know that facing the Home Park club gives them the ideal opportunity to back up their claim to be the Division's number one side.

Last season's success when City finished as runners-up in the Fourth Division to Cambridge United, provides Exeter with their first sample of higher grade football for 13-years. All those years ago, the side was in the process of growing up together, and lacked the know how to cling to their hard fought status, but the same cannot be said of the present team, for on the evidence of last season, they are just about ready to move into their prime.

THURSDAY 11th AUGUST 1977

ROBERTSON FEE TOO MUCH FOR NORWICH
The Norwich City directors have vetoed an attempt by their manager John Bond to spend £8,000 to sign Exeter City's transfer listed midfielder, Lammie Robertson. Bond intended to complete the deal today, but the financial position at the Carrow Road club has not made it possible.

Robertson had been extremely impressive in the recent friendly fixture between the two clubs at St. James' Park. That prompted Bond to make his move to sign the player. and Exeter would have been prepared to have transferred him had Norwich met their £8,000 valuation.

FRIDAY 12th AUGUST 1977

RED CARPET FOR DEVON DERBY
Exeter City and Plymouth Argyle will get the red carpet treatment when they run onto the St James' Park pitch tomorrow. They will run along a red carpet laid courtesy of the match sponsors, John Holt Carpets of Exeter. A familiar

former Exeter City player will be present, Jimmy Blain, who now works for the sponsors.

SAXTON: HARD WORK AND THE DEVON DERBY
Exeter City player-manager has been speaking about the season ahead and tomorrow's Devon derby in The Football League Cup.

"It seems no time since we were all celebrating together our promotion to the Third Division," he said. "And whilst the pleasantries were most enjoyable, it soon became clear that a lot of hard work and dedication would be required to establish ourselves in the higher, and what is going to be a very tough division."

Commenting on the eagerly awaited League Cup tie with Argyle, Saxton added: "Local derbies are by tradition exciting affairs and I know that both sides will play with a flair and imagination to prove to the west country that football is alive and well.

"I hope supproters will contribute to the occasion with good behaviour so that at the end of the day everyone leaves St. James' Park happy in the hope that the excitement spills over to the second leg at Plymouth on Tuesday."

SATURDAY 13th AUGUST 1977

FOUR PENALTIES IN DERBY CUP TIE
Football League Cup: Round One: 1st Leg
Exeter City 2 Plymouth Argyle 2
Exeter City team: Baugh, Templeman, Hore, Weeks, Saxton, Hatch, Hodge, Kellow, Robertson, Beer, Jennings.
Plymouth Argyle team: Barron, Smart, Uzzell, Horswill, Foster, Craven, Delve, Johnson (Sutton), Austin, Trusson, Rogers.
Scorers: Exeter: Robertson (2); Plymouth: Trusson (2).
Attendance: 6,712.

This has to be one of the most dramatic local derbies ever. The game swung through a whole range of emotions, from anger and outrage to suspense and even humour, when it seemed in such short supply amongst the usual rabble rousers. Above all this was wonderful entertainment and a fitting start to a challenging season in which both clubs need to attract every customer they can get.

An amazing four penalty kicks were taken. The first came after 8 minutes and was awarded against Argyle. Their skipper, Craven, fouled Lammie Robertson, who naturally took the kick himself and duly scored, only for the linesman to spot an infringement. The kick had to be retaken and this time Robertson sent the ball in the opposite corner of the net and it counted.

The third penalty kick of the game came in the 55th minute and was given for a foul on Tony Kellow. Robertson again netted from the spot. Amazingly Robertson was denied hat-trick of penalties in the 76th minute when his third of the game was saved by Argyle keeper Barron.

Argyle had equalised after 38 minutes when an inviting Johnson centre was flicked home from the head of Trusson. Four minutes later Trusson scored again, with a snap drive to give his side he lead for the first time.

For a while all the initiative swung Plymouth's way, but Exeter weathered the storm and finally broke out of their shell again to cause more alarm and winning those last two penalties.

RIVAL FANS CLASH BEFORE CUP TIE
The football season kicked off in rowdy style in Exeter this afternoon as hundreds of rival fans surged through the city centre before the Football League Cup tie between Exeter City and Plymouth Argyle.

At least one fan was taken to hospital with a head injury after an incident two hours before the match, near the Guildhall. Trouble started as Argyle supporters poured into Exeter early for the game. Several shop windows were smashed and shoppers sought refuge in stores from the unruly crowd.

A Devon General bus was attacked, with windows and the sides of the vehicle being kicked, as the Plymouth fans continued with their disgraceful behaviour. Police made several arrests inside St. James' Park, as the Argyle contingent pushed over fences at the St. James' Road end.

NEWCOMERS TO WATCH
The Exeter City reserve team will be unrecognisable to supporters from last season's side, and two of the new signings include 21-year-old midfield man, Dick Forbes, who has played for the England Schools Under-18 team and has also represented the Western League XI. Full-back Tony Mitchell was formerly with Leatherhead in the Isthmian League and has also represented the Western League and Surrey County. Both players are currently studying at St. Lukes' College in Exeter.

Other young players to watch should be last year's youth team skipper, Jeff Weeks (brother of first teamer Graham), striker Andy White and the hard tackling Andy Rowden.

MONDAY 15th AUGUST 1977

FOOTBALL VIOLENCE IS CONDEMNED
Inspections were being carried out at St. James' Park this morning by club officials to find out the cost of the damage caused to the ground by Plymouth Argyle supporters during Saturday's Football League Cup tie.

There was extensive damage to fencing and advertising boards as a result of sheer hooliganism during the match. For the second successive season there was crowd trouble before, during and after the game. Fourteen people needed hospital treatment, including a Police officer who was detained with concussion.

The Exeter branch of Licensed Victuallers condemned the violence shown towards their colleagues, and said that in future football fans must be banned from public houses. Around £150 worth of damage was caused in one incident alone, when doors and windows were smashed at the London Inn.

Exeter City chairman Gerald Vallance said the damage he had seen at the ground this morning was something of a shock to him.

"We thought there might be trouble," he added. "We tried to do what we could, but they ripped down much of what we put up."

TUESDAY 16th AUGUST 1977

DEVON RIVALS CANNOT BE SEPARATED
Football League Cup: Round One; 2nd Leg
Plymouth Argyle 0 Exeter City 0
Plymouth Argyle team: Barron, Smart, Uzzell, Horswill, Foster, Craven, Johnson, Delve, Austin, Trusson, Rogers.
Exeter City: Baugh, Templeman, Hore, Weeks (Holman), Saxton, Hatch, Hodge, Kellow, Bowker, Beer, Jennings.
Attendance: 7,639.

A replay between these two great Devon rivals will be needed next Tuesday evening to settle who goes through to the second round of the Football League Cup. The third match will take place at Home Park, Plymouth, Argyle winning the right to stage the game on a toss of a coin.

The second leg never reached the same heights as the game at St. James' Park, but both teams had chances to break the deadlock. Exeter had openings in the first half when they played their best football, but some of their passing went astray after the interval. Keith Bowker did a good job in midfield in place of the injured Lammie Robertson.

Plymouth too had their openings, forcing Peter Hatch to twice clear off the City goal line, whilst at the other end, Alan Beer's speed caused problems for the Argyle defence. Credit should be given to City's well organised defence which just did not know when to give in.

Undoubtedly the Grecians deserved to fight again for a spirited performance, even if there was precious little excitement during the 90 minutes. It was a heartbreaking night for Argyle who frittered away their skills, while Exeter confidently repelled Argyle's attacks.

WHICH DRESSING ROOM?
Plymouth Argyle manager Mike Kelly speaking before the League Cup tie against Exeter City at Home Park, was hoping to reverse the result of twelve months earlier.

"I am sure, because of the local rivalry, it will be a very competitive cup tie. Exeter are one up in the League Cup on us,

because last year they won both legs and naturally we are all hoping that we reverse that situation this season. One or two of their players will have to be very careful about going into the right dressing room, and we are thinking of putting up a signpost reminder for them!
I am thinking particualrly of player-manager Bobby Saxton and Johnny Hore, who will seem so much at home at Home Park".

WEDNESDAY 17th AUGUST 1977

ARGYLE WIN THE TOSS
It was drama behind the scenes at Home Park following last night's Football League Cup tie between Plymouth Argyle and Exeter City. A replay was needed. But where? St James' Park? Home Park? Even the neutral ground of Torquay United's Plainmoor?

Exeter City player-manager Bobby Saxton and Plymouth Argyle manager Mike Kelly both quickly agreed to eliminate Torquay from their considerations and decided to settle for the toss of a coin by match referee Derek Nippard of Christchurch.

"Heads," called Mike Kelly. "Right" said Nippard. "Home Park it is!"

FRIDAY 19th AUGUST 1977

BRADFORD CITY OFFER TURNED DOWN
Exeter City midfielder Lammie Robertson has turned down a move to Bradford City. The Valley Parade club, promoted along with the Grecians to the Third Division at the end of last season, agreed to pay City's asking fee of £8,000 for the player.

However, following talks, Robertson decided against the move to Yorkshire. he wants to get involved in the coaching side of the game and is prepared to wait until the right offer and club moves in for him.

SATURDAY 20th AUGUST 1977

GOOD START FOR CITY
Third Division
Walsall 1 Exeter City 3
Walsall team: Kearns, Taylor, Caswell, Newton, Hynd, Serella, Shelton (Clarke), Bates, Evans, Buckley, Birch.
Exeter City team: Baugh, Templeman, Hore, Weeks, Saxton, Hatch, Hodge, Kellow, Bowker, Beer, Jennings.
Scorers: Walsall: Taylor; Exeter: Beer (2), Kellow.
Attendance: 5,174

Exeter City made the perfect start to life in the Third Division - the first time for thirteen years - as they beat the experienced and much fancied Walsall, to start off the new era for the St. James' Park club.

Alan Beer, who has been the subject of transfer speculation lately, was again watched by a Leicester City scout, who must have gone away from the game suitably impressed as Beer scored twice. Exeter could not have made a better start, taking the lead after eleven minutes. Tony Kellow pushed the ball through and Beer moved forward to crack a superb right foot shot into the corner of the net.

City withstood a great deal of pressure before they struck again in the 37th minute. Beer shrugged off all the efforts of Serella and hooked the ball in. The twin striking power of Beer and Kellow continued to cause Walsall problems in the second half, but Peter Hatch saved Exeter in the 77th minute when he stopped Buckley's header on the goal line.

Eight minutes later Kellow increased Exeter's lead following a cross by Bobby Hodge to make it 3-0. Walsall though, pulled a goal back in the 87th minute through Taylor, who netted with a fierce high cross shot into the corner of the City goal.

TUESDAY 23rd AUGUST 1977

CITY PROGRESS TO ROUND TWO
Football League Cup: Round One Replay
Plymouth Argyle 0 Exeter City 1

Plymouth Argyle team: Barron, Smart, Uzzell, Horswill, Foster, Craven, Johnson, Delve, Austin (Hall), Trusson, Rogers.
Exeter City team: Baugh, Templeman, Hore, Weeks (Robertson), Saxton, Hatch, Hodge, Kellow, Bowker, Beer, Jennings.
Scorer: Exeter:
Beer.
Attendance: 8,776.

Exuberant Exeter City now have a home date next Wednesday with Football League Cup holders Aston Villa, thanks to an opportunist goal from their ace striker Alan Beer, seven minutes from time at Home Park. The Grecians handed out a lesson to Plymouth who the harder they tried, the more baffled they became. The outcome of the match never looked like being anything other than a City victory.

City displayed the sort of conviction and cohesion that earned them promotion last season. They used the ball quickly and skilfully and were good enough to trouble Plymouth from the start. Continued over eagerness cost Argyle chances, whereas Exeter showed class as well as spirit and sometimes did as they pleased.

Alan Beer thundered a 25-yard shot against the Argyle crossbar in the first half, while Austin was equally unlucky to strike a City post after the interval with John Baugh well beaten. The only goal of the match followed a through ball from Bobby Hodge. Beer raced in and chipped it over Plymouth keeper Barron.

WEDNESDAY 24th AUGUST 1977

KELLOW LINKED WITH ARSENAL
Speculation that Exeter City striker Tony Kellow could be a target for First Division Arsenal was quashed today by player-manager Bobby Saxton. It had been rumoured that Arsenal were ready to make a bid in the region of £100,000. "I have not had an official approach from Arsenal for Kellow," said Saxton. "There has been plenty of speculation about several of my players. There will be no one leaving in the near future. I am trying to build a side equipped to go into the Second Division."

SATURDAY 27th AUGUST 1977

CITY HAND BURY A GIFT
Third Division
Exeter City 2 Bury 2
Exeter City team: Baugh, Templeman, Hore, Weeks, Saxton, Hatch, Hodge (Robertson), Kellow, Bowker, Beer, Jennings.
Bury team: Forrest, Annan, Kennedy, Thomson, Tucker, Hatton, Woolfill, McIlwraith, Rowland, Entwistle (Bailey), T Robins.
Scorers: Exeter: Hodge, Kellow; Bury: Thomson, Entwistle.
Attendance: 5,236

A sixty second lapse in concentration cost City dearly. For in that minute after the interval they forgot to defend and a previously dead and done Bury were let off the hook. The 71st minute saw City coasting home, two goals to the good, but then they dropped a major clanger when Thomson was given a gift goal six yards out after Keith Bowker's headed clearance went straight to him.

A minute later Woolfall turned John Hore and Graham Weeks inside out and crossed for Entwistle to slot the ball past John Baugh for the equaliser. It left such a disappointing taste after Exeter had eased into a two goal lead through Bobby Hodge after six minutes and Tony Kellow two minutes before the break.

In fairness to Bury, both goals had an element of luck about them. The first goal from Hodge was meant to be a cross but the ball sailed over the crowded goal area into the net. Then Kellow's goal got the faintest of touches to a Hodge pass and the ball screwed just inside the post.

It looked that all Exeter had to do was to keep their heads and a follow up from the wonderful start at Walsall last week was on the cards. It all seemed to go wrong when Hodge was carried off in the 55th minute with concussion. A more positive side than Bury may well have sneaked the points. An afternoon therefore, that had started brightly for Exeter, finished with them grimly hanging on for the draw.

CITY VICE PRESIDENTS CLUB
During the summer extensive alterations have taken place under the grandstand at St. James' Park.
The old boardroom and tea room have been converted into one large Vice Presidents Club Lounge.

The idea is to encourage supporters to become Vice Presidents, paying £50 per season. Already City have signed on 20 Vice Presidents, and all the signs point to the club that they will have at least 30 members by Christmas.

"The building of the Vice Presidents' Club has only been made possible by the incredible dedication and professionalism of a few supporters," said City Commercial Manager, Ray Ellis. "They have given up every weekend and most evenings through the summer, working voluntarily in order to complete the work for the start of the season."

FIFTY YEARS OF FOOTBALL AT TORQUAY UNITED
Fifty years ago today Torquay United played their first ever match in the Football League when they met Exeter City at Plainmoor. The Torquay Times newspaper reported that the influx of visitors began early, and as the day wore on numbers increased.

Men were selling souvenir programmes and black and white and red and white favours, the colours of Torquay United and Exeter City respectively. After lunch time, all roads led to Plainmoor. Many different vehicles and ways were utilised in reaching the ground, charabancs, private cars, tram, omnibus, taxis, motor cycles, bicycles and shanks' pony.

There were about 8,000 spectators present half an hour before kick off which was timed to begin at 3.30pm. When John O'Connor, the Torquay United captain led his team from the dressing room onto the pitch, there was reckoned to be over 10,000 spectators present. The honour of scoring Torquay's first goal in the Football League went to inside-right Herbert Turner, who netted from the penalty spot after Exeter City centre-half Alex Pool had handled the ball. Bill Vaughan was to equalise for the Grecians and fittingly, on this historic day, honours ended all square at 1-1.

WEDNESDAY 31st AUGUST 1977

GRECIANS DRAW PRAISE FROM LEAGUE CUP HOLDERS
Football League Cup Round Two
Exeter City 1 Aston Villa 3
Exeter City team: Baugh, Templeman, Hore, Weeks (Robertson), Saxton, Hatch, Hodge, Kellow, Bowker, Beer, Jennings.
Aston Villa team: Rimmer, Gregory, Smith, Phillips, McNaught, Mortimer, Deehan, Little, Gray, Cropley, Carrodus.
Scorers: Exeter: Robertson: Aston Villa: Gray (3).
Att 13768

Despite going out of the Football League Cup to holders Aston Villa, visiting manager Ron Saunders praised Exeter City for their 100 per cent commitment and admitted that at one stage the Grecians might well have snatched a draw and a replay. It was not until the last minute of the match that Villa made absolutely sure of going through. Until then Exeter had gone mighty close to equalising, being denied by the woodwork and the goalkeeping of Jimmy Rimmer.

It was a tremendous game, and a particularly memorable second half when Exeter did virtually everything but get that second goal. They forced Villa back for long spells and both Alan Beer and John Templeman went so close to getting an equaliser.

After a jittery and nervous start, City gradually gathered momentum to come more into the game and shatter any illusions Villa might have had of romping to victory. It proved to be a performance by City that deservedly earned praise form the highest level. Villa went ahead in the 22nd minute when Alex Cropley's long free-kick was headed in by Andy Gray from six -yards. City had more of the play as the first half went on, but right at the start of the second half they were lucky to see a Cropley cross hit the bar. In the 58th minute Villa struck again through Gray who finished off a neat one-two that had split the Exeter defence. It was then that City made a tremendous effort to get themselves back into the tie. Ken McNaught fouled Tony Kellow in the 65th minute and Lammie Robertson, who had subbed Graham Weeks, hit home the penalty.

City almost got their reward 13 minutes later, but Beer's header was touched onto the bar by Rimmer. The goalkeeper then made a tremendous save to keep out a volley from Templeman as City continued to attack and push forward. All hopes of a replay vanished in the last minute when Mortimer broke quickly and set up a pass for Gray to complete his hat-trick.

REMEMBER SIR FRANCIS DRAKE!
In his programme notes for the Football League Cup tie against Aston Villa, the Grecians player-manager Bobby Saxton, had a warning for the Midland visitors. "The magic name of Aston Villa, one of the oldest and most respected and revered clubs in the entire Football League come to Exeter as cup holders and therefore entrants into the UEFA Cup," he wrote. "It is also my privilege to especially welcome the Minster of Sport, Dennis Howell, a Villa supporter, to the game. . However, I would remind you that the west country people have never given way too easily - remember Sir Francis Drake!"

EXETER CITY F.C.
Official Programme
Todays Match Sponsored by
JOHN HOLT CARPETS
90 BULLER RD
ST. THOMAS
EXETER
for all your ● CARPETS ● BEDDING ● FURNITURE Tel: EXETER 70803
EXETER CITY v PLYMOUTH ARGYLE
1st Round 1st Leg Football League Cup
Saturday 13th August 1977
Kick-off 3.00p.m. Price 15p

ARGYLE
Football League Cup
1st Round 2nd Leg
Tuesday 16th August 1977
Kick off 7.30 p.m.
EXETER CITY
OFFICIAL MATCH-DAY MAGAZINE OF PLYMOUTH ARGYLE
Volume 1 Number 3
15p

EXETER CITY F.C.
Official Programme
EXETER CITY .V. MINEHEAD
Friday 5th August 1977
Kick-off 7.00 p.m. Price 5p

EXETER CITY F.C.
Official Programme
EXETER CITY v BURY
Football League Div 3
Saturday 27th August 1977
Kick-off 3.00p.m. Price 15p

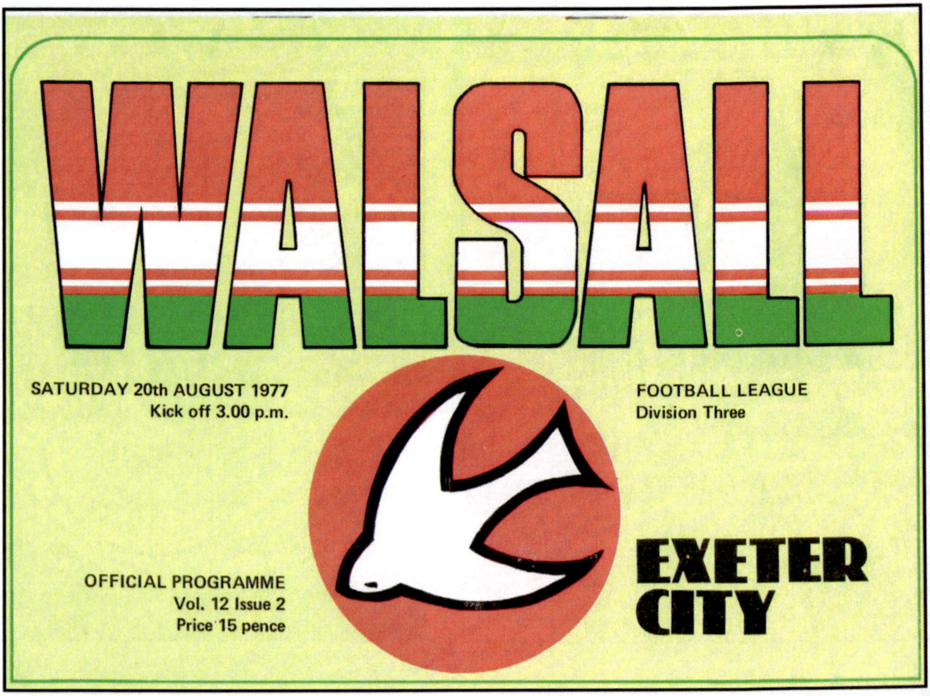
WALSALL
SATURDAY 20th AUGUST 1977
Kick off 3.00 p.m.
FOOTBALL LEAGUE
Division Three
OFFICIAL PROGRAMME
Vol. 12 Issue 2
Price 15 pence
EXETER
CITY

ARGYLE
Football League Cup
1st Round Replay
Tuesday 23rd August
1977
Kick off 7.30 p.m.
EXETER
CITY
OFFICIAL MATCH-DAY MAGAZINE OF PLYMOUTH ARGYLE
Volume 1 Number 5
10p

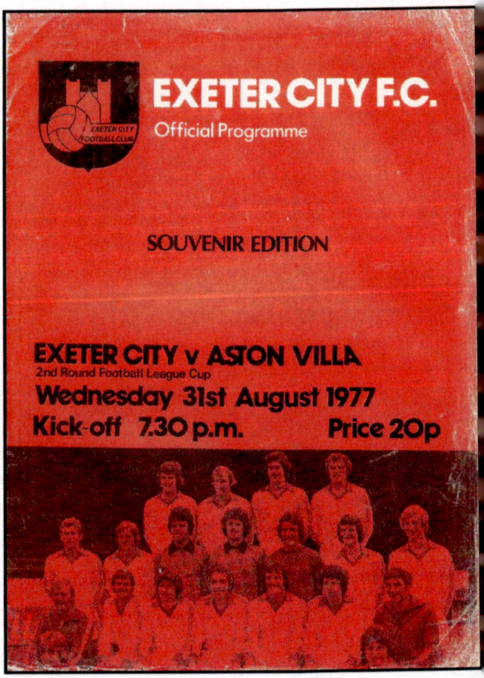
EXETER CITY
FOOTBALL CLUB
EXETER CITY F.C.
Official Programme
SOUVENIR EDITION
EXETER CITY v ASTON VILLA
2nd Round Football League Cup
Wednesday 31st August 1977
Kick-off 7.30 p.m.
Price 20p

PETERBOROUGH UNITED
VERSUS
EXETER
FOOTBALL LEAGUE DIVISION THREE
SATURDAY, 17th SEPTEMBER
K.O. 3.00 p.m.
15p
Mitre
PERMAWHITE
MAX

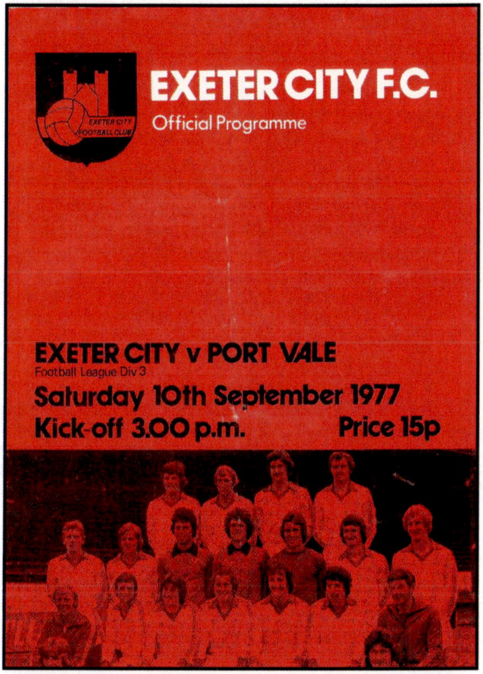
EXETER CITY F.C.
Official Programme
EXETER CITY FOOTBALL CLUB
EXETER CITY v PORT VALE
Football League Div 3
Saturday 10th September 1977
Kick-off 3.00 p.m.
Price 15p

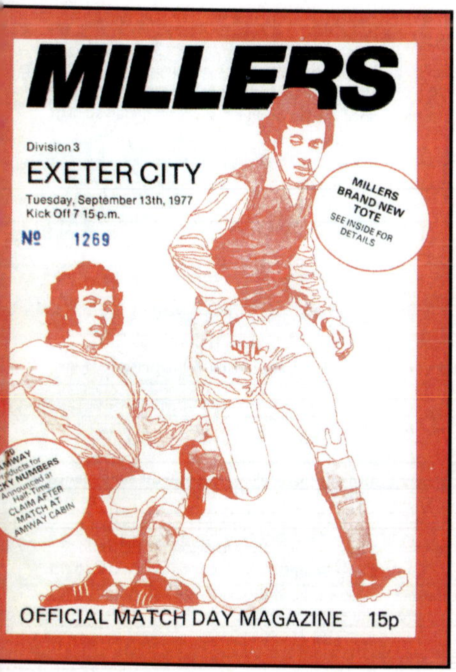
MILLERS
Division 3
EXETER CITY
Tuesday, September 13th, 1977
Kick Off 7 15 p.m.
№ 1269
MILLERS BRAND NEW TOTE
SEE INSIDE FOR DETAILS
OFFICIAL MATCH DAY MAGAZINE
15p

EXETER CITY F.C.
Official Programme
EXETER CITY FOOTBALL CLUB
EXETER CITY v CARLISLE UNITED
Football League Div 3
Monday 26th September 1977
Kick-off 7.30 p.m.
Price 15p

SATURDAY 3rd SEPTEMBER 1977

CITY IN CONTROL
Third Division
Shrewsbury Town 0 Exeter City 2
Shrewsbury Town team: Mulhearn, Leonard, Roberts, Turner, Griffin, Atkins, Nixon, Hornsby (Loughnane), Bates, irvine, Maguire.
Exeter City team: Baugh, Templeman, Hore, Hodge, Saxton, Hatch, Bowker, Kellow, Robertson, Beer (Holman), Jennings.
Scorers: Exeter: Beer, Kellow.
Attendance: 3,302

Who is to say that Exeter City cannot waltz through the Fourth and Third Divisions in successive seasons? The score line, albeit convincing by any standards away from home, did not relate the true story of the match. Even when Shrewsbury showed more of their hand in the second period, Exeter never looked in any real danger, because of their all round poise.

But for every home attack, there were three from City, with Lammie Robertson completely controlling the midfield show. Exeter often strung together as many as a dozen passes without a Shrewsbury player touching the ball.

Bobby Saxton posted the first warning to the home side in the 16th minute when his 40-yard pass over centre-half Griffin found Alan Beer, who rapped the ball into the side netting. Four minutes later and an almost identical move ended with Beer making no mistake this time.

It was Beer's shot that rebounded off the crossbar that led to Tony Kellow making it 2-0, pushing home the rebound. Beer limped off in the 34th minute, made a brief return, but went off for good nine minutes later. This reduced the effectiveness of the City attack, for Beer was in a class of his own, running the Shrewsbury defence ragged.

Keith Bowker and Bobby Hodge worked like beavers feeding the front men, whilst John Baugh made two fine saves in the second half from Bates and McGuire.

FRIDAY 9th SEPTEMBER 1977

LEE ROBERTS REJOINS CITY
Defender Lee Roberts has returned to St. James' Park on a permanent basis, the Shrewsbury Town player joining Exeter City today for a fee of £8,000. Roberts becomes player-manager Bobby Saxton's first signing since he took charge of the Grecians last January. Saxton had made several enquiries about Roberts since the player had a successful loan spell at Exeter towards the end of last season.

He played against Exeter last Saturday, but after the game Saxton reopened negotiations. The player has made no secret of the fact that he wanted to return to play for Exeter City.

SATURDAY 10th SEPTEMBER 1977

THIS WAS ALL TOO EASY FOR THE GRECIANS
Exeter City 4 Port Vale 1
Exeter City team: Baugh, Templeman, Hore, Hodge, Saxton, Hatch, Bowker, Kellow, Robertson, Holman, Jennings.
Port Vale team: Connaughton (Cullerton), McGifford, Harper, Ridley, Harris, Bentley, Lamb, Brownbill, Beamish, Baiey, Hemmerman.
Scorers: Exeter: Robertson (2), Hodge, Holman. Port Vale: Cullerton.
Attendance: 5,026

Exeter City will rarely harvest an easier two points than this. They were not so hot themselves, but at least they made hay while the sun shone, and have now only dropped one point in the opening four games.

They ever looked in trouble against a shabby Port Vale, who looked even shabbier when they lost goalkeeper John Connaughton in the 11th minute with a leg injury that required six stitches. Ken Beamish took over between the sticks. Exeter's main goal supply came from Lammie Robertson, and he turned goalscorer by grabbing the first City success from the penalty spot in the 28th minute when McGifford had upended Tony Kellow.

Bobby Hodge scored the second just before half-time with an angled shot that the recognised keeper would have been expected to have saved. Then up popped Robertson again to score from the second penalty 4 minutes from time, Harris having handled a Keith Bowker shot. The fourth City goal came from Harry Holman - his first in league football - accepted with relish after Kellow had flicked the ball on.

Vale got some reward for their troubles with a goal two minutes from time when John Baugh was all at sea with a Bentley cross and Cullerton punished his mistake. Exeter have played better, but tackled the match in intelligent stages. Once the second goal came, City switched into overdrive and were in total command.

BEER FAILS MEDICAL: TRANSFER FALLS THROUGH
The transfer of Alan Beer from Exeter City to First Division Leicester City has been dramatically halted after the striker failed a medical. It was revealed by City player-manager Bobby Saxton that a fee had been agreed with Leicester, only for a knee injury to Beer to show up in the medical. The player is currently out of action with a knee ligament injury. but Leicester City believe it to be a cartilage problem which will require an operation. Beer will now see an Exeter specialist and is naturally disappointed at the outcome of the decision

Leicester City manager admitted that Beer had not been his number one target when he watched the Grecians in action at Home Park in the Football League Cup, and that he gone along to watch fellow striker Tony Kellow. It was then that Beer caught McClintock's eye and Leicester have had the player watched ever since.

On Thursday night Leicester City contacted Saxton and Beer, and the player travelled to the Midlands yesterday for talks and medical prior to a possible transfer. The two clubs had agreed a fee of £70,000, plus a further £10,000 after Beer had completed 40 first team games.

The deal has now been put on ice for at least three weeks until Beer recovers from his knee injury.

"You cannot hold a player back when he has the chance of First Division football," said City chairman Gerald Vallance. "Neither could Exeter City, as a club, afford to turn down the sort of money that Leicester City were prepared to pay for the player."

His departure from St. James' Park would be a big blow for the clubs supporters who have seen Beer play himself on the verge of full Wales international honours. He was signed in November 1974 from Weymouth for a £4,000 fee.

TUESDAY 13th SEPTEMBER 1977

GRECIANS' UNBEATEN RUN COMES TO AN END
Third Division
Rotherham United 1 Exeter City 0
Rotherham United team: McAllister, Forrest, Breckin, Rhodes, Stancliffe, Spencer, Finney, Womble, Gwyther, Goodfellow, Crawford.
Exeter City team: Key, Templeman, Hore, Bowker, Saxton, Hatch, Hodge, Kellow, Robertson, Holman, Jennings.
Scorer: Rotherham: Finney.
Attendance: 4,889.

Thirteen proved to be unlucky for Exeter City. For 12 games and 87 minutes without defeat the Grecians' unbeaten sequence came to an end. It proved to be a personal tragedy for Richard Key - restored to the team in place of John Baugh - who failed to hold a fierce shot from Gwyther, and although John Hore had a chance to get the ball clear, Finney slipped it into an empty net.

Key and Exeter however, can have no regrets, for their confident, plucky, workmanlike performance won them many friends, if no points. Playing fast, attractive football, they more than held their own and came close to gaining both points. Even in the last minute Tony Kellow was denied an equaliser when the ball was cleared off the line. They earned the applause of the home crowd for their skilful play.

Both sides hit the woodwork in the first half. Rotherham's Crawford saw his header rebound off the bar, whilst a Lammie Robertson shot glanced off a post after Tony Kellow had set up the chance. The longer the game went on, the more menacing Exeter became, although the deadlock seldom looked like being broken. It was City who looked the more capable of breaking it though.

Keith Bowker had one effort cleared off the line, while man of the match Peter Hatch was denying Rotherham United time and time again at the back. Just as it seemed that Exeter had earned a point, Finney tapped the ball home for the winner. So Exeter City were defeated, and rightly so very disappointed. For they deserved better reward for their efforts.

BEER OUT FOR SEVERAL WEEKS
Leicester City are still interested in Exeter City striker Alan Beer, although manager Frank McLintock admitted that the latest injury news about the player made things a bit difficult. Beer was today having his injured knee put in plaster after a specialist had diagnosed ligament damage. It could be up to six weeks before Beer is expected to be fit to play again, a serious blow both to the player and the club.

ARGYLE MIDFIELDER SIGNS FOR CITY
Exeter City completed the £10,000 transfer today of 24-year-old midfielder Colin Randell from Plymouth Argyle. It ends two months of uncertainty for the player, as City boss Bobby Saxton first made a move for Randell in the close season, and after originally agreeing to join Exeter, Randell then changed his mind.

Negotiations were later reopened, only for Randell to be sidelined with injury, which he has now recovered from. The signing of Randell, together with Lee Roberts from Shrewsbury Town, brings City's spending in the transfer market in recent days to a not inconsiderable £18,000.

WEDNESDAY 14th SEPTEMBER 1977

FOLLOWING CITY TO ROTHERHAM
The chairman of the Exeter City Vice Presidents Club, Mr. P.E. Scatterfield, travelled with the City team to Rotherham United yesterday. Here is his impression of the day:-

"I had the pleasure of being invited to travel to Rotherham by one of the Exeter City directors, Clifford Hill. After I had accepted with enthusiasm, I was told it was rather a long journey. We left St. James' Park at 9am, on what was a bright and sunny morning.

The coach was soon underway speeding up the M5 towards the Midlands. The team, together with player-manager Bobby Saxton, trainer-coach Jack Edwards, physio Tony Long and Nip Dixon relaxing in their jeans and open neck shirts, either reading or playing cards. We arrived at the first stop just off the motorway in Birmingham, just before midday. As we alighted I asked Lammie Robertson how much he had won playing cards? His reply being: "We cannot afford to play for money. It's too long a journey."

Everybody was then asked by Mr. Dixon what we required to eat? A variety of different orders were given from cornflakes by Peter Hatch, to omelettes, scrambled eggs, or just toast. The rest of us had a very good and enjoyable three-course lunch and by 1pm we were on our way again, heading north towards Leicester.

Arriving at a motel just outside Leicester at around 2pm, where a booking had been previously made, Bobby Saxton had the players and himself off to their allotted bedrooms for a two-hour sleep and rest. At 4.15pm sharp, Jack Edwards had all the players assembled in the lounge, together with a large blackboard for a team talk and discussion by Bobby Saxton. Tea was then served, or rather Nip Dixon, Jack Edwards ad Bobby Saxton served, as there were no staff on duty at that hour, while the receptionist was cooking the eggs and making the toast.

By 5pm we were on the road again. Heading for Sheffield. The team were now smartly dressed with jackets and ties. We arrived outside Rotherham United's ground at 6.30pm. The team went straight to the dressing room. Clifford Hill and myself were met by one of the four Rotherham United Directors and escorted to their Boardroom. Everything looked neat and tidy, with the pitch in first class condition. Over a cup of tea we were told that Rotherham were hoping for promotion this season, after only missing it last year by goal average to Crystal Palace, and that they were looking forward to returning to the Second Division as they had been there for 12-years at one period.

We were escorted upstairs behind the main grandstand to their supporters lounge and introduced to their Chairman. This was a most impressive club, with a bar in one corner and lounge seating and tables worthy of a four star hotel. We were then asked if we would like to see the gym? We were taken by a director underneath the stand to one end of the ground where the indoor gym was situated.

What an eye opener it was! It was about three-quarter size of a football pitch, with a fine maple wood floor. Five goal posts were marked out on one side of the wall, with the Rotherham players already stripped and warming up with shooting practice. It did pass through my mind that we were going to have hard match. So it turned out, But what a game!

At half-time I had the pleasure of seeing the crowd standing and applauding the players from the pitch. In the boardroom at half-time everybody was full of praise at the quality of the football and at Exeter's attacking game. It had been thrilling end to end stuff, with perhaps the highlight being a save by Richard Key at point blank range.

The second half was excellent with City creating, if anything, more chances than the Millers, and then it happened in the 87th minute. Rotherham scored and the crowd erupted. Our heads went down, but not the City players. From the kick off they attacked and how we missed scoring I shall never know.

The hospitality afterwards was in true northern style, like their praise for Exeter's performance. Their honest opinion was that we deserved a point and that this was by far the best game they had witnessed for a long time. It was 10pm. Time to leave. After our farewells and thanks to the Rotherham United directors, we were back on the coach.

As we got on board we were handed a parcel by Nip Dixon, which turned out to be delicious fish and chips! So we set off in the long journey home through the streets of Rotherham eating fish and chips with our fingers. After an hour we stopped for a brief while for a wash and bush up. Then we were away again heading for Bristol.

I fell asleep to awake once more at around 2am, as we were pulling into Gordano Services at Bristol. All out for a cup of tea, and for the hungry players, eggs, sausage, bacon and chips was the favourite dish.

2.30am and we were away again on the last lap of the journey, arriving in Exeter at 3.45am. With a cheerful goodbye, wishing the team better fortune at Peterborough United on Saturday. I was at home by 4.30am and went straight to bed. I thought ... "And this is the end of a hard day's work."

THURSDAY 15th SEPTEMBER 1977

ROBERTSON TRANSFERRED TO LEICESTER
First Division Leicester City have signed Exeter City's transfer listed midfielder Lammie Robertson, who has been seeking a move since last January. The player travelled to Leicester today to complete the £8,000 deal which will enable him to make his debut on Saturday against Arsenal. Robertson is the third City player to catch the attention of Leicester manager Frank McLintock.

His initial targets were Tony Kellow and Alan Beer, but whilst watching these two, he was impressed with the skills of Robertson. Exeter City player manager Bobby Saxton speaking about the transfer said: "It is the chance of a life time move for Lammie."

SATURDAY 17th SEPTEMBER 1977

KEY PENALTY SAVE IS CRUCIAL
Third Division
Peterborough United 1 Exeter City 1
Peterborough United team: Waugh, Hindley, Lee. Doyle, Turner, Rose, Slough, Butlin, Camp (Cozens), Carmichael, Robson.
Exeter City team: Key, Templeman, Hore, Bowker, Saxton, Hatch, Hodge, Kellow, Holman, Randell, Jennings.
Scorers: Peterborough: Robson; Exeter: Kellow.
Attendance: 5,016

A goal in the 21st minute from Tony Kellow earned Exeter City's new look side a point at Peterborough United, for just as City looked to have a grip on the game they were shaken by Robson's 43rd minute equaliser.

As the match wore on the crowd were treated to a fine display by Grecians goalkeeper Richard Key, who also saved a 76th minute penalty taken by Lee, after he had brought Cozens down in the area. New signing Colin Randell had a quiet match and not surprisingly City lacked their recent rhythm. They created few chances and their man of the match was Peter Hatch.

Both sides played some neat football and once Kellow had headed City into the lead, Exeter displayed a good deal of composure, although at times the defence looked slightly vulnerable against the high ball. Peterborough looked far from out of the game, and their equaliser came when Doyle sent over a deep cross, which Robson headed in as Key scrambled to cover his near post. As the second half progressed it looked increasingly likely that City would have to fight a rearguard action, but their chances were made better by Peterborough's inability to finish off promising attacks.

The home side pushed forward in a bid to take the lead, but Exeter could not make use of the extra speed they had. City depended more and more on their defensive performance to hold onto the point.

SATURDAY 24th SEPTEMBER 1977

FIRST DEFEAT FOR TEN MONTHS
Third Division
Exeter City 0 Portsmouth 1
Exeter City team: Key, Templeman, Hore, Bowker, Saxton, Hatch, Hodge, Kellow, Randell, Holman (Roberts), Jennings.
Portsmouth team: Middleton, Roberts, Wilson, Piper, Foster, Denyer, Gilcrhist, Kemp, Stokes, Mellows, Barnard.
Scorer: Portsmouth: Kemp.
Attendance: 5,875.

Despite enjoying plenty of pressure, Exeter City failed to break down the Portsmouth defence and as a result lost their first home league match since the beginning of last December. The visitors grabbed a first half goal when they beat the offside trap, whilst Exeter could not get the vital breakthrough needed against a side playing with just two men up front.

They employed the method expected by City's player-manager Bobby Saxton, but it was a bad result for the first of two home games in 48-hours. Portsmouth had in fact arrived late at St James' Park, their coach being held up in traffic in the Honiton area.

Exeter looked the more aggressive side early on and almost took the lead when Keith Bowker crossed for Tony Kellow to head narrowly wide. City continued their efforts to get through in the pouring rain and after half an hour one of the advertising hoardings behind the St, James' Road goal broke as the large contingent of Portsmouth supporters pushed forward.

A minute later they certainly had plenty to cheer about as Kemp tucked the ball past Richard Key when totally unmarked. Despite Exeter's second half pressure they had nothing to show for it in terms of goals. They failed to look sharp enough to capitalise on any chances that presented themselves.

Portsmouth packed their defence in the last 15 minute. A powerful drive by John Hore was headed away for a corner and from it, Randell hit a superb 20-yard volley that was brilliantly turned away by Middleton.

CITY BOSS HAPPY WITH PROGRESS SO FAR
When Exeter City gained promotion to the Third Division at the end of last season, Grecians' manager Bobby Saxton said that he was confident that his team would hold their own at the higher level and need not fear the challenge of higher grade football.

"Our results so far this season have been most encouraging," added Saxton prior to City's match with Portsmouth this afternoon. "When you consider that four of the first six matches have been away from home, for which we have taken 5 points, then it is obvious that I am very satisfied with our performances. Two home games have produced 3 points from a possible 4."

"Whilst it is very early days, some cynics who suggested that we would be out of our class, notably some national newspapers, must surely be looking at the overall position with tongue in cheek. Being a realist I know only too well that early form and results do not mean that we have nothing to fear and that everything in the garden will be rosy. However, we must be confident in our ability to maintain progress and look to the future with extreme optimism."

MONDAY 26th SEPTEMBER 1977

ANOTHER BLANK FOR CITY

Exeter City 0 Carlisle United 1
Exeter City team: Key, Templeman, Hore, Bowker, Saxton, Hatch, Hodge, Kellow, Randell, Holman (Roberts), Jennings.
Carlisle United: Swinburne, Hoolickin, McCartney, Carr, MacDonald, Parker, McVitie, Ludlam, Tait, Rafferty, Lathan.
Scorer: Carlisle: Rafferty.
Attendance: 5,106

In a sort of encore Exeter City did not want to hear, Carlisle United beat them in a match that was virtually a carbon copy of Saturday's defeat against Portsmouth. Two home defeats in one weekend was certainly a disappointing discord of discontent for the Grecians.

Once again it was a case of City having the lions' share of the play. Carlisle rarely attacked dangerously, but still produced the goods when it counted, and that was enough to win the match.

City need to get goals. They have now scored only once in the last four matches. There was clearly growing frustration for Exeter and that was not helped when they had shots blocked and a couple of chances missed. Tony Kellow as usual got through an immense amount of work, but too often he was challenging up front without support. City lost his game simply because their firepower was neither strong enough or ruthless enough. It has to be put right if they are to stand any chance of winning matches.

The goal that won the game came in the 75th minute and was lashed into net by former Plymouth Argyle man, Rafferty, from a Hoolickin cross. Shortly before this City could have taken the lead, but a stinging shot from Nicky Jennings was blocked on the line.

Carlisle were not as defensively minded a side as Portsmouth, and showed a willingness to try and open the game up, but each time they were pushed back. Their approach work tended to be too complicated.

THIRD DIVISION LEAGUE TABLE							
	P	W	D	L	F	A	Pts
Shrewsbury Town	9	5	2	2	17	11	12
Gillingham	9	4	3	2	18	14	11
Oxford United	9	4	3	2	16	12	11
Bury	8	4	3	1	12	9	11
Colchester United	9	4	2	3	13	7	10
Tranmere Rovers	8	4	2	2	9	6	10
Chesterfield	9	5	0	4	12	12	10
Rotherham United	8	4	2	2	12	12	10
Walsall	9	2	5	2	11	10	9
Cambridge United	8	3	3	2	13	13	9
Chester	9	2	5	2	12	13	9
Swindon Town	9	3	3	3	13	14	9
Peterborough United	9	3	3	3	8	10	9
EXETER CITY	8	3	2	3	12	8	8
Carlisle United	9	2	4	3	9	9	8
Pylmouth Argyle	8	2	4	2	8	8	8
Wrexham	9	2	4	3	12	13	8
Port Vale	8	3	2	3	9	13	8
Portsmouth	8	2	3	3	5	7	7
Preston North End	8	1	5	2	5	7	7
Lincoln City	9	2	2	5	7	10	6
Bradford City	9	2	2	5	11	15	6
Hereford United	9	2	2	5	7	12	6
Sheffield Wednesday	8	0	4	4	3	9	4

GRECIANS TO GIVE INGHAM AND JACKSON A TRIAL

Highly rated striker Fred Ingham is to have a trial with Exeter City in the hope of breaking back into the Football League. Ingham, now 22, played for Stockport County as a 16-year-old in their first team, and was attracting offers in the region of £10,000 when he had the misfortune to break a leg.

He drifted into non-league football where he became one of the top goalscorers in the Cheshire League for Witton Albion. Moving to the South West to live, Ingham then linked up with Dawlish Town, before Western League champions, Falmouth Town signed him.

A second trialist to arrive at St. James' Park is Bob Jackson, who has recently been with Nottingham Forest on a similar basis.

FAIR PLAY AWARD SCHEME
Negotiations have been completed for the introduction of a brand new form of sponsorship involving all three of Devon's Football League clubs. Allbright Fastenings have agreed to pay each club £20 per match providing they do not have anyone booked or sent off during the game.

For each player sent off, the club will lose £10, and for a booking a deduction of £5 will be made. The pounds will be added up during the season and the Devon club with the most will receive a bonus of £50 and the Allbright Fastenings Fair Play Trophy.

The scheme will only operate for league matches and has been backdated to the start of the season.

SATURDAY 1st OCTOBER 1977

GOAL DROUGHT WORRIES FOR CITY
Third Division
Chesterfield 0 Exeter City 0
Chesterfield team: Ogrizovic, Tartt, Burton, Kowalski, Cottam, O'Neill, Jones (Fern), Dearden, Green, Parker, Heppollette,
Exeter City team: Key, Templeman, Hore, Bowker, Saxton, Hatch, Hodge, Kellow, Randell, Roberts, Jennings.
Attendance: 3,771

Exeter City continued to put their home record to shame with this their sixth point from five away games since their arrival in the Third Division. One issue that must concern player-manager Bobby Saxton though is the weakness at both home and away to turn superiority into match winning goals. Opportunities were there against Chesterfield, but they failed to take them. Bobby Hodge did get the ball in the net, but the goal was disallowed for a foul on the goalkeeper.

Keith Bowker had a header hooked off the Chesterfield line by Tartt, whilst Tony Kellow hoisted a good chance over the crossbar and Lee Roberts scooped a fine chance in the same direction 15 minutes later. Peter Hatch powered a goal bound header that struck Ogrizovic and bounced off the crossbar, while Kellow chased magnificently and full backs John Hore and John Templeman were never shaken out of their composure.

There were of course moments when City's goal mouth was subjected to a Chesterfield siege. Yet no City defender shirked the challenge and in the end the home sides flowing football was reduced to an up and under variety. The conditions were extremely cold, with driving rain, but Exeter were doing well as they anticipated a good result from the first of their two games in the North this weekend.

NEW CITY F.C. LOTTERY SCHEME
Exeter City are launching a new fund-raising lottery which they estimate will bring in another £12,000 per year to the club.

In addition to the existing competitions, a monthly lottery called "The City Lottery" will be inaugurated next week and the first draw for the £1,000 top prize will be made later this month.

The existing Supporters Association lotteries help towards raising a net total profit for the year of about £35,000. The new lottery will be run by the Centre Spot Social Club. The first tickets go on sale next week at various points in the city and surrounding districts.

"This is a similar scheme to the one run by Plymouth Argyle," said City commercial manager Ray Ellis. "It is an exciting new venture in the history of Exeter City Football Club. We need the money to finance various improvements that have been made within the social club complex. The club has made a tremendous difference to our annual turnover. Fund raising plays a major part in soccer and it is our intention to increase this even further by this new scheme which will be beneficial to the public and Exeter City."

Each ticket costs 20p, and everyone who buy one has the chance of winning the monthly top prize of £1,000. There will also be cash consolation prizes ranging from £5 to £500 each month.

MONDAY 3rd OCTOBER 1977

GRECIANS HIT BY DOUBLE GOAL SALVO
Third Division
Tranmere Rovers 2 Exeter City 1
Tranmere Rovers team: Johnson, Mathias, Flood, Parry, Philpotts, Evans, Peplow, Palios, Moore, Tynan, Allen.
Exeter City team: Key, Templeman, Hore, Bowker, Saxton, Hatch, Hodge, Kellow, Randell, Roberts, Jennings.
Scorers: Tranmere: Moore, Peplow. Exeter: Roberts.
Attendance: 3,807.

Determined and efficient from the outset, Exeter City made Tranmere Rovers look anything but a top of the table side. They were rocked, however, by two goals in as many minutes and a brave fightback just failed to bring any reward.

Tranmere often looked sluggish and unenterprising as City stole the initiative from the start. The Exeter defence apart from one wild period after an hour, gave precious little away, with Bobby Saxton and Peter Hatch in outstanding form.

Colin Randell, Nicky Jennings and John Templeman all produced worthwhile shots as Exeter pushed forward, yet it was Tranmere who should have snatched a 41st minute lead, but somehow Palios managed to hook the ball over the bar from close range. Richard Key pulled out a wonder save in the 54th minute from a Tynan volley, and this was the first sign of better things to come from the home side as City were suddenly hit by a goal burst.

In the 60th minute Moore picked his spot past Key following a pass from Tynan, then 60 seconds later Peplow raced in to put an unstoppable shot into the net as City appealed in vain for offside.

Exeter might have been excused for calling it a day, but instead they hit back with vengeance. Bobby Hodge hit the bar, then in the 76th minute Lee Roberts headed home from a neat flick on by Tony Kellow. Two minutes from time City almost salvaged a point as Tranmere defender Mathias cleared a shot from Saxton off the goal line.

SATURDAY 8th OCTOBER 1977

FREE TRANSFER DIXIE IS A MATCH WINNER
Third Division
Exeter City 0 Wrexham 1
Exeter City team: Key, Templeman, Hore, Bowker, Saxton, Hatch, Hodge, Kellow, Randell, Roberts, Jennings.
Wrexham team: Davies, Evans, Dwyer, Davis, Roberts, Whittle, Shinton, Sutton, McNeil, Cartwright, Griffiths (Thomas).
Scorer: Wrexham: McNeil.
Attendance; 4,722.

The player given a free transfer by Exeter City a few years ago, returned to St. James' Park and proved to be the match winner for Wrexham. Dixie McNeil waited until the very last minute of the match to score, as the referee signalled the goal and then blew for full time. McNeil scored with a sharp header following a free-kick, and in that one move taught Exeter a lesson in what finishing was all about.

The defeat has now stretched City's dismal run to seven games without a win, which has become a worrying trend. In the first half neither side gave anything away in a tight dour struggle. City almost took the lead on the half hour when a Nicky Jennings shot hit goalkeeper Davies without him knowing too much about it.

Exeter drove forward, but some of their passing was being cut out by an eager Wrexham side and it looked as if patience was going to be the virtue against the visitors who rarely threatened the Grecians. There were appeals from Exeter supporters for a penalty when both Lee Roberts and Tony Kellow went down in the area in the same incident, but the referee waved play on. Kellow had the chance to break the deadlock shortly before the end but missed from close range. It was to be a costly miss.

Wrexham threatened when Shinton hit the top of the crossbar, but then came McNeil's goal which left City with no time to hit back.

CITY BOSS IS DISAPPOINTED
Exeter City player-manager Bobby Saxton has been disappointed with the points return in recent matches.

"Having suffered two home defeats against Portsmouth and Carlisle United by the narrowest of margins, it was important we bounced back against Chesterfield," he said. "We became the first team this season to take a point from Saltergate. No one would argue that those two home defeats were, to state the obvious, very disappointing, and with a difficult away programme we knew we had to redeem ourselves."

"In the last six games, prior to today, we have managed only two points from a possible twelve, a record which is not encouraging. I am disappointed, but not too dispondent."

CONFUSION OVER CITY LOTTERY AVOIDED
Exeter City are to change the headings on their lottery draw tickets and associated publicity posters from "The City Lottery" to "The City F.C. Lottery." This is being done to avoid confusion with the lottery run by the Exeter City Council. City commercial manager Ray Ellis said that as from next month the tickets would bear the new title.

This follows an amicable meeting between council officials and the club when it was agreed to alter the football club lottery tickets purely to avoid confusion between the two schemes

"Thanks to the tremendous amount of goodwill between the council and the city football club the matter has now been sorted out," said Richard Van Oppen, leader of Exeter City Council. The current batch of 25,000 football club lottery tickets will continue to be sold this month as originally printed.

CITY SIGN YOUNG PROSPECT
Exeter City have added to their youth squad of players by signing local lad, Paul Clatworthy, 14, who has appeared for the Exeter Schools side. Clatworthy has signed on schoolboy forms with the Grecians, despite attracting the interest of a number of other clubs.

WEDNESDAY 12th OCTOBER 1977

DRAMATIC VICTORY FOR GRECIANS
Exeter City 2 Sheffield Wednesday 1
Exeter City team: Key, Roberts, Hore, Bowker, Saxton, Hatch, Hodge, Kellow, Randell, Holman, Jennings.
Sheffield Wednesday team: Turner, Walden, Rushbury, Dowd, Cusack, Mullen, Leman, Johnson, Tynan, Wylde, Bradshaw (Gregson).
Scorers: Exeter: Jennings, Holman; Sheffield Wednesday: Tynan.
Attendance: 4,564.

There could not have been a more dramatic finish to the game with Exeter City scoring the winning goal in the very last seconds. The referee signaled the goal and then blew the final whistle. So at long last the Grecians have broken that spell of games without a win and there must have been a sigh of relief big enough to have shaken the St. James' Park foundations. It had been a game of fast, furious action and full of excitement

The first half was played at an electrifying pace with plenty of incidents in both goalmouths. Wednesday were a tough and big side, but they did not play defensive football expected from them. It was such a vial win for Exeter who began with Harry Holman missing the target early on, and then have a Nicky Jennings overhead kick cleared off the line.

It was Wednesday though who took a 21st minute lead. Richard Key produced a brilliant save. Jennings hooked the ball clear, but it hit Tynan and rebounded into the net. Exeter hit back within a minute to equalise. A cross from Tony Kellow hit the bar and Jennings headed home the rebound.

Not surprisingly the pace was not as strong in the second half, but Exeter kept their shape and patience. With the seconds ticking away and a draw seemingly the result, City won a corner. John Hore took the kick, Kellow chipped the ball back into the middle for Holman to score with a header.

CITY DEVELOPING THEIR OWN PLAYERS
As one of the smaller clubs it is obviously logical for Exeter City to try and find their own players rather than paying a transfer fee for them from other clubs. This is of course the reason for operating a youth policy, but there is more to be gained than the mere saving of a transfer fee.

By concentrating on the cream of local talent as City are doing, they hope to be able to develop players who have a feeling for their local club and who produce the qualities which Exeter think are important in professional football.

When the club sign on a youngster on schoolboy forms a great deal of work has already taken place by Chris Davey, the reserve team manager, and especially chief scout and physio Tony Long. The boys are watched several times, parents visited and only then do the club sign a youngster.

The latest batch of 14-years old to sign for the Grecians are Ian Cole, Mark Bowen and Paul Clatworthy. The lads undergo a regular coaching and training sessions with Chris Davey and reserve team coach Ken Ramsden. The process is a long and demanding one and many fall by the wayside after promising much as schoolboys.

City are hoping that Bobby Hodge, Graham Weeks and Harry Holman, all youngsters brought through by the club may be joined in the first team by the current apprentice professionals, Roy Ireland and Paul Smythe, or even one or two of the younger ones in the not too distant future.

COMMERCIAL ASSISTANT APPOINTED
Following the recent launch of the City Lottery, a new member of staff has been appointed to the commercial department. "Stafford Spurway will need very little introduction to the majority of supporters," explained Commercial Manager, Ray Ellis. "He has been the Supporter of the Year for the past two seasons and on merit justifies his appointment as Commercial Assistant."

"Stafford will be concentrating mainly on the club's Three & Easy competition, looking for new agencies and recruiting more members."

SATURDAY 15th OCTOBER 1977

NEWMAN WATCHES EXETER CITY VICTORY
Third Division
Lincoln City 1 Exeter City 2
Lincoln City team: Grozier, Neale, Leigh, Booth, Wigginton, Crombie, Hubbard, Fleming, Graham, Smith, Harding.
Exeter City team: Key, Hore, Roberts, Bowker, Saxton, Hatch, Hodge, Kellow, Randell, Holman, Jennings.
Scorers: Lincoln: Graham; Exeter: Randell, Kellow.
Attendance: 4,704

Exeter City have at last laid their Sincil Bank bogey. After years of poor results at Lincoln City's ground they grabbed victory after taking an early lead. City were visited in their dressing room before the game by former Exeter manager John Newman, now in charge at Grimsby Town.

The Grecians went ahead after just four minutes when Bobby Hodge crossed for Keith Bowker to chest the ball down to Colin Randell, who hit a 20-yard shot that Grotier allowed to squirm through his hands into the net. Lincoln also had the ball in the net after 15 minutes, but Hubbard's long range effort was disallowed for offside. City were operating with just Harry Holman and Tony Kellow up front and having players funnelling back to cover as Lincoln drove forward.

The home side equalised in the 41st minute when a corner taken by Booth fell to Graham in a hectic goal mouth scramble, who hooked the ball past Richard Key. City survived some early second half pressure and then regained the lead in the 56th minute. A long clearance out of defence found Kellow in space, who calmly slotted the ball home. This goal spurred Exeter onto better things, because they had not been at their best until that point. The Grecians pushed forward as they strung their game together much better by going at Lincoln, The home side started to give the ball away time and time again and by the final whistle Exeter were worthy winners.

WEDNESDAY 19th OCTOBER 1977

SETBACK FOR ALAN BEER
Exeter City striker Alan Beer's knee has broken down again in training. And this big setback means he could be out of action for some considerable time.His knee gave way in yesterday's training session, just 24-hours after he had been given the all clear to start again.

The knee has once more been put in plaster and he will see a specialist early next week. Beer has been a big loss to the Grecians this season, and he felt his knee give way when he had to pull up after a challenge in a 5-a-side match at the Cat and Fiddle training ground.

FRIDAY 21st OCTOBER 1977

THIRD DIVISION LEAGUE TABLE

	P	W	D	L	F	A	Pts
Tranmere Rovers	12	7	2	3	17	8	16
Gillingham	13	6	4	3	25	20	16
Colchester United	13	5	5	3	17	9	15
Wrexham	13	5	5	3	19	15	15
Shrewsbury Town	13	6	3	4	23	20	15
Bury	12	5	5	2	15	12	15
Rotherham United	13	6	3	4	20	18	15
Peterborough United	13	5	5	3	11	11	15
Oxford United	13	5	4	4	19	16	14
Preston North End	12	4	6	2	12	9	14
EXETER CITY	13	5	3	5	17	13	13
Walsall	13	3	7	3	13	14	13
Swindon Town	13	4	4	5	20	19	12
Plymouth Argyle	13	3	6	4	14	16	12
Chesterfield	13	5	2	6	12	14	12
Cambridge United	12	4	4	4	16	19	12
Hereford United	13	4	4	5	10	13	12
Chester	13	2	8	3	14	20	12
Portsmouth	12	2	7	3	9	11	11
Lincoln City	13	4	2	7	14	16	10
Bradford City	13	3	4	6	15	19	10
Port Vale	12	3	4	5	13	21	10
Carlisle United	13	2	5	6	13	18	9
Sheffield Wednesday	13	1	6	6	9	16	8

SATURDAY 22nd OCTOBER 1977

BOXING CHAMP PRESENT TO SEE CITY DELIVER KNOCKOUT BLOWS
Third Division
Exeter City 2 Preston North End 0
Exeter City team: Key, Templeman, Hore, Bowker, Saxton, Hatch, Hodge, Kellow, Randell, Holman, Jennings
Preston North End team: Tunks, Cameron, Wilson, Doyle, Baxter, Cross, Coleman, Haslegrave, Thomson (Burns), Elwiss, Smith.
Scorers: Exeter: Jennings, Kellow.
Attendance: 5,444.

Exeter City continued their climb back into the top of the Third Division with a well deserved victory over Preston North End, who arrived at St. James' Park without an away win this season, but nevertheless possessing a good defensive record.

It was an historic match for the Grecians, for it was the first time they had played Preston in a league fixture. City opened in aggressive style, keeping the visitors defence extremely busy and very little of the Preston attack was seen early on. It was no surprise when City took a 25th minute lead. A Peter Hatch long throw in was helped on to Nicky Jennings who scored with a close range shot. This was the signal of some hectic City pressure. Harry Holman had a header cleared off the line and Tony Kellow had a goal disallowed.

The centre of attraction at half-time was the appearance of the British boxing Champion, Alan Minter, who was a guest of City director Clifford Hill, before officially opening the new Vice President's Club.

After 61 minutes Exeter confirmed their superiority with a second goal. It came after one of the many fouls during the afternoon on Holman. Bobby Saxton took a quick free-kick which caught out the Preston defence and Kellow headed over Tunks who was off his line. Exeter continued to dictate the play, although Cameron had a chance to reduce the arrears, but his shot was way off target which summed up the trouble with Preston - woeful finishing.

TUESDAY 25th OCTOBER 1977

KNEE OPERATION FOR BEER
Exeter City striker Alan Beer entered hospital today for an operation on his damaged right knee which has kept him from playing for most of the season. It is unlikely that the player will return to action for at least three or four months which is bad news for player-manager Bobby Saxton.

SATURDAY 29th OCTOBER 1977

THERE WAS NEVER A FOUR GOAL DIFFERENCE
Third Division
Swindon Town 4 Exeter City 0
Swindon Town team: Roberts, Ford, Trollope, McLaughlin, Aizlewood, Prophett, Moss, Stroud, Kamara, (French), McHale, Anderson.
Exeter City team: Key, Templeman, Hore, Bowker, Saxton, Hatch, Hodge, Kellow, Randell, Holman, Jennings.
Scorers: Swindon: Anderson (2), McHale, Moss.
Attendance: 7,021.

There must be a lengthy inquest into why Exeter City conceded goals when until the late stages there was never a great margin between the two sides. The game in effect, was won and surrendered, in the first half when a Anderson header in the 19th minute and a Moss shot after 32 minutes gave Swindon a comfortable interval lead.

City had their moments with Nicky Jennings striking a post to give Swindon a reminder that a hard afternoon still lay ahead. In the second half there were times when the Grecians looked completely out of their depth as Swindon stroked the ball about and individuals such as Kamara and Moss threatened to take City apart.

To their credit, Exeter never relinquished their belief in their own neat football and in the 60th minute hit the woodwork again, this time Tony Kellow's shot struck the foot of the post. Both Bobby Hodge and Jennings also saw shots fly narrowly over the crossbar as City tried to find a way back.

McHale was Swindon's hero in the 79th minute striking a spectacular shot from 30-yards that sailed high and to the left of a bewildered Richard Key. Exeter were punished again five minutes from time when Anderson scored his second goal of the game with a neat cross shot. The score line was a little flattering from the Swindon point of view, but any team who take chances in the way Swindon took theirs, deserve to win.

NB - Vintage adverts from the 1970s - do not respond!

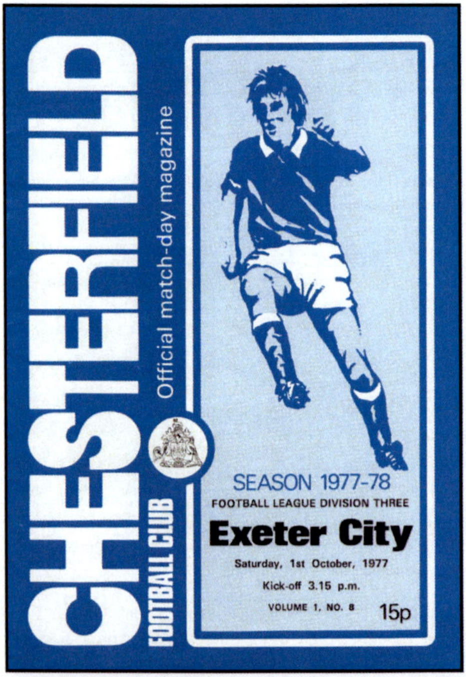

BACK ROW (L-R) Keith Ford, Keith Bowker, Harry Holman, Bobby Saxton MIDDLE ROW Lammie Robertson, John Templeman, John Baugh, Richard Key, Phil Howe, Bobby Hodge, Peter Hatch. FRONT ROW Jack Edwards, Nicky Jennings, Graham Weeks, John Hore, Tony Kellow, Alan Beer, Tony Long. IN FRONT Paul Smythe, Roy Ireland

WEDNESDAY 2nd NOVEMBER 1977

WESTERN LEAGUE STRIKER FOR CITY

The Western League's most talented striker, Fred Ingham, has been in full time training with Exeter City this week in an effort to earn a full professional contract at St. James' Park. The 23-year-old joined the Grecians as a non-contract player in September and has played in several reserve team matches.

At the age of 16, Ingham made his Football League debut for Stockport County. From there he moved to Blackburn Rovers where he had the misfortune to break a leg. He was released at the end of the season and Ingham then signed for Witton Albion in the Cheshire League, where he became their joint leading goalscorer.

FRIDAY 4th NOVEMBER 1977

HAPPY SO FAR SAYS CITY BOSS

With a third of the season gone Exeter City find themselves in twelfth position in the Third Division.

"At the beginning of the season I said that we had the players within the club capable of holding their own on the higher grade of football. Nothing has happened to make me change my mind," explained Grecians' player-manager Bobby Saxton.

"We started very well and occupied the third spot at one time having taken seven from a possible eight points, and at that time I said we should set our sights on the Second Division. I still maintain that this is what we must aim at, even though we are newly promoted and not expected to do more than hold our own in the Third Division."

"During the course of a season things can change, some for the benefit of the club, some to the detriment. Such changes can have an effect on the team. We have already suffered with the loss of Alan Beer for what looks like a lengthy period. However, good teams overcome setbacks like this and we shall do the same."

AND THE FIRST WINNER IS .....

The first winner of the newly launched Exeter City Football Club lottery is David Moore of Exeter. He will be presented with his cheque for £1,000 by City chairman Gerald Vallance during the half-time interval at tomorrow's game with Oxford United.

SATURDAY 5th NOVEMBER 977

GRECIANS WIN BATTLE IN THE RAIN

Third Division

Exeter City 2 Oxford United 1

Exeter City team: Key, Templeman, Hore, Bowker, Saxton, Hatch, Hodge, Kellow, Randell, Holman, Jennings.

Oxford United team: Burton, Kingston, Fogg, Bodell, Clarke, Jeffrey, McGrogan, Briggs (Seacole), Foley, Curran, Taylor.

Scorers: Exeter: Hodge, Bowker. Oxford: Curran.

Attendance: 4,830

Exeter City had a real fight on their hands before overcoming Oxford United. Both sides could have had more goals, but from City's point of view the game was decided when they lit the blue touch paper in an explosive ten minute first half period during the first half when they scored twice.

The match was played in heavy rain, so heavy that the guttering along part of the main stand was spilling over onto the track around the pitch. City went ahead after 15 minutes from the penalty spot. Nicky Jennings beat one man and was then promptly brought down by Briggs. Bobby Hodge hammered the spot kick high into the net.

There was no stopping Exeter at this point, and nine minutes later they went further ahead. John Templeman set the goal up as he exposed the Oxford defence with a pass to Hodge. He crossed to Keith Bowker who had the easy task of tucking the ball away from close range.

Oxford pulled a goal back after 33 minutes through Curran, and it proved to be heavy going after the interval on the treacherous surface. City had the ball in the net again when Harry Holman fed Tony Kellow, but his shot did not count for an offside decision.

Oxford searched eagerly for an equaliser and on one occasion John Hore almost conceded an own goal when trying to cut out a cross. Kellow missed a good chance of increasing Exeter's advantage in the closing stages, but nonetheless it had been a very hard earned victory.

CITY APPOINT A FULL TIME SCOUT
Exeter City have appointed former Plymouth Argyle goalkeeper, Jim Furnell, as the club's full time scout. Confirming the appointment yesterday, Furnell wasted no time in starting work for the Grecians as he went to watch the Western League match at Frome Town.

Furnell, who has also played for Rotherham United, Arsenal and Liverpool, has been involved in assessing players and opposition for Bobby Saxton this season. Following a board meeting of the Exeter City directors, Furnell has now been appointed on a full time basis. He was a team mate of Saxton whilst playing for Argyle.

INGHAM SIGNS FOR CITY
23-year-old striker Fred Ingham, who has been training with Exeter City this past week, has now signed a full professional contract with the club. This follows impressive performances whilst playing for the City reserve team.

VANDALS AT THE PARK
Police are investigating a case of vandalism at St. James' Park which occurred overnight. The newly painted doors of the main entrance to the ground have been daubed in yellow paint with the words – "Oxford United."

FRIDAY 11th NOVEMBER 1977

MILLWALL WANT KELLOW
Exeter City have confirmed that Millwall have been in touch with them over the transfer of striker Tony Kellow. "Millwall manager Gordon Jago has been in touch with me over the future of Tony Kellow," said City player-manager Bobby Saxton. "They have been in touch on several occasions, but I have told him he is not for sale. I also refute rumours that Millwall have offered £100,000."

SATURDAY 12th NOVEMBER 1977

CITY FAIL TO DEAL WITH A CORNER
Third Division
Gillingham 1 Exeter City 0
Gillingham team: Hillyard, Knight, Burrows, Overton, Shipperley, Crabbe, Nicholl, Hunt (Wetherley), Price, Westwood, Richardson.
Exeter City team: Key, Templeman, Hore, Bowker, Saxton, Hatch, Hodge, Kellow, Randell, Holman, Jennings.
Scorer: Gillingham: Price.
Attendance; 5,714

Exeter City's inexplicable weakness in dealing with corners cost them once again. They lost two goals in the previous away match at Swindon Town because of them - and they were exploited once more.

Gillingham only had four throughout the game, yet from the final one, snatched the goal that was to separate the sides. Centre-forward Price applied the coup-de-grace with a header that was perfectly placed in the top corner of the net with eight minutes of the match remaining. Apart from the Price goal there was only one real winner. That being the wind which gusted to gale force speeds at times. It reduced the game to a lottery.

Arguably Gillingham should really have cashed in during the first half when Richard Key made a string of fine saves to keep the scores level. Yet Exeter also experienced their share of misses, particularly in the second half when Burrows deflected a goal bound Harry Holman shot to safety without knowing what time of day it was. Keith Bowker was unlucky to see his 77th minute close range shot hooked off the line by Nicholl.

For much of the time though the game developed into a battle of the midfield where City were in control without being on top. It was up front where Gillingham held the aces over City, although the longer the game went on, the more disillusioned their forwards became in trying to outwit them.

TUESDAY 15th NOVEMBER 1977

TESTIMONIALS
Exeter City have been asked to provide seven players for tonight's match at Plainmoor between Torquay United and a combined Exeter City and Plymouth Argyle side. The match is a benefit for Torquay United's central defender David

Stocks, who gave up playing football last season following an ankle injury.

Former Exeter City full-back, Alan Goad, now with Hartlepool, had his testimonial game last night, when Nottingham Forest were the visitors. The game ended 2-2.

SATURDAY 19th NOVEMBER 1977

PENALTY SETTLES THE MATCH
Third Division
Exeter City 1 Bradford City 0
Exeter City team: Key, Templeman, Hore, Bowker, Saxton, Hatch, Hodge, Kellow, Randell, Holman, Jennings.
Bradford City team: Downsborough, Hardcastle, Podd, Ratcliffe, Middleton, Fretwell, Smith, Dolan, Cooke, Wright, Hutchins.
Att 4747

Exeter City had to rely on a Bobby Hodge spot kick 20 minutes from time to beat Bradford City, and it has to be said the decision looked to be somewhat harsh. Middleton and Hodge challenged for the loose ball. Hodge fell and the referee immediately awarded the penalty. It was enough to break the deadlock between two of last season's promoted teams.

After a pathetic first half, Exeter stepped up their game a little after the interval, but overall this was a poor match, from which City must have been relieved to have salvaged both points. It was a pretty scrappy affair with too many passes going astray and there was not any cohesion to the game.

Tony Kellow tried to break the deadlock with a deceptive 30-yard shot that was only just over the bar. Exeter pushed forward more in the second half, but there was little sign of a breakthrough with Bradford City dealing capably with the City attack which seemed to lack ideas. Even when the Grecians took the lead with a penalty, there was little to enthuse over. Both sides seemed to be sadly out of touch.

Peter Hatch had a superb game in defence for City, hardly putting a foot wrong, whilst Hodge was City's best forward. His colleagues though failed to bring Hodge into the game enough, as his pace caused problems at times to the Bradford City defence.

FURNELL TO BENEFIT CITY
In the months ahead there should be even more activity on the City youth scene with the arrival of Jim Furnell as full time chief scout. The club is sure to benefit greatly from his work. Already City have signed Heavitree United's talented forward, Micky Hunns, on youth forms, who along with another City youngster, Trafford Tasker, has been selected for the Devon County youth side.

PRAISE FOR CITY FANS
There has been nothing but praise for the travelling Exeter City fans who follow the team up and down the country. Player-manager Bobby Saxton and his players have already expressed that the City fans vocal support certainly lifts them at away fixtures.

The coach company used to transport the supporters have also complimented the Grecians on their behaviour both on the coaches and at Motorway Service Stations. Hooliganism, that we hear and read about elsewhere, is not tolerated in any shape or form by the club, so it is refreshing to hear the praise being heaped upon the City away followers.

MONDAY 21ST NOVEMBER 1977

EXETER CITY ANNOUNCE PROFIT FOR YEAR
Promotion has paid dividends for Exeter City Football Club as they announced a profit of £4,411 in the 1976-77 season, compared with losses of £22,451 and £30,909 respectively in the previous two years. The increases in net income from home gates and club fundraising are the two major items shown in the trading profit and loss account of the annual statement issued by the club today.

Home gate receipts were up from £25,653 to £49,813. Fundraising increased from £26,560 to £40,857. Exeter's tremendous run in to promotion obviously snowballed throughout the club, and the profit follows a sharp warning a year ago from chairman Gerald Vallance when he said that the club could not stand another substantial loss.

Vallance did, however, forecast that the club would come out of another year, even with a small profit, and this has been proved right. Share of away gate receipts was £15,918 compared to £14,328. Share of the F.A. and Football League pools was £35,975 as against £34,306.

Season ticket sales were also up slightly. Transfer fees received were way down at £3,250 as against £18,000. Wages and signing on fees were slightly down. Transfer fees paid showed a drop of £1,500, but travelling and hotel expenses rose by nearly £4,000. Maintenance of the ground and premises went up by nearly £3,000, but administration expenses showed a slight drop.

The directors are of the opinion that the value of the land and buildings at St. James' Park exceeds the book value of £40,674. They have taken no account of the potential tax liability which would arise in the event of the realisation of the land and buildings at this value. The debit balance at 31st May 1977 was £118,934.

FRIDAY 25th NOVEMBER 1977

COUNTY HOPING FOR REVENGE!
Exeter City travel to Newport County tomorrow for their first round F.A. Cup tie, and County boss Colin Addison has been talking about the game.

"The FA Cup match is a bit special for us because we're out for a bit of revenge against Exeter City, as they were the last team to win at Somerton Park," said Addison. "They are a very good footballing side and we shall have to be at our best if we are to go through to the next round. The FA Cup always means a little bit extra to me, because I know from my days at Hereford United what a good run can mean to a club and the district that supports it."

It is the sixth occasion that Newport County and Exeter City have been paired together in the F.A. Cup. The first encounter was way back n 1919-20 when both clubs were members of the Southern League, with County winning the sixth qualifying round tie at Somerton Park by 1-0.

However, in 1924-25 it was the Grecians turn to go through by the only goal in a second replay at Ashton Gate. In the 1945-46 two-leg competition, Newport coasted through winning both games, 5-1 at Somerton and 3-1 at St. James' Park. Exeter gained some revenge themselves though in the first round of 1968-69, when in a replay at Newport they won 3-1, two of the goals being own goals!

The most recent F.A. Cup meeting between the respective clubs was in November 1974 when City lost 2-1.

SATURDAY 26th NOVEMBER 1977

GRECIANS EARN A REPLAY AT SOMERTON PARK
F.A. Cup Round One
Newport County 1 Exeter City 1
Newport County team: Plumley, Derrett, Bell, Emanuel, Walker, Aizlewood, Guscott, Goddard, Clark, Vaughan, Williams.
Exeter City team: Key, Templeman, Hore, Bowker, Saxton, Hatch, Hodge, Kellow, Randell, Holman, Jennings.
Scorers: Newport: Goddard. Exeter: Bowker.
Attendance: 6,227.

If Exeter City win the replay on Wednesday evening they will have to thank goalkeeper Richard Key for two saves in the first match between the sides that would have graced the final itself, and both came in the final crucial last ten minutes of the tie. Fortunately for Exeter, a last minute shot from Goddard hit the post, rolled along the line, and hit the other post before the ball was cleared.

Newport County's efforts were such that they would consider themselves unlucky in having to replay at St. James' Park. City rarely moved out of bottom gear and resigned themselves to a backs to the wall struggle after losing Bobby Hodge with a knee injury after 75 minutes.

The Grecians took the lead on the hour when Nicky Jennings opened the way for Keith Bowker to score with a perfect header from six-yards. Following that success, Exeter shook off their cup-tie blues for the first time in the match and they moved forward with confidence and a purpose.

Exeter's feathers were well and truly ruffled in the 74th minute when they conceded a penalty and Newport equalised from it. Player-manager Bobby Saxton had brought down Clark in the area and up stepped Goddard to score. Several scuffles broke out behind the railway end of the ground and some Exeter supporters were ejected.

There has been a long history of such incidents between the two groups of supporters at Newport County's Somerton Park ground, and Police had to move in to restore order. City were reduced to ten men for the final 15 minutes, and hardly moved outside their own half, as they hung on grimly for a replay.

MONDAY 28th NOVEMBER 1977

CITY LOAN MOVE TURNED DOWN

Exeter City player-manager Bobby Saxton had to admit defeat in an attempt to get Tottenham Hotspur striker Martin Robinson on loan. Saxton has watched the player four or five times, but Spurs have refused to send the player out on loan. Exeter then asked how much Spurs wanted for the player on a transfer, and were told £30,000 to £40,000, which is way above what the Grecians are prepared to pay.

WEDNESDAY 30th NOVEMBER 1977

CITY REACH ROUND TWO

F.A. Cup Round One Replay

Exeter City 4 Newport County 2

Exeter City team: Key, Templeman, Hore, Bowker, Saxton, Hatch, Weeks, Kellow, Randell, Roberts, Jennings.

Newport County team: Plumley, Derrett, Bell, Emanuel, Walker, Aizlewood, Guscott, Goddard, Clark, Vaughan, Williams.

Scorers: Exeter: Roberts, Hatch, Kellow, Templeman. Newport: Clark, Goddard.

Attendance: 5,713.

In an exciting and dramatic cup tie, Exeter City, against all the odds, won through to round two after fighting back from a half-time deficit. Cruelly hit by injury, Tony Kellow was forced to play with his leg heavily strapped, but City showed courage and utter determination aplenty.

They refused to be knocked out of their stride and came back with a vengeance in the second half to stun a Newport side who must have thought by then that they, and not Exeter, were safely into the next round. City did in fact take the lead in the 16th minute. Kellow crossed for Nicky Jennings to nod the ball down to Lee Roberts to volley into the net.

Five minutes later it was all square again as Clark headed in a corner. Then in the 26th minute Newport edged in front. Once more it was from a corner which City failed to clear and Goddard lashed the ball home from the edge of the area. No one could have predicted what was going to happen in the second half though as City stormed back into the game.

Three minutes into the second half a Jennings corner was knocked on by John Templeman and Peter Hatch equalised with a diving header. Two minutes later City were in front with a tremendous four man move that ended with Kellow shooting into the net. The fourth Exeter goal came in the 67th minute. Templeman collected a throw in, weaved past two defenders, and shot low and hard into the net. City should have made it 5-2, but Keith Bowker's penalty kick was saved by Plumley in the 79th minute.

THURSDAY 1st DECEMBER 1977

DIFFICULT DECISION FOR NEWMAN

John Newman can end 18-months of painful self examination if Grimsby Town find their way straight back to Division Three by the end of the season. He has been fighting back self doubts since the day he decided to move from Exeter City just about one year ago.

Newman had spent seven years building an Exeter side he felt good enough to escape from the Fourth Division, when Grimsby Town offered him control of a side already established in the Third Division. The temptation was too great and he moved across to Grimsby, but was unable to check their slide into Division Four.

To rub in the irony, Exeter City gave him a promotion wave as they passed by onto Division Three.

"It was a difficult decision to leave City because they had a good chance of going up," says Newman.

When Exeter were promoted, it crossed Newman's mind that perhaps he had made a mistake on leaving St. James' Park. Newman does not resent Exeter City's success and is delighted that they got promotion and are doing so well now. The only thing that went wrong from his point of view was that Grimsby Town were relegated. Only time will tell whether he has made the correct long term decision.

CITY SIGN LUTON TOWN STRIKER

Exeter City have completed the signing of Luton Town striker, Gary Heale, on a one month loan deal. Grecians' secretary Pat Wakeham travelled to Luton today and then onto London to register the signing with the Football League so that Heale can play on Saturday against Cambridge United.

The injury to Bobby Hodge meant that City's chief scout, Jim Furnell, and player-manager Bobby Saxton have spent time searching for a loan player as a replacement.

SATURDAY 3rd DECEMBER 1977

GRECIANS ARE OUTCLASSED
Third Division
Exeter City 2 Cambridge United 4
Exeter City team: Key, Templeman, Hore, Weeks, Roberts, Hatch, Jennings, Kellow, Bowker, Randell, Heale.
Cambridge United team: Hansbury, Batson, Smith, Stringer, Fallon, Streete, Watson, Buckley, Morgan, Finney, Biley.
Scorers: Exeter: Kellow (2). Cambridge: Fallon, Watson, Morgan, Key o.g.
Attendance: 4,932.

Exeter City can surely not attempt to dream up an excuse for this rock bottom performance. They were quite simply outplayed by Cambridge United. The visitors worked harder, reaped dividends from two free kicks and generally exposed City's alarming frailty at the back.

They passed the ball with more accuracy and their only mistake was in giving away two needless penalties that boosted Tony Kellow's tally for the season to 8. It really was a little ironic seeing Kellow chasing a hat-trick in such an outclassed side as Exeter City. Cambridge got their first goal after 17 minutes from a Watson free kick that Fallon dived forward to meet and head past Richard Key.

Kellow equalised 10 minutes later from the penalty spot after Batson had handled, but United were back in front within 3 minutes. Key half stopped a Morgan close range header, but in trying to scoop the ball to safety only succeeded in hooking it into his own net.

Lee Roberts completely sold himself in the tackle to get beaten by Watson for the visitors third goal after 50 minutes. Morgan increased Cambridge's lead after 61 minutes sliding the ball home from close in, as City were being outplayed. Loan signing Gary Heale, who had an undistinguished debut, was brought down in the penalty are in the 79th minute and Kellow hammered home his second spot kick.

TUESDAY 6th DECEMBER 1977

MINEHEAD CUP TIE: ALL TICKET

Exeter City's F.A. Cup second round tie at Southern League, Minehead is to be all ticket, and the Somerset club are gearing themselves up for a ground record crowd of 4,000. Minehead have made special arrangements for 1,400 to be seated, 400 in the existing stand and a further 1,000 in two temporary stands. Exeter have agreed to meet half the cost of erecting the temporary stands.

They will receive 1,200 ground tickets at 80p each, and a further 100 main stand tickets at £1.75p. They will also have 500 temporary stand tickets on sale at £1.20p.

FRIDAY 9th DECEMBER 1977

CITY MISS THEIR CHANCES
Colchester United 3 Exeter City 1
Colchester United team: Walker, Cook, Wignall, Dowman, Williams, Leslie, Packer (Foley), Garwood, Gough, Froggatt, Allinson.
Exeter City team: Key, Templeman, Hore, Bowker, Roberts, Hatch (Jennings), Weeks, Kellow, Randell, Heale, Holman
Scorers: Colchester: Dowman, Gough, Garwood. Exeter: Holman.
Attendance: 3,267

Exeter City were somewhat unlucky to lose by the margin they did in this all action match at Layer Road. City had as much of the play as Colchester United, but failed to put vital chances away, and that finally was the difference between the two teams.

The Grecians started brightly enough, even though they paid the penalty by giving too much space to young Colchester defender Dowman, who always caused problems to the City defence from set pieces and corners. It was Dowman who headed Colchester into an 18th minute lead from a Garwood corner.

Things looked bleak for City just before half time when Peter Hatch was taken off to hospital with what looked like a serious ankle injury, but proved to be heavy bruising. City fought back well in the second half and Colin Randell crashed a first time shot against the crossbar. In the 61st minute Harry Holman equalised, slamming home a rebound off Walker, following a free-kick taken by Nicky Jennings.

Colchester regained the lead after 65 minutes. Packer floated in a free-kick and bad marking left Bough to hit a right foot volley into the net. Seven minutes later Allinson swept past Graham Weeks, John Templeman and John Hore, before pulling the ball back for Garwood to score his 100th league goal, to clinch the game for Colchester. City continued to have as much of the game as Colchester, and Gary Heale was unlucky to see his shot pushed up onto the bar by Walker.

TUESDAY 13th DECEMBER 1977

SAXTON BIDS FOR GILES
Exeter City player-manager Bobby Saxton was today waiting for a reply from Charlton Athletic after making a firm bid for former Grecians defender, Jimmy Giles. Charlton's asking price of £10,000 is probably more than City can afford, but Saxton is hoping his lower bid will be accepted. Giles joined Charlton in a £10,000 deal in June 1976 after four successful years at St. James' Park, and the player is understood to be very interested in a move back to Exeter.

FRIDAY 16th DECEMBER 1977

MINEHEAD'S BIG F.A. CUP DAY
Minehead FC club secretary, Tony Milton, has described tomorrow's F.A. Cup second round tie as Minehead's big red letter day.

"We have every reason to expect a record attendance as we stand on the threshold of another soccer milestone, being only 90 minutes away from cup glory and a place in the third round for the very first time," he said. "Similarly Exeter City have high hopes pinned upon reaching the round which sees the big fish make their entry."

"With the added cup fever that has gripped the town of Minehead in the past few days. I feel sure that tomorrow's game has all the ingredients for being a memorable cup tie. "As members of the Southern League, we are ambassadors for non-league football and you can be assured that our club and players are well aware of the prestige which such a big day brings to the club and even more so to the town of Minehead."

SATURDAY 17th DECEMBER 1977

CITY CRUISE INTO ROUND THREE
F.A. Cup Round Two
Minehead 0 Exeter City 3
Minehead team: Macey, Impey, Clausen, Carter, Boyd, Brown, Freeman, Bryant, Leitch, Jenkins, Durbin.
Exeter City team: Key, Templeman, Hore, Bowker, Saxton, Hatch, Randell, Kellow, Holman, Roberts, Jennings.
Scorers: Exeter: Randell (2), Kellow.
Attendance: 3,200

Cup fever descended upon the town of Minehead. Their Irnham Road ground, situated in a public park, was packed to capacity as a record all ticket crowd awaited the entry of the two teams.

A temporary stand had been erected at the ground to accommodate the crowd, and the television cameras were present to record the proceedings. Exeter City found it all so simple though, as Minehead really only flickered into life at odd moments.

City's tactics were more than the non-leaguers could cope with. They used Harry Holman and Nicky Jennings as orthodox wingers, and the width they created left big holes in the Minehead defence. Tony Kellow gave City just the start they were looking for, by heading home after just ten minutes, following a Jennings corner, which had been flicked on by Lee Roberts. Minehead had a chance to equalise in the 27th minute, but a header from Leitch was superbly saved by Richard Key at full stretch.

Exeter ran the midfield, where Colin Randell and Keith Bowker gave the Southern League team little chance to create anything for their front runners. Exeter might well have had more than one goal by half-time, and if Minehead still had thoughts of a giant killing act, then they had to play a lot better after the interval.

City stretched their lead in the 67th minute when a superb 30-yard free kick flew into the net, as Randell's right foot shot took Macey by surprise. It was all over for Minehead and with ten minutes remaining they conceded a third goal and again it was from a free kick. Randell beat the the defensive wall with a swerving free kick to complete a comprehensive demolition job on Minehead, who had quite frankly, disappointed.

MONDAY 19th DECEMBER 1977

GILES RETURNS TO ST. JAMES' PARK
As expected Jimmy Giles is an Exeter City player again. The central defender agreed to sign for a second spell at Exeter City and put pen to paper in a £7,000 transfer today. Charlton had wanted £10,000 for the player, but Giles was keen to return to Exeter, and they accepted City's lower offer.

TUESDAY 20th DECEMBER 1977

EX-GRECIAN ACCUSED OF MURDER
Former Exeter City player, Alvan Williams, 45, was yesterday remanded in custody accused of the joint murder of a student outside his public house in Tottenham, North London. Williams, who played for the City in the 1960s, and once managed Southend United and Hartlepool, now runs the Robert E. Lee pub in Tottenham High Road. The charge was later reduced to one of affray.

WEDNESDAY 21st DECEMBER 1977

100 PER CENT TICKET PRICE INCREASE SHOCK
Exeter City supporters were shocked to learn that the Grecians are to increase the cost of admission by up to 100 per cent for their forthcoming F.A. Cup third round tie against Wolverhampton Wanderers. Grandstand tickets will be £3, double the normal price for a league fixture. A place in the Cowshed will be £1.50p compared to 80p., and the rest of the ground will be £1.20p instead of 80p.

The tie will be all-ticket, with a crowd limit of 16,000. It seems certain to break the club's gate receipts record set against Aston Villa earlier this season in the Football League Cup. City are setting up a special programme voucher scheme to ensure that the fans who turn up for the Hereford United match on 27th December will be able to obtain tickets.

Anyone who produces a programme from that game is guaranteed a ticket. Programmes will only be on sale inside the ground for the Hereford game and will be limited to one per person. Exeter City's Board of Directors decision to increase prices and cash in on the F.A. Cup is sure to anger the regular faithful fans who turn up every week for Third Division matches. The board felt, however, that they wanted to make as much money as possible out of the tie.

"Football at our level is all about survival," commented City secretary, Pat Wakeham. "A game like this will hopefully pay for new signings like Jimmy Giles."

MONDAY 26th DECEMBER 1977

ALL SQUARE AT HOME PARK
Third Division
Plymouth Argyle 2 Exeter City 2
Plymouth Argyle team: Barron, Smart, Uzzell, Megson, Foster, Craven, Johnson, Harrison (Taylor), Austin, Horswill, Rogers.
Exeter City team: Key, Templeman, Hore, Bowker, Saxton, Hatch, Jennings (Heale), Kellow, Randell, Roberts, Holman.
Scorers: Plymouth: Johnson, Craven. Exeter: Roberts, Kellow.
Attendance: 12,349.

This was good Christmas entertainment with plenty of excitement and a draw was a fair result at the end of it all. It was real end to end stuff, packed with attacking football and memorable saves by both goalkeepers. City almost won, but Argyle snatched an equaliser in the closing minutes.

Tony Kellow was always a threat to Plymouth, having his best game for some time. It was a battle for both sides which the spectators enjoyed immensely. Lee Roberts gave Exeter a 35th minute lead, at which stage they lost Nicky Jennings, who went off with severe discomfort after being struck in the face by the ball.

There was no shortage of excellent goalkeeping, with Richard Key making a superb double stop from Horswill and Rogers. At the other end, Barron saved spectacularly three times from Kellow. Plymouth scored an equaliser right on half-time, as Johnson finished off a fine move involving Horswill and Harrison. Johnson was unlucky to hit the City woodwork twice in the second half before Kellow, who confirmed his astonishing virtuosity, headed Exeter back into the lead when the Argyle defence failed to cut out a corner. Three minutes from time Craven powered a header past Key to earn Plymouth a deserved share of the points, to end the best local derby match between these two sides for a very long time.

TUESDAY 27th DECEMBER 1977

BOWKER IS CITY'S MATCH WINNER
Third Division
Exeter City 1 Hereford United 0
Exeter City team: Key, Templeman, Hore, Bowker, Saxton, Hatch, Heale, Kellow, Randell, Roberts, Holman.
Hereford United team: Mellor, Price (Proudlove), Burrows, Layton, Jefferson, Sheedy, Stephens, Briley, Davey, Marshall, Emery.
Scorer: Exeter: Bowker.
Attendance: 6,722.

Exeter City will be happy enough with their holiday points haul, but their performance in this match lacked the polish and purpose that they displayed against Plymouth Argyle. No doubt the conditions, a heavy pitch and torrential showers, did not help. But even allowing for that, much of Exeter's play was scrappy with a lot of loose passing and off target passing.

There was just not the same pattern, composure or drive to their approach work that they had shown at Home Park. It was a match that produced little excitement and at one time it looked as if there might be more bookings - four - than concrete shots at goal. Both sides battled away in the midfield mud and in spells Hereford looked better equipped to overcome the conditions.

For Exeter it was a case of a patchy performance. Sometimes they showed flashes of their true form, but not until the last twenty minutes did they demonstrate any real authority. The deadlock was broken in the 68th minute when John Templeman's free kick was turned into the penalty area by Colin Randell and Keith Bowker was on the spot to head home.

Early in the game City had been let off the hook when Davey with only Richard Key to beat incredibly hooked his shot over the bar. Equally, Exeter should have taken the lead themselves just before half time, but Kellow's penalty kick hit the post.

JACKSON LEAVES FOR WESTON
Exeter City have transferred Bob Jackson to Western League club, Weston-Super-Mare. Jackson, a non-contract player, had come to the club following trials with both Bristol Rovers and Nottingham Forest. Things did not work out as well as he would have liked and he was not offered a full professional contract by the Grecians. As Jackson lives in Weston-Super-Mare, the move to his local club was a sensible one for him, as he had to drive to Exeter for both training and matches.

EXETER CITY'S PROGRAMME - 1947 STYLE
Did you know that in August 1947 there were over 250 Lewis tobacco shops, including two in Exeter, all selling French briar pipes that could be filled with Afrikander, costing about three shillings and fourpence an ounce? For a cash outlay of £365, a mobile caravan home, two rooms, four berth fully furnished would be delivered. These gems of information were found in an old Exeter City match programme of August 1947. A glimpse through its pages reveals much more and stirs memories to keep one chattering away for some considerable time.

Just over 30 years ago, the cost of this mine of information was three old pennies. The cover, red and white, depicted a player in the then City colours, red and white hooped shirts, happily booting a ball in the manner of Third Division South forwards of the day. The visitors to St. James' Park were Reading. Page two revealed four spaces for advertising, two of which were empty! Further on we read that chairman Sid Thomas, headed the board of directors, with secretary George

Gilbert assisting manager George Roughton in organising the club's affairs.

After a few words on the previous season came another advert, this time for Central Garages, along with a photograph of their latest charabanc. A few more blank spaces, then we reach an article about the arrival of two new signings, Cyril Johnstone and Bill Fallon. The centre pages reveal an absence of empty spaces surrounding the square containing the City and Reading team line ups.

A further turn of the page reveals the Grecians' Association notes, pointing out that the subscription of two shillings fell due on 1st August and could be paid at the hut on the St. James' Road side of the covered bank.

GOOD NEWS FOR TRAVELLING GRECIANS
Exeter City have just ended considerable negotiations with British Rail. This has meant that the club have agreed terms on rail travel for away trips. In the past British Rail had priced themselves so high that it was either far too expensive for City fans to travel, or the risk taken by the football club was too high, often requiring 800 travellers to avoid losing money on a hired train.

Now it has been agreed that the club can issue their own tickets to be used on existing services. The fares will in most cases will be lower than existing cheap day returns. The club will steward the travelling fans themselves, who must be members of the Travelling Grecians. The first trip will be to Oxford in 31st December. The train will leave Exeter at 10.07. The fare is £2.75p return, with tickets available from the Near Post club shop. For an additional 75p travellers can also enjoy a packed lunch.

SATURDAY 31st DECEMBER 1977

GOALLESS AT THE MANOR GROUND
Third Division
Oxford United 0 Exeter City 0
Oxford United team: Milkins, Fogg, Drysdale, Bodell,
Stott, Jeffrey (Curran), McGrogan, Taylor, Foley, Seacole, Duncan.
Exeter City team: Key, Templeman, Hore, Weeks (Jennings), Giles, Hatch, Randell, Kellow, Bowker, Roberts, Holman.
Attendance: 4,688.

Ignore the result. Exeter City have figured in far worse games this season and won. They have also figured in better games and won. It was a bit like that. A lot of good football and some that might as well be forgotten. Oxford United were defending an unbeaten record at the Manor Ground which stretched back over ten games.

Exeter placed too much emphasis on defence and midfield to make it count where it really matters in front of goal. Having said that, there were still two moves late in the game that might have sent Exeter home with two points instead of one.

In fairness a winning goal for either side would have been an injustice on an afternoon when City player-manager dropped himself to make way for new signing Jimmy Giles. Oxford, like Exeter, did have their rare chances, but found Richard Key in brilliant form. He made two superb saves in the opening half hour. City suffered a setback in the 27th minute when Graham Weeks sustained a badly cut knee and was helped off to be replaced by Nicky Jennings.

Tony Kellow who had been struggling with knee ligament trouble for several games ended this match hobbling quite badly. Exeter though kept battling away at a tough Oxford defence. But the home side came more into the game in the second half, although the City defence dealt capably with any threat.

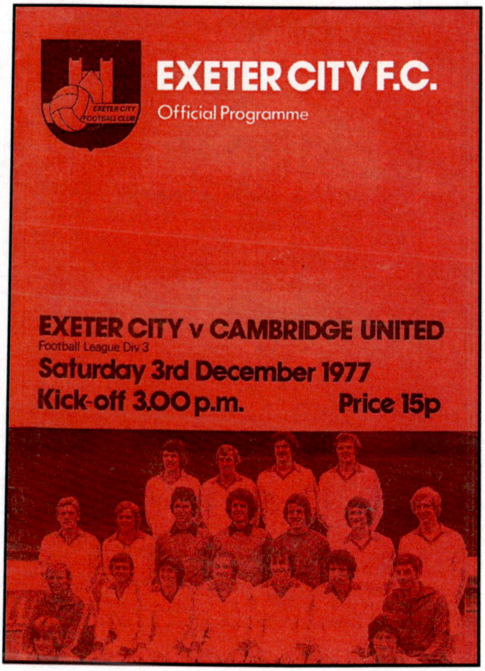
EXETER CITY F.C.
Official Programme
EXETER CITY v CAMBRIDGE UNITED
Football League Div 3
Saturday 3rd December 1977
Kick-off 3.00 p.m.
Price 15p

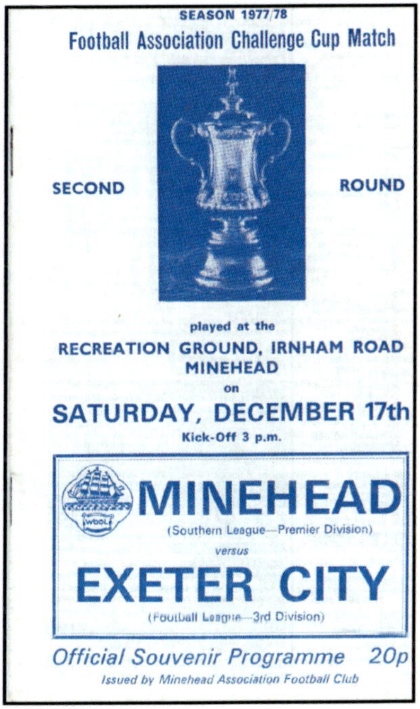
SEASON 1977/78
Football Association Challenge Cup Match
SECOND
ROUND
played at the
RECREATION GROUND, IRNHAM ROAD
MINEHEAD
on
SATURDAY, DECEMBER 17th
Kick-Off 3 p.m.
MINEHEAD
(Southern League—Premier Division)
versus
EXETER CITY
(Football League—3rd Division)
Official Souvenir Programme 20p
Issued by Minehead Association Football Club

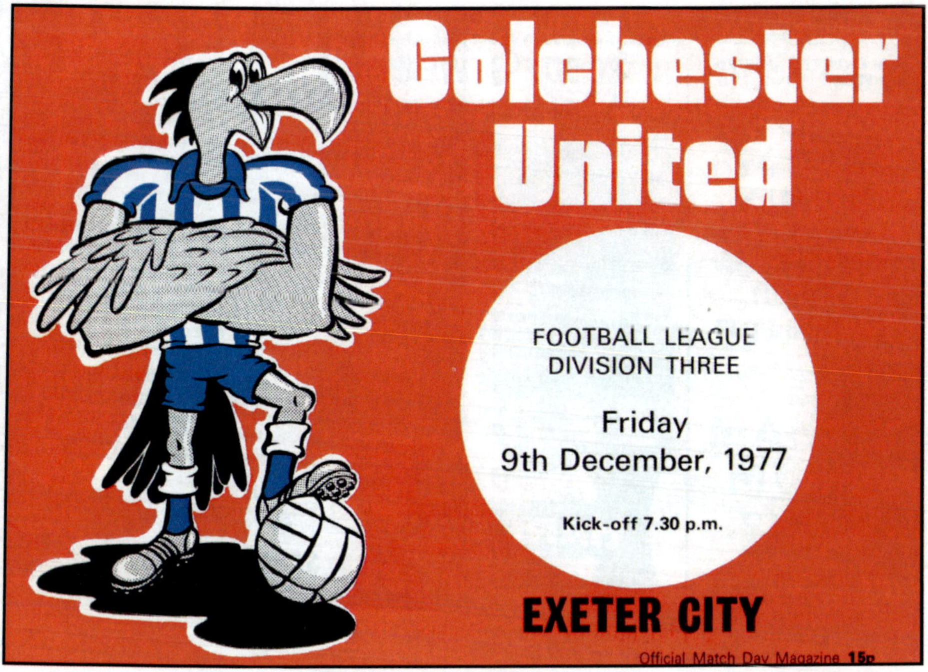
Colchester
United
FOOTBALL LEAGUE
DIVISION THREE
Friday
9th December, 1977
Kick-off 7.30 p.m.
EXETER CITY
Official Match Day Magazine 15p

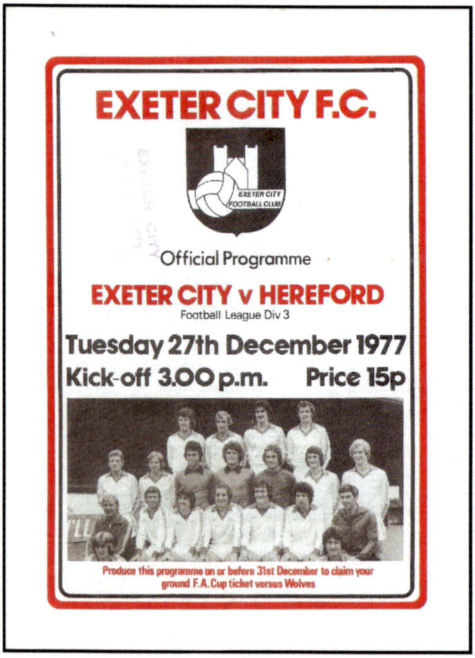
EXETER CITY F.C.
Official Programme
EXETER CITY v HEREFORD
Football League Div 3
Tuesday 27th December 1977
Kick-off 3.00 p.m.
Price 15p
Produce this programme on or before 31st December to claim your ground F.A. Cup ticket versus Wolves

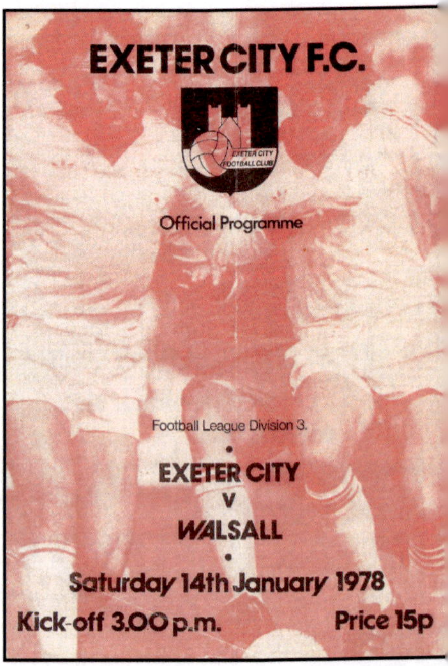
EXETER CITY F.C.
Official Programme
Football League Division 3.
EXETER CITY
v
WALSALL
Saturday 14th January 1978
Kick-off 3.00 p.m.
Price 15p

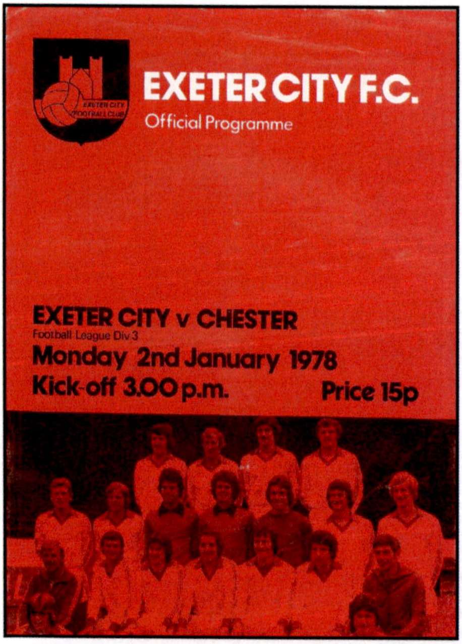
EXETER CITY F.C.
Official Programme
EXETER CITY v CHESTER
Football League Div 3
Monday 2nd January 1978
Kick-off 3.00 p.m.
Price 15p

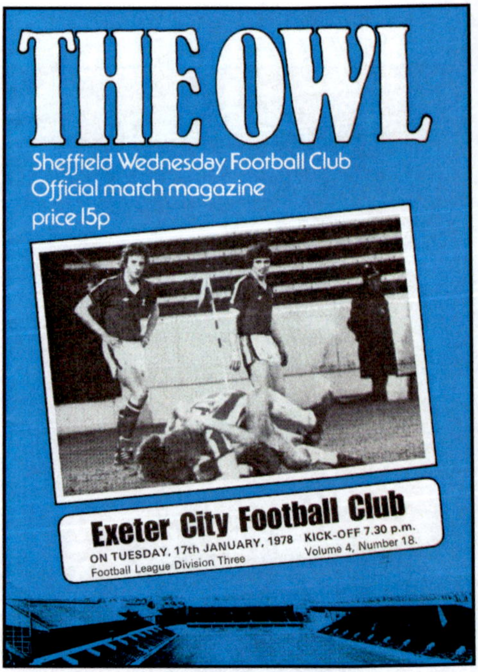
THE OWL
Sheffield Wednesday Football Club
Official match magazine
price 15p
Exeter City Football Club
ON TUESDAY, 17th JANUARY, 1978
KICK-OFF 7.30 p.m.
Football League Division Three
Volume 4, Number 18.

MONDAY 2nd JANUARY 1978

DREAM DEBUT FOR INGHAM
Third Division
Exeter City 1 Chester City 1
Exeter City team: Key, Templeman, Hore, Bowker, Giles, Hatch, Jennings, Kellow, Ingham, Roberts, Holman.
Chester City: Lloyd, N.Edwards, Walker, Nickeas, Delgado, Oakes, Crossley, Livermore, L.Edwards, Jones, Phillips.
Scorers: Exeter: Ingham. Chester: Crossley.
Attendance: 6,193.

Fred Ingham crowned his debut by grabbing a 54th minute equaliser. The 24-year-old, who only signed professional forms for the City in November after playing for Dawlish Town in the Western League, rounded off a heading match in the Chester goal mouth with a neat shot into the net.

He saved lacklustre City with that decisive blow and combined bursts of enthusiasm with some impressive touches. His debut was otherwise the only bright spot on a disappointing afternoon. Chester had not won an away match in eleven months, but could well have ended that dismal run had they taken their chances at St. James' Park.

In the first half Exeter City were ineffective and sadly unimpressive. Not until after the interval did the Grecians really start to link their game into any sort of pattern that resembled authority. Even allowing for players missing form the side through injury, this was a very much below par performance by Exeter. Chester shocked City by grabbing a 21st minute lead. A free-kick was rolled short to Crossley who thumped a 25-yard shot into the net.

After that Exeter looked jittery and Chester should have made more of the chances they created. Although Exeter played a lot better after Ingham's equaliser, Chester never let up and with only five minutes remaining Crossley fired wide with only Richard Key to beat.

SHOULD CITY RESERVES PLAY IN HIGHER LEAGUE?
As clubs become more and more professional off the field, so the inevitable question is being asked – "Why are Exeter City reserves not competing in the Football Combination?"

The answer is probably a very complex one with many considerations, such as finance and travelling expenses. Finance because of the number of professional players needed, and of course being accepted in the in Combination, Exeter's geographical position could lose them a few votes on that score. Perhaps there will be a revision of the present structure of the Football Combination league so that it operates on a regionalised basis.

Several players have blossomed in the City reserves so far this season, but none deserves more credit than amateur players, Dick Forbes and Tony Mitchell. Signed from St. Lukes College, they have both achieved a consistently high standard, both in training and in matches. Forbes, who skippers the reserve team from midfield, has become a firm favourite with supporters for his skilful and tricky play. Mitchell, normally a full-back, but very much a utility player, is a real players' player and much of his ability goes unnoticed.

CITY HOLD SCHOOLBOY TRIAL MATCHES
During the Christmas school holidays, Exeter City held their first schoolboy trial matches of the season, which Chief Scout, Jim Furnell hopes will be the first of many.

"Because of the financial state of Exeter City, and of the game in general, we feel it is imperative that we produce our own young players through a sound youth policy," said Furnell. "This we are attempting to do on our own doorstep by holding these trial matches in an effort to unearth possible stars of the future. I have watched scores of games since joining Exeter City as Chief Scout, looking at players at all different levels and have returned home very disappointed at the standard I have seen."

"I am sure there must be boys in the South West who, given the right opportunity and coaching can make a name for themselves in the game. We will be very critical in assessing the boys in the trial matches, but once we agree that a boy has a bit of something special then he will be given every encouragement to fulfil his ambition to become a professional footballer."

SATURDAY 7th JANUARY 1978

NO MISTAKING IT'S F.A. CUP DAY
Exeter City gave a mixed welcome to the estimated 3,500 Wolverhampton Wanderers supporters who invaded the city today for the third round of the FA Cup.

Public houses closed for the fear of what might happen, and there were 120 Police on duty to prevent any trouble that may arise. There was an official welcome from the Deputy Mayor of Exeter, John Levers, who said he hoped it would improve relations between the two sets of supporters.

No fewer than 37 coaches were parked in Union Road and Prince of Wales Road, as the Wolves fans were escorted to St. James' Park. The first to arrive were a group of 20, who had travelled overnight, slept in a railway waiting room at Bristol Temple Meads, whilst waiting for a connection that reached Exeter at 6am. The communication cord was pulled on one train arriving in Exeter this morning, but despite enquiries being made by the Railway Police, the culprits have not been found.

In another incident a mini car was overturned in Longbrook Street by a crowd of Wolverhampton Wanderers fans. One of the many messages wishing Exeter City success in the F.A. Cup was a telephone call received by City secretary Pat Wakeham. This was from former Grecians' manager John Newman, now in charge at Grimsby Town, who still watches with great interest the news coming from St. James' Park.

Former Exeter City secretary Mike Cosway, now secretary at Aldershot, was in Exeter today to watch the game. A lifelong supporter of City, Cosway took his holidays to specially attend the match.

GRECIANS ROBBED OF F.A. CUP SUCCESS
F.A. Cup Round Three
Exeter City 2 Wolverhampton Wanderers 2
Exeter City team: Key, Templeman, Hatch, Bowker, Giles, Saxton, Randell, Kellow, Holman, Roberts, Hore.
Wolverhampton Wanderers team: Bradshaw, Palmer, Parkin, Daley, Hazell, McAlle, Hibbitt, Carr, Richards, Bell, Kelly (Daly).
Scorers: Exeter: Roberts, Holman. Wolves: Carr, Daly.
Attendance: 14,377.

Exeter City, give or take a little time for a mass pitch invasion, were just three minutes away from F.A. Cup glory.

That is all that remained on the watch when Wolves substitute Gerry Daly hit a terrific volley from the edge of the penalty area that screamed into the net to save his side from a giant killing act. Wolves may have been a First Division side, but on the day Exeter City looked more worthy of that crown, with a display that captivated the crowd and allowed their players to walk off at the end with their heads held high.

City were not just Wolves equal, they were better on the day, and they were cruelly robbed of deserved glory by that Daly goal. Wolves took the lead in the 24th minute and Richard Key must take some of the blame for it. Carr seeing the Exeter keeper off his line, cleverly flighted his free-kick into the net. Six minutes later though, City equalised. Lee Roberts beat two defenders before unleashing an 18-yard shot past Bradshaw.

The fact that Exeter called the tune before and after the equaliser was due in no small measure to Keith Bowker, John Hore and Colin Randell. They completely ran the show from midfield and blocked their more illustrious visitors of Carr, Daley and Hibbitt. Exeter strung together some very good moves and did not look overawed by their First Division visitors.

City went ahead in the 67th minute following a scramble in the Wolves penalty area, and as the ball bobbled around, Harry Holman fired home from close range. The subsequent scenes were ecstatic and although Wolves poured extra men forward in attack in search of a face saving equaliser, there looked no way that Exeter's competent defence would be pierced. Yet beaten they were in the 87th minute. The look of dejection on every City face, players and supporters, told the story, for it was something that was not deserved.

THIRD DIVISION LEAGUE TABLE

	P	W	D	L	F	A	Pts
Wrexham	23	13	6	4	39	24	32
Tranmere Rovers	24	12	6	6	39	22	30
Gillingham	24	10	10	4	40	30	30
Peterborough United	23	10	9	4	19	15	29
Cambridge United	23	11	6	6	40	28	28
Preston North End	23	9	9	5	27	20	27
Shrewsbury Town	24	10	6	8	40	31	26
Colchester United	23	13	7	4	32	22	25
Swindon Town	23	8	8	7	40	33	24
Bury	23	7	10	6	25	30	24
EXETER CITY	23	9	5	9	28	28	23
Walsall	23	7	9	7	27	27	23
Chester	23	6	11	6	25	32	23
Chesterfield	23	9	4	10	24	25	22
Oxford United	24	7	8	9	33	35	22
Carlisle United	23	6	9	8	30	31	21
Rotherham United	23	6	8	9	29	35	20
Port Vale	23	4	12	7	25	33	20
Bradford City	23	6	7	10	26	36	19
Plymouth Argyle	23	5	8	10	26	32	18
Lincoln City	23	5	8	10	24	34	18
Hereford United	23	5	8	10	16	26	18
Sheffield Wednesday	23	5	7	11	20	29	17
Portsmouth	23	3	11	9	23	39	17

SUNDAY 8th JANUARY 1978

WOLVES' FANS WRECK CITY'S BIG DAY
Gangs of soccer hooligans marred Exeter City's day of glory yesterday, after they had held First Division Wolverhampton Wanderers to a draw at St James' Park in the third round of the F.A. Cup.

Wolves fans raced onto the pitch at the end of the game and broke the crossbar of the goal at the Big Bank end, and then tried to deliberately smash the goal posts to the ground. The wanton destruction was carried on outside the St. James' Park, when hooligans ripped up pieces of masonry to use as weapons and missiles, smashing windows of nearby houses.

Exeter City now face a costly bill to repair the damage at the ground, whilst local residents have complained bitterly that they too have been left with pounds worth of repairs. In Well Street and Victoria Street, terrified residents ducked for cover as their windows were broken by flying bottles, bricks and beer cans as the Wolves fans made their way back to their coaches.

Within minutes the club found themselves besieged by a group of very angry residents demanding that their windows be replaced at Exeter City's expense. Immediately officials found two builders among the Vice Presidents Club, and they began the work of boarding up the windows.

In the ground itself, trouble began before a ball was kicked. Wolves supporters at the St. James' Road end smashed down crash barriers and flowed onto the pitch, starting a running battle with City supporters. Twice during the match play was halted by pitch invasions by Wolves fans, this despite a blue line of 35 Police officers trying to hold them back. A total of 29 arrests were made and City Commercial Manager, Ray Ellis, estimated the damage to the crash barriers alone, would cost £1,000 to put right.

MONDAY 9th JANUARY 1978

WOLVES SUPPORTERS CLUB ARE ASHAMED
Supporters of Wolverhampton Wanderers are likely to organise a collection for the people living near St. James' Park, whose property was damaged after Saturday's F.A. Cup tie. A group within the Wolverhampton Wanderers Supporters Club were ashamed of the hooligan fans who went on the rampage after the game.

They are planning a whip round to send money to Exeter to pay for the damage, and replace the windows that were smashed. The news from Wolves was welcomed by Robert Marshall, who is leading a residents campaign to win compensation for the damage.

"Many residents feel bitter that we have not yet seen any definite action," he said. "This if the first offer of compensation we have had and is a fine gesture by the true supporters of Wolverhampton Wanderers."

TUESDAY 10th JANUARY 1978

NO CUP SHOCK FOR CITY
F.A. Cup Round Three Replay
Wolverhampton Wanderers 3 Exeter City 1
Wolverhampton Wanderers team: Bradshaw, Palmer, Parkin, Daley, Hazell, McAlle, Hibbitt, Carr, Richards, Bell, Daly.
Exeter City team: Key, Templeman, Hatch, Bowker, Giles, Saxton, Randell, Kellow, Holman, Roberts, Hore.
Scorers: Wolves: Richards, Hibbitt, Daley. Exeter: Kellow.
Attendance: 20,000

Exeter City's exit from the F.A. Cup at Molineux was neither inglorious or glorious. They never looked like springing a shock as in the first match at St. James' Park. However, Wolves lack of finishing early on meant that there was always a chance, albeit a slight one, that Exeter might just cause an upset.

Really though, Wolves were in command throughout with their midfield strong men the rigidly controlling force. The times that Exeter came close to scoring could be counted on the fingers of one hand as the Grecians attack were firmly held in check.

Wolves came forward with purpose and peppered a stream of shots at the Exeter goal. Many times, however, they were not on target, with the result that although they went ahead in the 40th minute through Richards, hopes of a dramatic comeback by the City were kept alive until ten minutes from time. It was mostly an uphill battle for Exeter, fighting to contain Wolves. Richard Key, Peter Hatch and Bobby Saxton were outstanding in a hard pressed City defence.

In the second half Colin Randell sent a couple of efforts over the Wolves crossbar, but it was still the home side making most of the running. After Key had made two fine saves, Hibbitt was sent away by McAlle in the 80th minute to lash the ball into the net. Six minutes later Tony Kellow headed in a Lee Roberts cross to give Exeter brief hopes of a comeback.

A minute later though Wolves had regained their two goal lead. City lost possession and Daley raced away out on his own to score and earn his side a place on the fourth round.

WOLVES MANAGER CONDEMNS SENSELESS BEHAVIOUR
In the match programme for the F.A. Cup replay between Wolverhampton Wanders and Exeter City, the Wolves manager Sammy Chung wrote about the scenes that had marred the first match at St James' Park.

Chung wrote:- "There was one aspect of the atmosphere at Exeter which thoroughly depressed me. I refer to the senseless and stupid behaviour of a certain so called group of Wolves supporters. I can only apologise to all Exeter City directors, players and supporters, and assure then that the vast percentage of our supporters are well behaved and sensible followers of our great sport."

CITY DIRECTORS DISCUSS THE TROUBLE AT THE PARK
The Exeter City directors held a board meeting last evening to discuss the trouble at the F.A. Cup tie with Wolverhampton Wanderers. Afterwards, City chairman Gerald Vallance expressed sympathy to nearby residents whose windows were broken by the Wolves fans, but said that the club could not accept any liability for the damage. He added that the broken railings in the ground would be repaired with stronger ones and that the work would be done in such a way that a cage could be constructed above them if necessary.

THURSDAY 12th JANUARY 1978

COURTS FINE THE HOOLIGANS
Exeter city magistrates imposed fines totalling nearly £2,500 on the hooligans who appeared in court following the F.A. Cup tie against Wolverhampton Wanderers. Fans from the Midlands also terrorised residents in Tewkesbury on their way home on Saturday night, where they caused trouble in pubs and smashed the window of a fish and chip shop.

FRIDAY 13th JANUARY 1978
IT WAS PURE LUNACY SAYS EXETER POLICE CHIEF
The head of Exeter Police, Chief Superintendent John Proctor has defended the way in which his officers handled the troubles at Exeter City's F.A. Cup match with Wolverhampton Wanderers. He said that the Police were not expecting trouble because they were told that Wolves fans were well behaved. Nevertheless, there were more men on duty than for any other football match in the city. He praised the way his men, who were under considerable pressure, tackled the unprecedented situation.

"It was frightening to be among the Wolves fans," he said. "It was pure lunacy. There were about 1,750 people behind the St. James' Road goal, but only about 500 of them were out for trouble."

It was Mr. Proctor, in consultation with Exeter City Football Club officials who decided to impose a crowd limit of 16,000 at the ground for the match, but he saw no reason to reduce this for future games. "Despite the fact that barriers were broken, there was still plenty of room inside the St. James' Road enclosure," he added. "Exeter City can in no way be blamed for what happened."

SATURDAY 14th JANUARY 1978

SECOND TIME LUCKY FOR KELLOW
Third Division
Exeter City 1 Walsall 1
Exeter City team: Key, Templeman, Hatch, Hore, Giles, Saxton, Randell, Kellow, Bowker, Roberts, Holman.
Walsall team: Kearns, Macken, Caswell, Shelton, Serella, Harrison, Dennehy, Bates, Wood, Buckley, King.
Scorers: Exeter: Kellow. Walsall: Buckley.
Attendance: 5,149

Home form is still, costing Exeter City a high price in the Third Division where they seem to struggle to get into their stride. It was an uneventful first half during which neither side looked likely to score, and it was only thanks to Tony Kellow that City earned a point from the match.

Both sides were guilty of giving the ball away as the game became a midfield battle with neither team threatening where it mattered - in the penalty area. There was not enough combination in the Exeter side between the players to really expose Walsall, and the Grecians' attack lacked width.

The second half livened up belatedly on and off the field. The Walsall assistant manager was booked for a remark he made to the referee from the bench. There was more fire in the game as Exeter began to push forward with more authority, but they had nothing to show for it, despite forcing three successive corners.

Walsall were awarded a penalty in the 70th minute when Jimmy Giles brought down Caswell, and Buckley made no mistake with the spot kick. Nine minutes later, Exeter equalised. It followed a corner taken by Colin Randell which Kellow knocked home for this thirteenth goal of the season. It was the second time in the match he had the ball in the net, the first occasion the goal was disallowed for an infringement.

NEWS OF FORMER GRECIANS
Several former Exeter City players have been in the news recently and it is of interest to keep tabs on them.

Campbell Crawford, who left City in 1974 on a free transfer, is now assisting Kidderminster Harriers in the Southern League in a coaching capacity, after having played for them.

Micky Fudge, who had one season at St. James' Park in 1967-68, has signed for Midland Combination outfit, Malvern Town. He joined Wellington Town (now Telford United) on leaving City and had a successful spell there appearing in the F.A. Trophy Final at Wembley. He was the club's leading goalscorer on a couple of occasions, then moving to Kidderminster Harriers in June 1976.

John Henderson, who arrived at Exeter City in November 1962 from Charlton Athletic was transferred last month from Halesowen Town to Dudley Town, both sides playing in the West Midlands League. Henderson made 46 appearances and scored 6 goals for Exeter before leaving in 1964 and signing for Doncaster Rovers.

Henderson then went on to play for Chesterfield, Kidderminster Harriers and Stourbridge.

One of last seasons loan signings, Geoff Gay, who played 5 full games for City before returning to Bolton Wanderers, is a regular fixture in the Southport side this season. He recently scored his fifth goal for Southport against Rochdale, who themselves included another former Exeter City player in their side, Tony Morrin.

TUESDAY 17th JANUARY 1978

THE GRECIANS DESERVED BETTER
Third Division
Sheffield Wednesday 2 Exeter City 1
Sheffield Wednesday team: Bolder, Walden, Grant, Rushbury, Cusack, Mullen, Wylde, Porterfield, Tynan, Johnson, Leman.
Exeter City team: Key, Templeman, Hore, Bowker, Giles, Hatch, Saxton, Kellow, Randell, Roberts, Holman.
Scorers: Sheffield Wednesday: Rushbury, Wylde. Exeter: Bowker.
Attendance: 9,596.

Before the match Exeter City player-manager Bobby Saxton, who as a boy, used to watch Sheffield Wednesday from the Hillsborough terraces declared: "I know they will give 100 per cent."

However, he was not counting on the home sides confidence receiving a boost as a 27th minute penalty put them ahead. It seemed a harsh decision as Jimmy Giles was ruled to have handled. Rushbury's spot kick gave Richard Key no chance.

The goal seemed to rouse City's determination though. The equaliser for which they fought so hard for eventually came in the 75th minute when Keith Bowker headed in a high cross from Harry Holman against the crossbar and the nodded the rebound into the net from almost on the goal line. Five minutes later Wednesday were ahead again through Wylde, who drove the ball into the net after Richard Key had stopped a header from Mullen, but could not hold it.

Wednesday could count themselves lucky with both goals. Exeter played some good football and their defence with Peter Hatch producing consistently good form, generally stood firm. However, this 10th defeat of the season seriously dented Saxton's hopes of a challenge to the Division Three pace setters. At the other end of the table, Wednesday moved off the bottom. Exeter had done enough in the game to have earned a draw, but it was not to be.

SATURDAY 21st JANUARY 1978

SECOND HALF COLLAPSE
Third Division
Bury 5 Exeter City 0
Bury team: Forrest, Keenan, Kennedy, Hatton, Tucker, Bailey, Stanton, Suddick, Rowland, Robins, McIlwraith.
Exeter City team: Key, Templeman, hatch, Hore, Giles, Saxton, Randell, Kellow, Bowker, Roberts, Holman.
Scorers: Bury: Rowland (2), McIlwraith (2), Suddick.
Attendance: 3,730.

Seemingly in with a chance when they were a goal behind, after playing some neat football. Exeter City collapsed in the second half and in the end were lucky to get away with only a five goal beating.

The Grecians' defence were totally overwhelmed, but Exeter still managed to keep themselves territorially in the game, and if they had been as positive in their finishing as they were neat in their build up, they would have got on the score sheet. Both sets of players made light work of the waterlogged surface until the second half when the testing conditions sapped much of the strength of the City defence.

Bury had taken the lead in the 13th minute when Richard Key failed to cut out a corner taken by Suddick, and Rowland turned the ball in from close range. Not until Suddick added to Bury's lead in the 60th minute did the Exeter defence fold. Bury tore into City, creating gaps that just had to lead to more goals. McIlwraith netted twice with headers in the

66th and 73rd minutes, and then Rowland scored his second of the game and Bury's fifth in the 87th minute.

Key was again at fault for the fifth goal when the ball passed through his legs. It was not a happy day for Key, but he was not the only City player to be blamed for his side's defeat. It was simply, that in addition to lack of firepower, the defence wilted badly, and Bury took full advantage.

Exeter must have wished the game had been called off, as it had been in some doubt before the kick off, and only a magnificent effort by the Bury groundstaff, who forked away the surface water, allowed the fixture to go ahead.

SATURDAY 28th JANUARY 1978

THAT ELUSIVE FIRST VICTORY
Third Division
Exeter City 1 Shrewsbury Town 1
Exeter City team: Key, Templeman, Hatch, Hore, Giles, Saxton (ingham), Randell, Kellow, Bowker, Roberts, Holman.
Shrewsbury Town: Mulhearn, King, Griffin, Turner, Keay, Lindsay, Irvine, Hornsby, Loughnane, Maguire, Nixon.
Scorers: Exeter: Kellow. Shrewsbury: Hornsby.
Attendance: 3,906.

Exeter City are still seeking their first win this year, as they struggle to find the right formula to lift themselves away from the Third Division relegation zone It looked as if they might break their duck as they led through a Tony Kellow goal, right up to the 87th minute. However, Shrewsbury, who worked and ran so hard during the second half, snatched the equaliser when Hornsby headed in a cross from Maguire.

It provided the game with a fair result n front of a crowd that included former F.I.F.A. President, Sir Stanley Rous, and the Sports Minister, Dennis Howell, both in Exeter to attend a dinner function. The cloying mud always restricted the two sides known for their short passing movements. Yet the end to end play helped compensate for the lack of good football.

Exeter played without a recognised winger with Harry Holman forsaking his role on the left to tuck in behind strikers, Kellow and Lee Roberts. Kellow's goal came in the 38th minute. Jimmy Giles stole in on the blind side of the Shrews defence for Peter Hatch's free-kick and Kellow swept the ball in when Giles headed it down to him.

Shrewsbury responded well to the challenge of the second half and deserved their goal, a just reward for their endeavours. City player-manager Bobby Saxton limped off the field in the 68th minute with a pulled thigh muscle, and he must now regard the remaining 18 games as a major uphill struggle if Exeter are to steer a course for Third Division safety.

SAXTON CALLS FOR SUPPORTERS TO RALLY BEHIND THE TEAM
With Exeter City entering the final third of the season and promotion and relegation issues becoming a reality to most clubs, player-manager Bobby Saxton wants the fans to get behind the team to ensure that Third Division football will once again be played at St James' Park next season.

"We find ourselves in a battle to pick up as many points as possible in order to ensure that we maintain a respectable position in the top half of the division," said Saxton.

"We have now been pushed into the lower half and this is a position we obviously do not wish to occupy for any length of time. The games we face will have a bearing on whether will have a nail-biting end to the season, or sit comfortably in the top half of the table, a position we will naturally be aiming for. During this period we need the supporters to give the team every encouragement. Sometimes things will not be as rosy as we would like, but they have shown in the past that when we hit a sticky patch they have given us all the encouragement to lift us. Believe me, it is very important to the players who want to do well for you and the club. We need the encouragement of the fans, the people who matter."

CITY LOTTERY SUCCESS
The month of February will see the introduction of a fortnightly Exeter City Lottery. When the club launched the lottery back in October last year, it was thought that the monthly draw would be a short enough period between lotteries. However, owing to the tremendous support the club has received, they have now decided to have a fortnightly draw.

The ticket price will remain at 20p, and the draw will be made at various venues away from the Centre Spot social club. The first new venue will be at St. Loyes Hotel in Exeter on 31st January.

WEDNESDAY 8th FEBRUARY 1978

CITY'S MISERABLE RUN CONTINUES
Third Division
Port Vale 4 Exeter City 0
Port Vale team: Connaughton, Beech, McGifford, Ridley, Harris, Bentley, Sutcliffe, Lamb, Froggatt, Beamish, Bailey.
Exeter City team: Key, Templeman, Hore, Bowker, Giles, Hatch, Weeks, Kellow, Randell, Roberts (Ingham), Jennings.
Scorers: Port Vale: Froggatt, Sutcliffe, Beamish, Griffiths.
Attendance: 3,333

This latest heavy defeat at Port Vale sent Exeter City plunging into the Third Division relegation zone, in a match in which they never got started. They suffered a disastrous start falling behind after just 15 seconds. The scorer, Froggatt, was making his debut for Port Vale.

Exeter struggled to get into the game as Vale were inspired by their dream start. The hosts pressed for more goals and only a tremendous flying save by Richard Key prevented Beamish from increasing the Grecians' troubles. Colin Randell was desperately unlucky not to pull a goal back just before the break, when a 25-yard shot hit the inside of the post. However, just as City seemed to be getting their game together they gave away another goal in the 52nd minute.

Keith Bowker's terrible back pass was cut off by Beamish who sent Sutcliffe away to beat Key from close range. It was all over for Exeter who slipped back into their habits of the first half and in the 67th minute Beamish made it 3-0, after Peter Hatch had failed to clear a header from Froggatt.

The Grecians could make no inroads against the Vale defence and their night of misery was complete three minutes later when Jimmy Giles tripped Beamish just inside the area. Sutcliffe scored form the penalty spot. It was a defeat that the City had only themselves to blame for. Too many players made elementary mistakes and were punished for them.

MEETING WITH THE SCHOOLS
Exeter City held an informal meeting in the Vice Presidents Lounge at St James' Park, with Headmasters and Sportsmasters of the schools in the Exeter and district last evening.

It was a lighthearted discussion posing the qustion: "How can Exeter City Football Club help the schools and vice versa?"

A lot of positives came from the meeting on the question of recommendation of boys, coaching in schools and more importantly, the continued furtherance of the boys education should they join the club. With better relationships and increased co-operation between the Grecians and the schools, the club's youh policy should improve which will be to the benefit of everyone.

SATURDAY 11th FEBRUARY 1978

AT LONG LAST: CITY WIN A GAME!
Exeter City 1 Peterborough United 0
Exeter City team: Baugh, Templeman, Hore, Weeks, Giles, Roberts, Hodge, Kellow, Holman, Bowker, Randell.
Peterborough United team: Barron, Hughes, Lee, Ross, Turner, Carmichael, Slough, Butlin, Doyle, Mc
Ewan, Anderson.
Scorer: Exeter: Holman.
Attendance: 4,017.

At long last! Exeter City have won their first game at St. James' Park in 1978. It was badly needed. The all important goal came in the 58th minute when Harry Holman punctured the Peterborough United defence with a superbly struck left foot shot. It was a costly mistake by goalkeeper Barron which led to the goal. He was penalised for taking too many steps ad Colin Randell rolled a short free-kick to Holman who did the rest.

There had been a lack of goal mouth action in the first half as play was mainly confined to midfield.

Peterborough were being caught offside in their build up play, but slick moving Exeter defence were also creating some promising moves, only for these to break down in and around the visitors penalty area. There was an immediate let off for City at the start of the second half when a header from Slough beat John Baugh, only to rebound off the crossbar.

After the Holman goal, City's confidence visibly grew and they almost increased their lead in the 68th minute. Again it was Holman whose shot flew inches over the bar. Then following a quick throw out by Baugh, Exeter swept into attack and Barron saved well from Bobby Hodge.

This welcome victory should surely give City a boost in their efforts to scramble away from the bottom end of the Third Division.

SATURDAY 25th FEBRUARY 1978

BLANK WEEKEND FOR CITY
After a thorough inspection of the St. James' Park pitch, and a check with the weather forecasters, referee Alex Lees from Bridgwater was forced to call off Exeter City's match with Chesterfield.

Many areas of the playing surface were in a waterlogged state, after the snow had melted and left pools of water.

TUESDAY 28th FEBRUARY 1978

THIS WAS AWFUL TO WATCH
Third Division
Portsmouth 1 Exeter City 1
Portsmouth team: Figgins, Roberts, Taylor, N.Piper (Pullar), Cahill, Denyer, S.Piper, Kemp, Gilchrist, Mellows, McCaffery.
Exeter City team: Key, Templeman, Hore, Weeks, Giles, Roberts, Hodge, Kellow, Randell, Bowker, Holman.
Scorers: Portsmouth: Cahill. Exeter: Cahill (o.g).
Attendance: 10.260.

Both Portsmouth and Exeter City combined to produce a truly appalling first 45 minutes and two scrappy goals in the second, both of which were scored by Pompey defender, Cahill, which summed up a dreadful Third Division match. In the opening 19 minutes Exeter forced two corners, both taken by Colin Randell, and both kicked straight out of play.

It was 23 minutes before Portsmouth produced the first shot of the match when a 25-yard effort by Denyer went narrowly wide The rest of the half was instantly forgettable. It took a 50th minute own goal by Cahill when he headed Randell's corner past his own goalkeeper to put any life into the match.

Fifteen minutes later Piper watched Bobby Hodge chest his shot off the City goal line, and then John Hore stopped the follow up effort from Piper again. The same Portsmouth player then rattled the crossbar in the 73rd minute and although Richard Key grabbed the rebound, and Cahill appeared to kick the ball out of his hands into the net, the referee gave the goal.

Three minutes later Exeter put together their best move of the match, when John Templeman combined with Hodge to cross for Harry Holman, City's best player, to turn the ball against the post.

A draw was a fair result with the Portsmouth performance testimony as to why they began the game at the bottom of the table, and Exeter showing that they need to improve greatly on this display. The elementary skills can be seen on any local pitch, and were sadly lacking from both sides at Fratton Park, as relegation, on this display, seemed more likely for both clubs.

Football League. Division 3. Kick-off 3.00 p.m.
SATURDAY, 4th MARCH 1978
WREXHAM v. EXETER CITY
Official Programme — 15p.
WREXHAM

EXETER CITY F.C.
EXETER CITY FOOTBALL CLUB
Official Programme
Football League Division 3.
EXETER CITY
v
ROTHERHAM UTD
Wednesday 8th March 1978
Kick-off 7.30 p.m.
Price 15p

PRESTON NORTH END F.C.
PNE
Exeter City
League Division 3
SATURDAY, 18th MARCH, 1978, at 3.00 p.m.
OFFICIAL PROGRAMME 15p
PP

EXETER CITY F.C.
EXETER CITY FOOTBALL CLUB
Official Programme
Football League Division 3.
EXETER CITY
v
SWINDON TOWN
WEDNESDAY 22nd March 1978
Kick-off 7.30 p.m.
Price 15p

EXETER CITY F.C.
EXETER CITY FOOTBALL CLUB
Official Programme
Football League Division 3.
EXETER CITY
v
PLYMOUTH ARGYLE
Tuesday 28th March 1978
Kick-off 7.30 p.m.
Price 15p

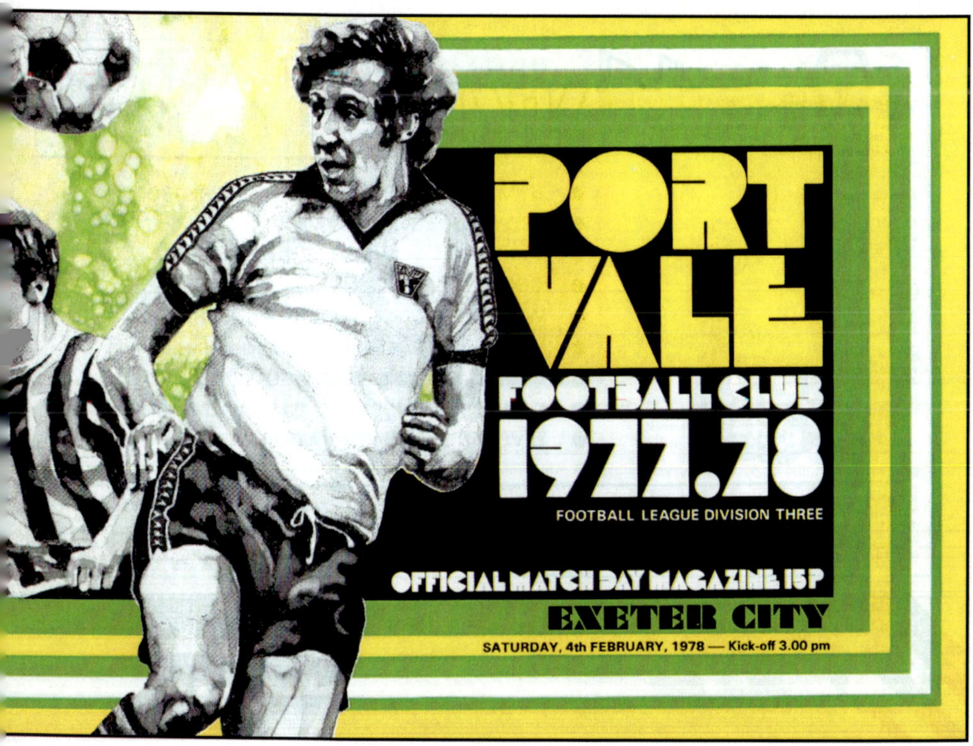
PORT VALE
FOOTBALL CLUB
1977.78
FOOTBALL LEAGUE DIVISION THREE
OFFICIAL MATCH DAY MAGAZINE 15P
EXETER CITY
SATURDAY, 4th FEBRUARY, 1978 — Kick-off 3.00 pm

THURSDAY 2nd MARCH 1978

THIRD DIVISION LEAGUE TABLE

	P	W	D	L	F	A	Pts
Cambridge United	32	16	8	8	56	40	40
Gillingham	32	13	14	5	55	39	40
Preston North End	31	14	11	7	44	27	39
Wrexham	29	15	9	5	46	30	39
Tranmere Rovers	32	14	10	8	44	27	38
Bury	30	11	12	7	43	35	34
Walsall	30	10	13	7	38	32	33
Swindon Town	28	11	10	7	48	38	32
Colchester United	31	10	12	9	40	34	32
Peterborough United	29	11	10	8	23	22	32
Chester	31	8	16	7	35	41	32
Chesterfield	29	12	7	10	34	27	31
Shrewsbury Town	32	10	11	11	45	41	31
Carlisle United	31	9	13	9	41	40	31
Oxford United	33	10	10	13	46	39	30
Lincoln City	32	9	11	12	33	40	29
EXETER CITY	31	10	9	12	34	43	29
Sheffield Wednesday	31	8	10	13	31	38	26
Port Vale	31	6	13	12	33	48	25
Plymouth Argyle	30	6	11	13	35	46	23
Bradford City	30	8	7	15	37	52	23
Rotherham United	27	7	8	12	32	43	22
Portsmouth	32	4	14	14	30	52	22
Hereford United	30	5	11	14	21	41	21

SATURDAY 4th MARCH 1978

LATE WINNER DENIES CITY
Third Division
Wrexham 2 Exeter City 1
Wrexham team: Niedzwiecki, Hill, Dwyer, Davis, Roberts, Thomas, Shinton, Sutton, McNeil, Whittle, Cartwright (Lyons).
Exeter City: Key, Templeman, Hore, Weeks, Giles, Roberts, Hodge, Kellow, Randell, Bowker, Holman.
Scorers: Wrexham: Whittle, McNeil. Exeter: Bowker.
Attendance: 15,317.

Former Grecian Dixie McNeil continues to haunt Exeter City with his last gasp goal acts. In October he scored in the dying seconds at St. James' Park to give Wrexham victory, and in this game he flung himself forward to head the winning goal in the 88th minute. It was a personal tragedy for City's man of the match Jimmy Giles, who until then had completely marked McNeil out of the game.

It was a deflection too that had put Wrexham into the lead after 38 minutes. Whittle's free-kick going in off the Exeter defensive wall, leaving Richard Key stranded. It had been a scrappy game until then, with the Exeter defence led by lee Roberts and Giles keeping a close watch on the Wrexham forwards. Colin Randell worked hard in midfield and it was from his corner 11 minutes from time that City got the goal that they thoroughly deserved.

Wrexham failed to clear and Keith Bowker got in a shot that went over the goalkeeper's head into the net. Wrexham who failed to produce the form that has taken them to near top of the table, should have had the game wrapped up as they struck at the City in the second half. Roberts sliced an open goal chance wide and McNeil also went close. However, City almost equalised in the last minute of the game, but Bowker sent his shot wide of the target.

City player-manager Bobby Saxton said that he was disappointed at the way the team had conceded the late goal, which was not for the first time this season.

MONDAY 6th MARCH 1978

ARGYLE MIDFIELDER SIGNS FOR CITY
Exeter City player-manager returned to his former club, Plymouth Argyle, not for the first time, to sign midfielder John Delve. It has created a milestone in the history of the club, as the transfer fee was paid for by the very successful City Lottery competition.

Delve came through the youth ranks at Queen's Park Rangers and was given his Football League debut in December 1972 at Luton. He played as a defensive midfielder, who along with another home-grown youngster, John Beck, seemed to be the perennial substitute for much of the 1972-73 season. For the next couple of season, Delve and Beck were Queen's Park Rangers midfield back ups - especially to Gerry Francis - either when Francis was injured, or if Francis played forward (as he did a couple of times when Stan Bowles was suspended!).

Delve made 15 league appearances before a £30,000 transfer to Plymouth Argyle in 1974. He was a member of the team that won promotion to the Second Division in 1974-75 and continued to feature regularly in the next two campaigns. Delve lost his place in the side to Gary Megson, and was therefore keen to rejoin his former team mate, Saxton at St. James' Park, having made a total of 151 league and cup appearances for Plymouth.

WEDNESDAY 8th MARCH 1978

GRECIANS VICTORY HELPS RELEGATION WORRIES
Third Division
Exeter City 1 Rotherham United 0
Exeter City team: Key, Templeman,
Hore, Delve, Giles, Roberts, Hodge, Kellow, Randell, Bowker, Holman.
Rotherham United team: McAllister, Pugh, Breckin, Rhodes, Forrest, Green, Finney, Phillips, Gwyther, Goodfellow, Nix.
Scorer: Exeter: Kellow.
Attendance: 4,016.

The only goal of the match gave Exeter City a crucial victory against Rotherham United to open a seven point gap between themselves and the bottom four. The crowd must have accepted the fact that it was going to be a goalless draw until Tony Kellow struck in the 88th minute. John Delve had a quiet debut, but it was from his pass that the goal emerged, when Kellow steered the ball home as McAllister came off his line.

It was, however, an uninspiring match. Exeter had more of the game, but failed to make it count. City's play did not have the fluency needed, with passes going astray and there was also a lack of control at times on the ball. Colin Randell was outstanding in midfield with his strong running and distribution.

With both sides needing the points for the same reason, this was always going to be a battle, and in the end it was Exeter's perseverance that saw them through. City did not really create much in the way of clear cut chances. Randell hit a 25-yard drive just past the post and Harry Holman had a shot saved by McAllister in the first half. After the interval Keith Bowker saw his header brilliantly saved and Randell sent in a blistering drive that just cleared the crossbar. Rotherham had a couple of chances to score, both falling to their danger man, Finney, but other than that, they looked sadly out of touch.

SATURDAY 11th MARCH 1978

POSITIVE CITY: BEST PERFORMANCE FOR SOME TIME
Third Division
Exeter City 3 Lincoln City 0
Exeter City team: Key, Templeman, Hore, Delve, Giles Roberts, Hodge, Kellow, Randell, Bowker, Holman.
Lincoln City team: Grozier, Guest, Leigh, Neil, Wigginton, Cooper, Jones, Hubbard, Hoult (Harford), Smith, Harding.
Scorers: Exeter: Holman (2), Bowker.
Attendance: 4,280.

Exeter City made it a maximum four points from their two home games in four days by defeating Lincoln City in style, especially in the first half when they swept into a two goal lead by the interval. They made the ideal start by scoring after just five minutes when John Templeman struck a low cross to Tony Kellow, who beat a defender to feed Keith Bowker. He rounded off the move superbly with a well struck left foot shot past the diving Grotier.

City were in a positive mood, aggressive and constructive, and they continued to put Lincoln under pressure for the rest of the half. The Lincoln defence was breached again in the 42nd minute when Jimmy Giles and Keith Bowker combined to set up a chance for Harry Holman to hit a low shot into the net. Exeter were given a standing ovation at half-time.

Although not quite so dominating in the second half, the Grecians still increased their lead after 58 minutes. Holman was the scorer once more, following a good piece of work by Kellow. Little had been seen of the Lincoln attack with Richard Key having hardly anything to do. This was the best performance by Exeter for some weeks and their relegation fears must surely now be over.

TUESDAY 14th MARCH 1976

NO BLAME ATTACHED TO THE GRECIANS
Exeter City have been completely exonerated at a meeting of the Football Association Disciplinary Committee, held yesterday in Birmingham. The committee were investigating the crowd trouble at the FA Cup tie, at St. James' Park, against Wolverhampton Wanderers.

Exeter were reported under F.A. Rule 33(A) regarding the responsibility of a club for its spectators, and they requested a personal hearing. City chairman Gerald Vallance and Police Superintendent Graham Burgess of the Exeter Police were in Birmingham to meet the committee.

The committee felt that Exeter City Football Club had taken all reasonable precautions to prevent misconduct by spectators and no further action would be taken. "The committee recommended that the club should put in some crash barriers behind the St. James' Road goal, and we will consider it," said Vallance. The Devon and Cornwall Police Chief Constable, John Alderson, also made his special report on the match available to the F.A. committee.

SATURDAY 18th MARCH 1978

CITY HOLD ON FOR A POINT
Third Division
Preston North End 0 Exeter City 0
Preston North End team: Tunks, McMahon, Cameron, Burns, Baxter, Cross, Coleman, Haslegrave, Thomson (Spavin), Elwiss, Bruce.
Exeter City team: Key, Templeman, Roberts, Bowker, Giles, Hore, Delve, Kellow, Randell, Holman, Hodge.
Attendance: 9,189

Exeter City became the first team to gain a point at Deepdale since last November. The fact that Preston failed to score for the first time since September gave a pointer to the way that the game went. Every credit must be given to the City defence for their sterling second half performance.

For nearly the whole of the second period the defence had to withstand an onslaught few other teams could have survived, with Richard Key the star man with a faultless goalkeeping display. In the first half the game switched from end to end, with Exeter just having the slight edge. John Delve put in a 30-yard snap shot that went just wide, while Preston's Thomson fired over the City bar when well placed.

Harry Holman appeared to be brought down in the penalty area, but amazingly the referee awarded a free-kick outside the box. Just before half-time City went close to taking the lead, when a long range shot from Bobby Hodge went narrowly wide.

Key made one of his outstanding saves in the 47th minute from Coleman. Key was still in the thick of things three minutes form the end when he again denied Coleman after the Preston player had dribbled past two City defenders. Manager Bobby Saxton was glad of the point, and was full of praise for his defence, but thought his teams passing abilities were weak up front.

WEDNESDAY 22nd MARCH 1978

A NIGHT TO FORGET
Third Division
Exeter City 0 Swindon Town 0
Exeter City team: Key, Templeman, Hore, Delve, Giles (Hatch), Roberts, Hodge, Kellow, Randell, Bowker, Holman.
Swindon Town team: Allan, McLaughlin, Ford, Stroud, Carter, Prophet, Moss, Kamara, Guthrie, Bates, Trollope.
Attendance: 4,449.

It was an unhappy night for Exeter City. They not only lost defender Jimmy Giles for the second half with a back injury, but also had John Delve booked, who could now face a suspension. To add to their misfortune City missed opportunities late in the game to snatch victory. It was not until well into the second half that the Grecians looked more like opening up the Swindon defence effectively. Until then it was a game of precious little goal mouth action and equally little excitement.

City should have scored 15 minutes from the end but somehow Keith Bowker, standing in front of goal, put a header well over the top from a Harry Holman cross. In the first half, Exeter's defence, after showing some hesitancy, tightened up and started to catch the Swindon attack in the offside trap.

Towards half time City started to show signs of getting their game running more smoothly, but they were still not sharp enough up front and all too often they spoiled moves with inaccurate passing. It took a good save by Allan to stop a shot from Holman, and then Delve, who on the night was Exeter's most probing and challenging player, dropped a chip shot over the bar.

Peter Hatch came on to replace Giles, but the pattern of the game remained the same and a deadlock looked more than likely the outcome. Stroud broke away for Swindon, but sent his shot well wide, whilst at the other end, Allan did well to drop onto a fierce drive from Tony Kellow.

PERMISSION GRANTED FOR CITY FANS

Over the course of the past two months, Exeter City's Commercial Manager Ray Ellis has received letters from all the motorway service stations informing him that all football supporters have been banned from using their facilities unless prior permission has been obtained.

Exeter, being one of the football outposts geographically speaking, felt it was very important to arrange a rest and eating venue for their travelling Grecians. Ellis has now come to an agreement with Gordano Services at Bristol on the M5 that all bona fide travelling supporters on organised trips can use all of their facilities. This permission has been granted mainly due to the well behaved Exeter City supporters who have previously used the Gordano stop.

SATURDAY 25th MARCH 1978

DISASTROUS FIRST HALF FOR CITY

Third Division

Hereford United 4 Exeter City 0

Hereford United team: Mellor, Price (Holmes), Burrows, Cornes, Layton, Sheedy, Stephens, Marshall, Crompton, Davey, Emery.

Exeter City team: Key, Templeman, Hore, Delve, Hatch, Roberts, (Weeks), Hodge, Kellow, Randell, Bowker, Holman.

Scorers: hereford: Crompton (2), Stephens, Davey.

Attendance: 4,436.

A three goal first half salvo from a lively Hereford United shook Exeter City, and they never recovered. There was a sensational start to the game with City conceding a goal after 31 seconds. John Delve failed to control a cross from Davey and the ball ran free to Stephens who had no difficulty in tucking it past Richard Key. It was the first goal that Stephens had scored for three years.

In blustery conditions and driving rain, the Grecians found it hard to make any headway and suffered a further blow in the 7th minute when Lee Roberts was stretchered off to be replaced by Graham Weeks. Before City's reorganised defence had time to settle, Hereford struck again. Crompton netting from ten yards. With 27 minutes gone Hereford added a third goal when Sheedy took an inswinging corner and Davey climbed above everyone else to head well out of Key's reach.

Exeter's defence was caught out in the 51st minute when they allowed Marshall to send a header onto the crossbar and from the rebound Crompton nipped in between Peter Hatch and Keith Bowker to nod it past Key. Sheedy had the ball in the net again 13 minutes later, but to Exeter's relief it was disallowed for offside.

It was not until the 71st minute that City won their first corner, but Tony Kellow's header was easily cleared.

MONDAY 27th MARCH 1978

THIRD DIVISION LEAGUE TABLE	P	W	D	L	F	A	Pts
Wrexham	33	19	9	5	57	33	47
Cambridge United	37	18	9	10	62	44	45
Preston North End	35	16	12	7	50	30	44
Gillingham	36	14	14	8	58	47	42
Walsall	35	13	14	8	44	36	40
Tranmere Rovers	36	14	11	11	46	38	39
Peterborough United	34	13	13	8	27	24	39
Bury	35	12	13	10	49	41	37
Chester	35	9	19	7	41	46	37
Colchester United	36	12	12	12	46	40	36
Carlisle United	35	10	16	9	45	43	36
Swindon Town	33	12	11	10	51	44	35
Chesterfield	33	13	9	11	41	34	35
Lincoln City	37	12	11	14	39	46	35
Shrewsbury Town	36	11	12	13	47	46	34
EXETER CITY	35	12	10	13	39	45	34
Oxford United	36	11	10	15	50	52	32
Port Vale	35	7	15	13	38	52	29
Rotherham United	32	10	8	14	38	46	28
Sheffield Wednesday	34	8	12	14	35	44	28
Plymouth Argyle	35	7	13	15	41	53	27
Bradford City	35	9	9	17	44	60	27
Hereford United	34	8	11	15	26	45	27
Portsmouth	36	5	15	16	33	58	25

TUESDAY 28th MARCH 1978

IT'S A DEVON DERBY STALEMATE AGAIN
Third Division
Exeter City 0 Plymouth Argyle 0
Exeter City team: Key, Templeman, Hore, Delve, Hatch, Giles, Hodge, Kellow, Randell, Bowker, Holman.
Plymouth Argyle team: Barron, Horswill, Uzzell, Bason, Foster, James, Megson, Taylor, Binney, Fear, Trusson.
Attendance: 8,334.

Two old adversaries battled it out, and a not unexpected goalless draw ensued. Few would argue that justice was not done in the heavy conditions at St. James' Park. The game and the result clearly show that there is little to choose between the two sides, as out of five meetings this season, this was the fourth time they had finished all square.

The Grecians will view this as a precious point earned in their bid to stay away from any possible relegation troubles. On the night Argyle could justly claim that out of all the incidents, and there were plenty going on in both goal mouths, that they came closest to scoring. Only two superb saves from Richard Key in the first half stopped Argyle from gaining an interval lead. Considering the conditions, following three pitch inspections by the referee, both sides produced some lively football.

In the end though, neither side, respecting each other and canny in their defensive work, could find the vital spark needed for a positive breakthrough. Perhaps it was typical that two of the Exeter players who stood out for their performances were former Argyle men, John Delve and John Hore. City missed a couple of chances to have grabbed victory, and indeed looked especially lively in attack early on. Argyle showed that they are a formidable side away from Home Park and really battled it out for the 90 minutes with Foster and Megson outstanding.

42 POINTS IS THE TARGET
Exeter City player-manager Bobby Saxton has set his side target which he feels will ensure Third Division football at St.

James' Park next season.

"I believe we need 42 points to be sure of Third Division safety," said Saxton. "Our performances up to the game against Swindon Town had improved considerably and we hope to maintain that throughout the remainder of the season. It is important that we acquire the points target as soon as possible, as the better it will be for all concerned at Exeter City."

SATURDAY 1st APRIL 1978

CITY SLITHER TO DEFEAT
Third Division
Chester City 2 Exeter City 1
Chester City team: Lloyd, Nickeas, Raynor, Jeffries, Storton, Oakes, Delgado, Livermore, Howat, Mellor, Phillips.
Exeter City team: Key, Templeman, Hore, Delve, Giles, Hodge (Jennings), Kellow, Randell, Bowker, Holman, Hatch.
Scorers: Chester: Mellor, Phillips. Exeter: Holman.
Attendance: 1996

Exeter City's relegation anxieties are not yet over. After an unhappy afternoon at Chester, not only were they decisively beaten, but they also had Bobby Hodge stretchered off in the 20th minute with a hip injury. City could never master the difficult conditions caused by torrential rain shortly before kick off and during the match.

It was not until three minutes from time that Harry Holman made the scoreline look more respectable when he hammered a fine shot past Lloyd. The centre of the pitch was a quagmire as the rain continued to fall, but the small crowd had an early goal to cheer when Mellor gave Chester the lead with a low drive in the ninth minute.

Little was seen of the Exeter attack, but both sides were doing well to keep their feet and produce any worthwhile football on the waterlogged surface. Four minutes before half time, Phillips turned a cross into the City net to increase Chester's lead.

The Grecians could not make any headway against a strong Chester defence. To make matters worse there was a second injury scare for City, when Tony Kellow, who had been carrying a shoulder injury for several games, damaged it again, but he carried on after treatment.

It was Kellow who put in City's first shot of any note in the 70th minute, only to see Lloyd make a brilliant save, tipping the ball over the top. City, who came to life after Holman's goal, almost grabbed an equaliser in the closing seconds when an effort from Keith Bowker went close.

MONDAY 3rd APRIL 1978

UNHAPPY LONG WEEKEND UP NORTH
Third Division
Carlisle United 2 Exeter City 0
Carlisle United team; Swinburne, Collins, McCartney, MacDonald, Sawyers (McLean), Parker, McVittie, Bonnyman, Tait, Kemp, Hamilton.
Exeter City: Key, Templeman, Hore, Delve, Giles, Hatch, Saxton (Jennings), Kellow, Randell, Bowker, Holman.
Scorers: Carlisle: Kemp, Bonnyman.
Attendance: 3,693.

Carlisle United put three successive defeats behind them to overpower Exeter City with a goal in each half. Exeter never really got going against a strong, blustery wind, which made good football impossible.

Carlisle pressed right from the start and John Delve had to clear from McVitie after a free-kick on the left. Harry Holman managed a shot into the side netting after a good City build up after 15 minutes, but sixty seconds later Carlisle were ahead. A McCartney cross was met by Kemp who headed home from 8-yards.

At the other end Tony Kellow forced a corner and Jimmy Giles got up to head goalwards but Swinburne produced the first of a series of fine saves to deny City the equaliser. Carlisle continued to force the pace in the second half and Kemp fired wide from close range when he should really have scored. The Cumbrians had better luck in the 65th minute when Bonnyman put the result beyond doubt with a header from ten-yards which had Richard Key easily beaten.

After that, the game became somewhat ragged and three players were booked. Towards the end Colin Randell got in perhaps the best position of the match for Exeter, but again Swinburne produced a tremendous save to turn his shot over the bar. City's long weekend up north has been far from happy and they must now aim for a point a game in their last six matches to be sure of playing Third Division football again next season.

FRIDAY 7TH APRIL 1978

NOTHING TO SHOW FOR IT
Player-Manager Bobby Saxton has been comenting on his teams trip to the north of England last weeked when they played at Chester and Carlisle United in the space of 48-hours.

"It must be said that our long weekend away in the North proved to be fruitless and we certainly did not do ourselves any favours," he said. "Two away games, travelling the length of the country and finally arriving back home, tired and weary, in the early hours of Tuesday, having motored through the night and with nothing to show for it was not great. Everyone was bitterly disappointed to have returned empty handed, for I felt we deserved to return with at least two points, and this would certainly have been a bonus in terms of the survival target I have set of 42 points."

"You are probably asking why 42 points? What is so significant about that number? I say 42, because no club has ever been relegated with that number of points. I cannot see this season being the exception to the rule. If we can collect six points from our remaining games, I believe we can be assured of Third Division football again next season, and we must then plan a renewed effort to climb out of the Division and march on into the Second."

SATURDAY 8th APRIL 1978

CITY OVERCOME THE TEN MEN OF GILLINGHAM
Third Division
Exeter City 2 Gillingham 1
Exeter City team: Key, Templeman, Hore, Weeks, Giles, Hatch, Randell, Kellow, Bowker, Holman, Jennngs.
Gillingham: Hillyard, Knight, Buttress, Overton, Young, Crabbe, Nicholl (Walker), Weatherley, Price, Westwood, Richardson.
Scorers: Exeter: Bowker, Kellow. Gillingham: Nicholl.
Attendance: 3,982.

Exeter City inched another two points towards Third Division safety in a game that will be remembered for the tough line that the referee took, rather than the standard of play. He booked no fewer than seven players and sent off Gillingham centre half Young after 26 minutes for a foul on Harry Holman, having been shown the yellow card two minutes earlier for a foul on the same player.

Gillingham were eager to sustain their promotion challenge and City were similarly anxious to win because of their suspect position in the bottom half of the table. Exeter won in the end because they snapped up two of the half a dozen chances that fell their way, while the Gills took advantage of only one of the same number of goalscoring opportunities.

The visitors took a shock lead in the first minute when Nicholl rifled in a shot from 25-yards. Less than 60 seconds later City equalised. Keith Bowker's shot cannoned off the crossbar on its way past Hillyard following a cross from John Templeman. City went in front after 26 minutes, and again it was a Templeman centre that did the damage. Tony Kellow netted with a glancing header past Hillyard.

Kellow had another chance seven minutes into the second half, when after beating two defenders his shot was cleared off the line. Bowker also had an effort scrambled away from Colin Randell's 66th minute corner, yet it was always touch and go whether the ten man Gills side would equalise in the second half.

SATURDAY 15th APRIL 1978

EXCELLENT AWAY WIN FOR THE GRECIANS
Third Division
Bradford City 1 Exeter City 2
Bradford City team: Downsborough, Podd, Spark, Johnson, Middleton, Fretwell, Dolan, Wright, Cooke, McNiven, Hutchins.
Exeter City team: Key, Templeman, Hore, Weeks, Giles, Hatch, Hodge, Kellow, Bowker, Holman, Randell.
Scorers: Bradford City: Dolan: Exeter: Holman, kellow.
Attendance: 4,924

Battling Exeter City earned full marks against a poor Bradford City team at Valley Parade to further ease any fears of being dragged into the relegation zone. The Grecians produced the more progressive football and always looked the more likely to score. After a quiet start by both sides in which City's soundness at the back was a feature in limiting Bradford's threats to a minimum, Keith Bowker sent in a 25-yard drive that smacked against the crossbar.

Two minutes before the break Exeter deservedly went into the lead when Harry Holman scored to crown a concerted move in which the Bradford defence was left helplessly flat footed. The home side had to suffer constant barracking from the crowd, although they did carry a certain amount of threat in a succession of attacks, far more desperate than creative.

City's back four continued to give Richard Key first class cover, and the keepers' anxieties were kept to a minimum. Just when Exeter looked to be well on the way to a victory, a fiery surge of aggression by the Yorkshiremen brought a 70th minute equaliser when Dolan ran through the Grecians defence to score. This development disturbed Exeter temporarily, but they recovered and turned on commendable spirit in going all out to regain the lead four minutes later.

Tony Kellow headed home Colin Randell's perfectly flighted free-kick to confirm that City's overall team work continued to be superior to anything that came from Bradford.

MONDAY 17th APRIL 1978

INJURIES HAVE HIT CITY THIS SEASON.
The Grecians have suffered more than their fair share of players being missing through injury, some of them long term casualties.

"During our run in last season with only a staff of fourteen professionals, we were fortune enough to be injury free, apart from Richard Key. This obviously helped us gain promotion," said City boss Bobby Saxton. "if it had been anyone else than Key being injured, for instance one of our strikers, for any length of time, then it would have been very difficult to have maintained the type of results we were getting at the time, and we would have possibly missed out on promotion. This season the exact opposite has occurred and we have suffered because of it. Seven times the stretcher has had to be called upon."

"Long term imjuries have been Alan Beer, missing since the start of the season. Bobby Hodge out for three months following a cartilage operation. Lee Roberts out with knee trouble until the end of the season, and John Baugh out with a broken finger. To go through a season and not get any players injured is rare, but to lose key players for long periods at a time makes life difficult at the top level, so you can imagine what it does to the teams in the lower divisions."

TUESDAY 18th APRIL 1978

CITY EDGE CLOSER TO SAFETY
Third Division
Exeter City 0 Chesterfield 0
Exeter City team: Key. Templeman, Hore, Weeks, Giles, Hatch (Jennings), Hodge, Kellow, Randell, Bowker, Holman.
Chesterfield team: Tingay, Tartt, Burton, Pollard, Cottam, O'Neill, Cammack, Fern, Simpson, Walker, Kowalski.
Attendance: 3,200

Nearly, but not quite. That was the story for Exeter City in what proved to be a colourless stalemate. They needed a win to be sure of Third Division safety, but the goalless draw means one more point is still required. City's worries are only a matter of statistical possibilities rather than a football probability.

The more concerning feature about this game was City's mediocre performance. Throughout they never really stamped any authority on the play, although there were moments when they might have got a vital goal. Those occasions were only fleeting and rare though, as it was Chesterfield who could have snatched victory, and only a superb save by Richard Key, who kept out a header from Walker, denied them.

Exeter rarely looked like a combination that was going to construct a comfortable win. Their play was ragged, lacked fluency, construction, and planning. Some of their passing was atrocious. Too often only the tireless Tony Kellow was the only man taking on the Chesterfield defence.

Kellow badly needed support and City required confidence to produce some football of initiative and adventure. Even so, despite the disappointments of this match, Exeter with their points tally, must surely guarantee Third Division football next season.

FORMER GRECIAN LEAVES CLUB
Bobby Nash, who played one league match for Exeter City in the 1966-67 season, has just relinquished the post of manager to Southern League, Ashford Town. Nash, who joined the Grecians from Queen's Park Rangers, later had spells playing for Hastings United and Folkestone Town.

SATURDAY 22nd APRIL 1978

ANOTHER GOALLESS DRAW FOR CITY
Third Division
Exeter City 0 Colchester United 0
Exeter City team: Key, Templeman, Hore, Delve, Giles, Bowker, Hodge, Kellow, Randell, Ingham, Holman.
Colchester United team: Walker, Cook, Williams, Leslie, Packer, Dowman, Foley, Gough, Dyer, Allinson, Wignall.
Attendance: 3,853.

Exeter City are safe. They made sure of Third Division football next season with another goalless draw at St. James' Park, this time against Colchester United. The result gave City their 42 point target which ensures their safety, but it was another disappointing performance from them following their midweek draw against Chesterfield.

In fact had Colchester been sharper in the opening 25 minutes they could well have made life difficult for the Grecians, having missed two clear cut chances. Just before half-time City went close to getting that vital goal when following a throw in, Fred Ingham crossed, and Tony Kellow went in with a brave header that went narrowly over the top. Several niggling off the ball incidents led to Wignall and John Delve - just back from suspension - to be booked.

Jimmy Giles sent a header just wide in the 64th minute as Exeter continued to push forward for the breakthrough. John Hore showed all of his experience and superb skill when he cleaned up in defence following a mistake by John Templeman, but it was still a stalemate in the sun. Giles headed over his own crossbar to clear a header from Allinson, and when Exeter counter attacked Ingham turned superbly to strike a shot from the edge of the penalty area that was easily saved by Walker.

WEDNESDAY 26th APRIL 1978

CITY HIT THE GOAL TRAIL AT LAST
Third Division
Exeter City 4 Tranmere Rovers 2
Exeter City team: Key, Templeman, Hore, Delve, Giles, Bowker, Forbes, Kellow, Randell, Ingham, Hatch.
Tranmere Rovers team: Johnson, Mathias, Flood, Parry, Philpotts, Evans, Craven, Cliff, Moore, Tynan, Allen.
Scorers: Exeter: Bowker (2), Hatch, Delve. Tranmere: Allen, Cliff.
Attendance: 3,156.

Exeter City cheerfully shook off their cares of the recent grim struggle to stay in Division Three, and celebrated their success in that venture by tearing Tranmere Rovers apart, with three goals in a hectic 15 minute second half spell. It was a game packed full of incidents and excitement in comparison to the two previous goalless home draws.

Perhaps the most pleasing aspect was the highly impressive debut of St. Lukes College midfielder, Dick Forbes. City did have an early scare when Allen put the ball in the net, but the goal was disallowed for offside. City took a 14th minute lead when Peter Hatch blasted home a free-kick. A defensive mix up then let in Allen for an equaliser twenty minutes later.

Jimmy Giles put a header against the crossbar at the start of the second half, but the Grecians almost immediately fell behind when Cliff ran the length of the field to place his shot wide of Richard Key. Exeter equalised on the hour as Keith Bowker headed home, and ten minutes later he did the same again, nodding in an accurate cross from Forbes. It was all over for Tranmere in the 76th minute when City struck again with John Delve weaving his way past three players to lash a 20-yard shot into the net. It was a shame that the supporters had to wait until the final home fixture of the season before witnessing what was the best match of the season.

SATURDAY 29th APRIL 1978

GRECIANS FAIL TO SPOIL THE PROMOTION PARTY
Cambridge United 2 Exeter City 1
Cambridge United team: Webster, Howard, Buckley, Stringer, Fallon, Hansbury, Cozens, Spriggs (Morgan), Sweetzer, Finney, Biley.
Exeter City team: Key, Templeman, Hore, Delve, Giles, Hatch, Forbes, Kellow, Randell, Bowker, Ingham (Hodge).
Scorers: Cambridge: Finney, Fallon. Exeter: Bowker.
Attendance: 8,741.

Club history was made by Cambridge United when they came from behind against Exeter City to secure the points that won them promotion to Division Two. Both goals were identical as they came in the 73rd and 84th minutes, following far post headers from corners, Finney and Fallon being the scorers.

Until then it seemed that the Grecians were heading for what would have been a well deserved and hard earned point at the very least. City in fact took the lead after 64 minutes from former Cambridge United player, Keith Bowker, who latched on to a long through ball from John Delve, sprinted past Stringer and hit a well struck cross shot into the corner of the net.

Cambridge had gone into the match unbeaten at home for 21 matches and there was rumblings in the crowd that their side had failed to show anything like their top form. Credit for that must go to Exeter though, who worked hard and it was obvious there was too much tension in the game for Cambridge.

The inevitable pitch invasion came after Finney's goal and there was immediately a different look about the home side as they surged forward at the City defence, who were busy for the first time in the match. Richard Key made a brilliant flying save to his left from a Biley shot, before Fallon sent the supporters wild. At the final whistle the Abbey Stadium pitch was a scene of massed ranks of fans calling for their promotion heroes.

NB - Vintage adverts from the 1970s - do not respond!

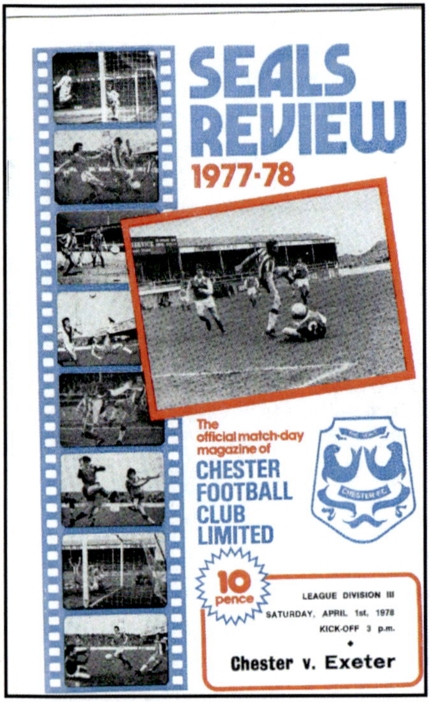
SEALS REVIEW
1977-78
The official match-day magazine of
CHESTER FOOTBALL CLUB LIMITED
10 pence
LEAGUE DIVISION III
SATURDAY, APRIL 1st, 1978
KICK-OFF 3 p.m.
Chester v. Exeter

SEASON 1977-78
C·U·F·C
CARLISLE UNITED
MONDAY, 3rd APRIL, 1978
EXETER
Kick-off 7.30 p.m.
Third Division
Sponsored by
CARPET DESIGN CENTRE (DUMFRIES) LTD.
OFFICIAL PROGRAMME 15p

Bradford City
a.F.C.
LEAGUE DIVISION THREE
Bradford City
VERSUS
Exeter City
Saturday, 15th April, 1978
Kick-off 3.00 p.m.
Official Programme 15p

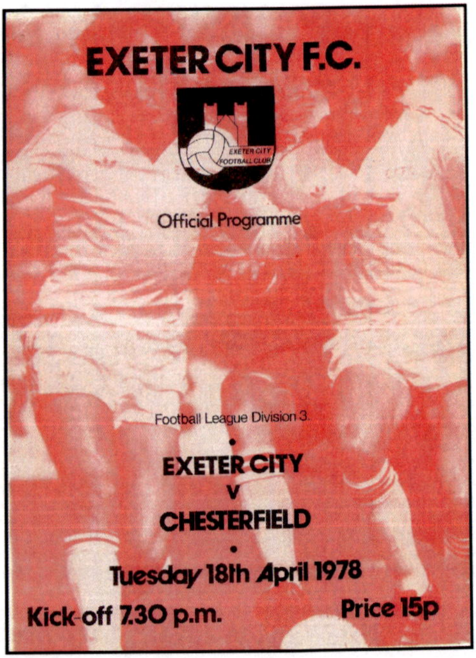
EXETER CITY F.C.
EXETER CITY FOOTBALL CLUB
Official Programme
Football League Division 3
EXETER CITY
V
CHESTERFIELD
Tuesday 18th April 1978
Kick-off 7.30 p.m.
Price 15p

NB - Vintage adverts from the 1970s - do

EXETER CITY PLAYERS AND MANAGEMENT - 1976-77 & 1977-78

THE MANAGERS

NEWMAN John, Henry, George (b. Hereford 13th December 1933)
Representing Herefordshire as a youth player, Newman played as a central defender, beginning his professional career with Birmingham City in March 1951. He was a member of the team that won the Second Division and was on the losing side in the 1956 F.A. Cup Final against Manchester City.

After 60 league appearances for Birmingham, Newman moved on to Leicester City in November 1957 and added a further 61 league outings, scoring two goals.

He signed for Plymouth Argyle in January 1960 where Newman became a firm favourite making 298 league outings and scoring nine goals.

In 1966 Newman played for the Football League side which beat the Irish League 12-0 at Home Park. He was in illustrious company for the Football League side consisted of seven players who played for England when they won the World Cup in the same year.

At the age of almost 34, he moved to Exeter City in November 1967. His first game for the Grecians in a disastrous 5-1 defeat at Brentford.

However, he went on to feature regularly in the side. On the departure of Frank Broome as Exeter manager, Newman was appointed player-manager in April 1969.

He handed in his resignation in October 1971 after some poor results, but was persuaded by the players to tear it up and stay on.

He remained in charge until December 1976 when he took over as manager of Grimsby Town.

Leaving Grimsby in July 1979, he was then assistant manager at Derby County, and also their manager between January and November 1982.

Newman was appointed manager of his home town club, Hereford United, in November 1983, and stayed in charge until September 1987.

Appointed assistant manager of Notts County in July 1988,; he then took a similar position with York City.

In 1991 he was coach and chief scout at Mansfield Town. Newman was living in Mickleover, Derbyshire in 2010.

SAXTON Robert (b. Doncaster 6th September 1943)
Saxton had a successful career both as a player and as a manager. He got his Football League chance with Derby County after signing for them in February 1962 from Denaby United.

He made 96 league appearances for the Baseball Ground club, and moved on after the arrival of Brian Clough as manager.

He signed for Plymouth Argyle in February 1968 for a fee of £12,000 and was an instant success going to feature in 231 league matches for the Pilgrims, scoring seven goals. Saxton was in the team that reached the semi-final of the Football League Cup in 1973-74.

He would have played a lot more for Argyle but for being sidelined for the 1969-70 season with a broken leg which he suffered in a car accident.

Saxton made the short move to Exeter City in September 1975 for £4,000, being signed by his former Argyle team mate John Newman.

He made his Grecians debut in a 2-2 home draw with Crewe Alexandra, scoring one of the goals,

When Newman left to take over as manager of Grimsby Town, Saxton became the Exeter City player-manager in January 1977, and guided the team to their second ever promotion by the end of that season.

Plymouth Argyle persuaded him to return to Home Park in January 1979 as their manager, succeeding Malcolm Allison, taking with him almost all of the Grecians' back room staff. He remained in charge until May 1981 when he was appointed the manager of Blackburn Rovers.

Saxton left Ewood Park in December 1986 and was then employed as an advisor at Preston North End in the following month.

His next managerial job proved to be a struggle, that being at York City in June 1987 and the team slipped to the bottom of the Fourth Division. He left York in September 1988.

His next port of call was at Blackpool, where he became a coach within days of leaving York.

He then became assistant manager at Newcastle United in 1989 and had a couple of months as caretaker boss from March 1991.

Saxton was then chief scout for Manchester City in October 1991, before going back to the North East as assistant to Peter Reid at Sunderland between 1995 and 2002.

In 2010 Saxton was living in Beamish, Co Durham and working as a scout for Sunderland.

THE PLAYING STAFF

BAUGH John, Robert (b. Uganda 23rd February 1956)
Baugh attended Aldenham School in Hertfordshire, before going to St Luke's College in Exeter, where he played in goal for the college team.

He was signed by Exeter City on non-contract forms in March 1977 and was thrust almost immediately into their promotion campaign in the old Fourth Division as regular Grecians keeper, Richard Key, broke an ankle in the 2-0 defeat at Crewe Alexandra.

Baugh played the final 15 games of the season, keeping 8 clean sheets as Exeter finished second and clinched promotion.

His debut came against Scunthorpe United and City crashed to a 4-1 defeat at the Old Show Ground.

After two seasons with City, Baugh decided to leave the game to pursue his career in teaching and eventually became Headmaster of The Dragon School in Oxford.

Over the years the school has had had some famous pupils such as John Betjemen, Leonard Cheshire, Hugh Gaitskell, Antonia Fraser, Tim Henman, Peter Jay, Hugh Laurie, plus generations of lawyers, businessmen, musicians and scientists. Baugh was living locally in Oxford in 2013.

BEER Alan, Desmond (b. Swansea 11th March 1950)
Had it not been for a knee injury, then the career of Alan Beer could have been very different to what it was.

The injury ended his playing days, just as he was on the verge of a £70,000 move to then First Division, Leicester City, and the winning of a full international cap for Wales.

A former Wales amateur international, Beer had played in local football in the Swansea area for Tower United and West End, before he signed professional forms for Swansea City in February 1971. He scored 3 goals in 15 league appearances for the Swans.

He dropped out of the Football League though when signing for Weymouth in August 1972, where his goalscoring ability was noted by Exeter City who duly paid a fee of £5,000 for him in November 1974.

Beer made his Grecians debut at Rochdale the same month and scored in the 1-1 draw, the first of many goals for City.

He was the club's top scorer in 1975-76 with 20 league goals in 46 appearances, and the following season played a prominent part, alongside Tony Kellow, in scoring the goals that took Exeter to promotion to the Third Division (21 goals in 38 league outings).

Beer was picked as one of the 24 players in the Welsh squad for the home internationals in the Summer of 1977, but didn't get a call up into the team.

A knee injury sustained in only the third league match of the 1977-78 season at Shrewsbury Town , having already scored two goals that season, ended his playing days. On medical advice he eventually retired from playing in August 1978.

In December 1978 Beer had a testimonial match played on his behalf between Exeter City and West Bromwich Albion.

He returned to the Swansea area and later worked for Bassetts Honda. Beer was living in Swansea in 2013.

BOWKER Keith (b. West Bromwich 18th April 1951)
Another player who has two spells with Exeter City - two productive spells in fact with a good goals per game ratio.

He started his career at Birmingham City as an apprentice and featured in the team that reached the final of the FA Youth Cup.

He became a full professional with Birmingham, then First Division side in August 1968.

Reaching first team level, Bowker made 21 league appearances, scoring five goals.

However, Exeter City decided the team needed a bit of a shake up and in December 1973 they paid fees on the same day, not only for Bowker, but for Peter Hatch from Oxford United as well.

Both players made the Grecians debut in front of just 693 spectators at Workington. (The author of this book was on the terraces that day!).

Bowker stayed until May 1976, during which time he had netted 38 league goals in 110 appearances.

He then signed for Cambridge United for a fee of £10,000, but his stay there was a short one and seven months later he had moved to Northampton Town.

After just four league appearances for the Cobblers, Bowker was on his way back to Exeter in August 1977, and this time he scored 28 goals in 102 league outings for the Grecians.

His final Football League club was to be Torquay United whom he joined in August 1980.

Bowker featured in 53 league matches for Torquay, scoring nine goals, being eventually released to link up with Western League club, Bideford.

He then became manager at Taunton Town until 1993. Bowker worked for the Royal Mail in Exeter, where he still lives.

CLAPHAM Keith (b. Fareham 9th September 1952)
Clapham didn't make his Football League debut until joining Exeter City in July 1972.

Prior to that he had been an apprentice at Bournemouth, signing a full contract with them in September 1970, but he didn't make a first team breakthrough.

However, he had been a regular in their reserve team, totalling 75 outings in two seasons.

He made his Grecians debut against Torquay United at Plainmoor on 23rd September 1972, a game City won 2-0.

For the next three seasons Clapham was a steady performer in the City defence.

He was transfer-listed in October 1976 and left St James' Park the following March so he could play in Australia.

DARKE Peter, George (b. Exeter 21st December 1953)
Darke is a member of the exclusive club of players who have played for three Devon clubs in the Football League.

Although Exeter-born, Darke gained a professional contract with Plymouth Argyle in December 1971, having joined the Home Park club as an apprentice.

He made 99 league appearances for Argyle, scoring two goals, but in October 1976, he played a small part in helping Exeter City win promotion as he joined the Grecians on loan, making his debut in a 3-1 home win over Southport.

Signing for Torquay United on a free transfer in July 1977, after turning down an offer from Exeter, Darke spent two seasons at Plainmoor adding a further 59 league games to his career total.

He signed for Minehead prior to the start of the 1979-80 season. he then played for Wellington, Saltash United and Liskeard Athletic before returning to Saltash United as their manager in 1985.

Darke is the son-in-law of Torquay United legendary striker, Tommy Northcott, whose brother George also played for Exeter City. Darke later worked as a salesman.

DELVE John, Frederick (b. Isleworth 27th September 1953)
A former England Schools international, Delve joined Queens' Park Rangers as an apprentice, earning a full contract in July 1971.

He made 15 league appearances for the Loftus Road club, before a £30,000 fee took him to Plymouth Argyle in July 1974.

A tenacious, busy midfielder, Delve helped Argyle win promotion in his first season at Home Park and completed 132 league appearances scoring six goals by the time he made the short move to Exeter City in March 1978 to rejoin his former Plymouth team mate, Bobby Saxton, who was player-manager at Exeter.

Making his City debut against Rotherham United, a game which the Grecians won 1-0, Delve assisted Exeter to their highest finish in the Third Division in 1979-80 when they ended the season in 8th place.

He also played his part in the club's run to the quarter-final stage of the FA Cup in 1981.

It was something of a shock to Exeter fans when Delve was allowed to move to Hereford United in June 1983 as he had hardly missed a game since he had signed for the Grecians.

His consistency again shone through at Hereford, where he enjoyed four good seasons playing in 118 league matches, scoring two goals. In 1986-87, Delve signed for Gloucester City, but was back at Exeter to assist with the club's lottery scheme and eventually signed as a player again in October 1987.

Delve had the job as caretaker manager after Exeter boss Colin Appleton left the club in December 1987, and remained in charge until the end of the season.

On the appointment of Terry Cooper as manager, Delve was again released and in 1987-88 played for Minehead.

He also had a spell with Elmore as player-coach in 1991-92, being released by them in January 1992.

He was appointed steward at the Centre Spot Social Club at St James' Park in 1988.

He became landlord of the Village Inn, Exwick, Exeter in March 1990. However, by 2010 he was working for the Royal Mail in Exeter.

FORBES Richard, John (b. Ashford 12th March 1955)
Formerly on the books at Woking, Forbes was studying at St Luke's College in Exeter when he signed for Exeter City in April 1978, although he had played for the Grecians' reserve team prior to that.

He featured in the last two matches of the 1977-78 season, at home to Tranmere Rovers and away at Cambridge United, and in a handful of matches the following two seasons.

Forbes won a regular place in the team during 1980-81 and played his part in the team as they reached the quarter-final of the FA Cup.

However at the end of that season, he signed for Bideford, and after a couple of seasons in North Devon, got a second Football League chance when signing for Plymouth Argyle in August 1983.

Forbes was to play just three league matches for Argyle though, and in the summer of 1984 moved back to Bideford, before playing for Tiverton Town, combining playing with teaching at the Clyst Vale Community College, Broadclyst. Forbes was appointed as coach to Cyst Valley FC in July 2010.

GAY Geoffrey (b. Romford 4th February 1957)
Gay has a unique record at Exeter City of being the only outfield player to have made his league debut for the club and ended up as a goalkeeper!

Gay replaced the injured Richard Key between the posts in the game against Crewe Alexandra at Gresty Road in March 1977.

A former apprentice with Bolton Wanderers, he signed a full contract in January 1975, but never made a first team league outing.

On loan to Exeter, and helping them go on and win promotion, he stayed until the end of the 1976-77 season.

Given a free transfer by Bolton, Gay signed for Southport in August 1977 where he was an almost ever present in their team during his one season stay at Haig Avenue.

He moved to Wigan Athletic in July 1978, but in complete contrast only featured in one league game for the newly elected Football League club, who had ironically replaced Southport as members of the Fourth Division.

Gay then moved to Macclesfield Town, who were then in the Northern Premier League, and subsequently played for Bangor City, Droylsden, Mossley (for whom he had two spells in 1984-85 and 1986-87), Chorley and Horwich R.M.I.

GILES James, Archer (b. Kidlington 21st April 1946)
Giles was playing for his village team, Kidlington, when he first joined Swindon Town in March 1965. He went on to play in 13 league matches for the County Ground side.

Transferring to Aldershot in October 1968, he was regular first teamer going on to make 82 league outings and scoring three goals, and was their Player of the Year in 1969-70.

Two weeks after Exeter City had played at Aldershot in game in where Giles had been introduced as a substitute and scored against the Grecians, manager John Newman managed to gain the signature of the defender for a fee of £4,000 and what a bargain it proved to be.

Making his City debut in a home fixture against Barrow, Giles went on to become a firm favourite of the St James' Park faithful missing only handful of games between his first and last appearance for the club which was in April 1975.

He was to become the first player to win the Player of the Year award for two seasons running at Exeter, in 1971-72 and 1972-73. He also won it in 1974-75.

Giles was then transferred to Charlton Athletic in June 1975 for £12,000 where he went on to score six goals in 93 League appearances.

The good news as far as Exeter fans were concerned, was that Giles signed for a second spell with the Grecians in December 1977 for £7,000.

Giles again missed few games, but in his final season with the club in 1980-81, he lost his place to Lee Roberts.

At the end of the season Giles moved to Yeovil Town as their player-manager, a position he held until the 1982-83 season.

Giles had a testimonial match played on his behalf in April 1985 when an Invitation XI faced Exeter City.

Continuing to live in the East Devon area and owning his own bricklaying business, Giles has become well known to Exeter City supporters in another sphere, namely co-commentator at Grecians' matches with BBC Radio Devon.

He also managed the Exeter City Legends team, along with Alan Banks. Giles was living in Ottery St Mary in 2014.

GREEN Michael, John (b. Southend 20th November 1957)

Green, who was part of the Exeter City 1976-77 Fourth Division promotion squad, was originally signed by the Grecians as an apprentice.

The diminutive midfielder earned a full contract in November 1975, having been on City's books since he was 15-years-old, whilst still at Hele's School. He had been playing for local youth side, Pilgrims, in the East Devon Youth League.

His only outing for the first team squad, was ironically at his home town of Southend on 23rd October 1977, when he replaced winger Bobby Hodge as a substitute a game which City lost 2-0.

Green later went on to play for Exmouth Town and used to work for Rawle, Gammon and Baker during the 1980s.

He later got a first class honours, then a BA and followed that up with a PHD. Latterly Green worked as a lecturer at Loughborough University. He sadly died in February 2009 after battling against cancer.

HATCH Peter, Derek (b. Wargrave 22nd October 1949)

Another long serving Exeter City player and what a bargain he proved to be when signing from Oxford United in December 1973.

Despite signing professional for Oxford in October 1966, in seven years with the club he only made 19 league appearances, scoring two goals.

All that was to change when he moved to Devon, as he made his debut for the Grecians in a 3-1 defeat at Workington watched by just 693 spectators. Keith Bowker made his debut for City in the same game.

Hatch played in the 1976-77 promotion winning team and also starred in the run to the FA Cup quarter-final in 1981, including one memorable performance against Newcastle United when he scored once and made two other goals in the 4-0 win. He was voted as Exeter City Player of the Year for 1976-77.

At the end of the 1981-82 season, Hatch was given a free transfer and he joined Bideford. Hatch also played for Taunton Town, Barnstaple Town as player-manager, Dawlish Town, Crediton United and Heavitree United.

Hatch had a testimonial match in October 1986 when Exeter City faced his former club, Oxford United.

He often appeared for the Ex-City professional team and later worked as a postman. In 2014 Hatch was living in Exeter.

HEALE Gary, John (b. Canvey Island 15th July 1958)

Heale began his career with his local club, Canvey Island in 1975. He moved to Luton Town in December 1976 and scored one goal in seven league appearances.

He was loaned to Exeter City in December 1977 making his debut in 2-4 defeat at home to Cambridge United. he retained his place in the three following matches, before returning to Luton.

Transferred to Reading in August 1979, he had the best spell of his career in the Football League as he netted 20 goals in 76 appearances for the Elm Park side.

In the summer of 1982 Heale linked up with Sparta Rotterdam, staying there for one season.

He then signed for San Diego Sockers of the North American Soccer League, later moving on to Tacoma Stars of the Major Indoor Soccer League.

In 1987, Heale signed for the Los Angeles Lazers, then the St Louis Storm in 1988.

He spent one season with Seattle Storm in the Western Soccer League and the Seattle Sounders of the A-League in 1994.

HODGE Robert, William (b. Exeter 30th April 1954)
Much was expected of a young Hodge when he made his Exeter City debut against Reading as a substitute in September 1974.

A steady, hard working winger, he had been awarded a full contract by the Grecians three months earlier.

He was to stay at St James' Park for just over four seasons, including playing his part in the 1977 promotion winning team, when he scored seven goals in 35 league starts.

After appearing in the opening four league matches of the 1978-79 season, Colchester United parted with a fee of £15,000 to take him to Essex. At Layer Road he added a further 92 league appearances and 14 goals.

Hodge returned to Devon when he signed for Torquay United in August 1981, but he only played in four league matches, scoring one goal.

Keen to take up an offer play in Norway, Hodge kept himself match fit by at first appearing in a few matches for Chelmsford City and then training at Fulham.

He enjoyed two years in Norway playing for Fredrikstad and still has many contacts in that country to this day.

On his return to England, Hodge became player-manager of Eastern Counties League side, Clacton Town.

After retiring from playing Hodge eventually moved back to Devon, living in West Hill, Ottery St Mary, where he runs his own carpentry business

HOLMAN Harold, William (b. Exeter 16th November 1957)
Although born in Exeter, Holman started his professional career as an apprentice with Chelsea, moving back to sign for Exeter City in July 1976.

The England Schools international made his Grecians debut in a goalless draw against Workington at St James' Park in October 1976.

He went on to play in the following six league games without finding the net, as Exeter went on to win promotion.

He won a regular place in the City side throughout 1977-78 playing in 37 league games, scoring eight goals, the first of which came in a 4-1 home win over Port Vale.

The following season he was restricted to just 8 league appearances and one goal.

Transfer listed at his own request in August 1978, four months later, Holman signed for Peterborough United, a month after he had a reported dispute with manager Bobby Saxton over his lack of first team opportunities.

He only stayed at Peterborough until the end of the season, scoring one goal in nine league starts.

Moving back to the Exeter area to live, apart from a handful of games for Exmouth Town, Holman then retired from the game. He was still living in Exeter in 2014.

HOOKER Alan, Thomas (b. Exeter 23rd June 1956)
From a well-known family based in Budleigh Salterton, Alan joined Exeter City as an apprentice, becoming a full professional in July 1974.

Hooker made his league debut for the Grecians in a 2-0 defeat at Brentford in December 1974. he went on to complete nine outings for the City that season.

He started the 1975-76 season off filling the left-back slot and added a further 28 league games to his tally.

He also featured in the first half of the 1976-77 promotion season, making a further 13 appearances.

After leaving the Grecians in the summer of 1977, Hooker signed for Bideford.

He was to later play a major part in the success of Exmouth Town in the 1980s, captaining the side on several occasions.

Hooker was playing for Weston-Super-Mare in 1992-93. Working for Clark's Shoes in Exmouth, he later transferred to their Street factory in Somerset and played for Bridgwater Town, where he became joint manager of the team in 1994, a position he held until the 1999-2000 season.

He then became player-manager of Street FC in the Western League and in 2013 was living in Street.

HORE Kenneth, John (b. St. Austell 10th February 1947)
After starring for the East Cornwall Schools side, Hore was signed by Plymouth Argyle as an apprentice, signing a professional contract in December 1964.

After making his debut for Argyle against Northampton Town in 1965, Hore went on to amass 400 league appearances and scored 17 goals.

Exeter City signed Hore, initially on loan in March 1976, thus linking up again with his former Argyle team mate and City player-manager, Bobby Saxton. He made his Grecians debut against Rochdale at St James' Park.

In the summer of 1976, the move was made permanent and Hore was an ever present in the Exeter promotion winning team of 1976-77.

He never missed a league game in the following season either, when he won the Exeter City Player of the Year award, only two in 1978-79, and played in all 46 league matches in 1979-80, such was his remarkable consistency.

Leaving the Grecians in the summer of 1980, he signed for Bideford, where he became player-manager.

Hore guided Bideford to two Western League championships as manager He also ran a successful health club business in the Guildhall Centre, Exeter.

Appointed manager of Plymouth Argyle in October 1983, he steered the club to the semi-final of the FA Cup losing narrowly to Watford.

He was rewarded with a two-year contract, only to be sacked four months later.

Hore returned to St James' Park in January 1985 to assist with coaching and was appointed caretaker manager in May of that year after Jim Iley was dismissed.

In 1989 he had joined Western League Torrington, as their manager, a position he held until midway through the 2002-03 season. Hore was living in Exeter in 2014.

INGHAM Frederick, Roy (b. Manchester 3rd April 1954)
An apprentice with Stockport County, Ingham moved into the full professional ranks in April 1972. He scored one goal in 19 league outings for County.

He was given a free transfer in August 1973 and signed for Blackburn Rovers. Ingham never made the Blackburn first team and had the misfortune to sustain a broken leg.

He was eventually released, and joined Witton Albion, where he became their leading goalscorer.

Signed by Exeter City on non-contract forms in September 1977, Ingham had by that time been playing for Dawlish Town and Falmouth Town. He was given a full contract by the Grecians two months later.

Ingham made a successful debut against Chester City, scoring in the 1-1 draw at St James' Park.

Retained for the 1978-79 season, Ingham only made two substitute appearances against Chester City and Tranmere Rovers respectively and at the end of the campaign left the club to play for Falmouth Town for a second spell at that club.

JENNINGS Nicholas (b. Wellington 18th January 1946)

A left-winger who began his professional career with Plymouth Argyle in June 1963, who had signed him from his home town club of Wellington in Somerset.

Jennings was to score 11 goals in 98 appearances for Argyle, before moving to Portsmouth in January 1967 for a fee of £25,000.

He was to prove so popular there that he won the Player of the Year title. Going on to make 207 league appearances for Portsmouth he netted 44 goals.

He also had a short loan spell with Aldershot in November 1973. However, given a free transfer in May 1974, Jennings returned to Devon to sign for Exeter City, who had faced competition from Aldershot, Charlton Athletic and Northampton Town for the players' signature.

He proved to be a huge success at St. James' Park, including appearing in the City team that won promotion in 1977.

Jennings stayed for four seasons, during which time he scored 15 goals in 124 league matches. He then became player-manager of Western League side, Wellington Town.

He had a testimonial match between Exeter City and Nottingham Forest in February 1979, a game which marked the debut of England's first £1million player, Trevor Francis.

Jennings later became a full time Probation Officer and then retired to live in Wimborne Minster, Dorset, before moving to Bournemouth, where he was in 2014.

JORDAN Michael, John (b. Exeter 8th January 1956)

Signing as a full professional in July 1975, he had been on the books at Exeter for the previous 18 months. Jordan made his Exeter City and Football League debut two months later as a substitute in in the 1-0 defeat at Workington.

Jordan had netted 21 goals for the City reserve side in 1974-75, even though he had missed the last two months through injury. He had formerly played for Clyst Valley in the Devon & Exeter League.

He went on to score three goals in 11 appearances that season, his first goal proving to be the winner (and only one of the game) at Cambridge United in January 1976.

Although he started off in the first team the following season, Jordan could only add another seven league appearances, before he was released in 1977 joining Bideford.

A knee injury restricted his appearances with the North Devon side, and he later played for Tiverton Town and Dawlish Town, before moving into the management side of the game in the Exeter area. Jordan was living in Exeter in 2014.

KELLOW Tony (b. Falmouth 1st May 1952)

A true Exeter City legend, Kellow enjoyed no less than three separate spells with the Grecians and was always a fans favourite.

He first signed for the Grecians from Falmouth Town in July 1976, where he had been a prolific goalscorer. Falmouth would also receive 10% of any future fee that Exeter received for the player.

Kellow had started his playing career with the Falmouth Docks team in the Falmouth & Helston league.

At the age of 15 he made his debut for the Docks first team in the Cornwall Combination League.

He later joined South Western League side, Penzance, playing for the Cornwall County side on five occasions.

Kellow moved to Falmouth Town in the summer of 1973 and netted 62 goals in his first season as his team won the South Western League title.

Kellow switched back to Penzance for the 1974-75 season, but twelve months later had signed for Falmouth Town once more, and in 1975-76 scored well over 50 goals for them.

Despite the higher level of football, Kellow netted twice on his league debut for Exeter, in a 2-2 draw against Hartlepool United at St James' Park.

In his first season he netted 19 league goals and formed a lethal partnership with Alan Beer (21 goals) which did much to earn Exeter promotion to Division Three.

He was Exeter's top scorer with 14 league goals in 46 matches in 1977-78, and had netted 7 in 17 games in 1977-78 before a move to Blackpool took place in November 1978 for a fee of £105,000 - a then club record.

Three months earlier City had turned down a bid of £40,000 from Chesterfield, as well as £70,000 from Fulham, £75,000 from Peterborough United and £45,000 plus a player from Watford.

Although Kellow scored 23 goals in 57 league appearances for the Seasiders he never really settled on the Lancashire coast and was pleased to return to Exeter for another club record fee of £65,000 in March 1980. He soon got back into the scoring groove, and became the Exeter City Player of the year in 1980-81.

This time he scored 61 goals in 143 league outings, before transferring to Plymouth Argyle in November 1983 for a fee of £5,000.

By the following October and having made only a handful of appearances for Argyle, Kellow signed for Swansea City.

He featured just the once as a substitute for the Swans, then moving to their near neighbours Newport County in November 1984, scoring 8 goals in 20 league matches.

Kellow started his third spell back at Exeter City in July 1985 and was to stay for another three seasons, once again becoming the clubs' leading scorer in 1985-86 and 1986-87.

He then became the Grecians' Promotions Manager, Commercial Manager and also ran the Centre Spot social club at St James' Park.

Kellow had a benefit match at St James' Park in August 1990, when Exeter City played Leicester City.

After finally leaving the Grecians in November 1991, Kellow became landlord of the Eagle Tavern in Howell Street, Exeter.

He was also appointed Crediton United's commercial manager in November 1992.

Later Kellow returned to his native Cornwall at Budock Water where he still lived in 2010. A weekly internet show,

"Kellows Bootlaces" was named after the player who many regard as one of the all-time Grecian legends and a terrific character. Kellow died in February 2011.

KEY Richard, Martin (b. Coventry 13th April 1956)
Key joined Exeter City as an 19-year-old, having previously been a junior at Coventry City.

He went straight into the Grecians' first team and made his league debut against Torquay United at Plainmoor in September 1975.

The keeper appeared for City 37 times in his first season at the club, and the following season, 1976-77, was a member of the Exeter promotion winning team.

Unfortunately he sustained a broken ankle in a game at Crewe Alexandra in March 1977, so missed the run-in.

He was back as first choice keeper in 1977-78 and added a further 41 league appearances to his tally.

He was then transferred to Cambridge United in August 1978 for a fee of £10,000.

Key made 52 league outings for Cambridge, and also had a loan spell with Northampton Town.

He then joined Orient in August 1983 and played a further 42 league matches for them.

Moving to Brentford in August 1984, he only featured in one league match for the Bees, and two months later joined Sunderland to provide goalkeeping cover for them.

During his time with the Black Cats, Key was loaned back to Cambridge United where he played 13 league games.

After being on the books as a non-contract player with Swindon Town, Key's Football League career came to an end when he signed for Brentford for a second spell with them in August 1985, making three league outings. Key then played for Southern League club, Cambridge City.

Key returned to St James' Park for a reunion of the promotion winning team of 1976-77 and more recently has been living in Freshwater Bay, Isle of Wight.

MORRIN Anthony, John (b. Swinton 31st July 1946)
After signing for Bury as an apprentice, Morrin gained his first full contract in October 1963 and played three league matches for the Gigg Lane side. He then moved to Burnley in July 1965, but never featured in their team.

Signing for Stockport County in October 1966, he made 31 appearances and scored 2 goals.

His career really took off when moving to Barrow in March 1969, featuring in 97 league matches and netting six goals.

Signing for Exeter City in July 1971, Morrin was to stay at St James' Park for nearly six years, during which time he was a member of the 1976-77 promotion winning squad.

After his Grecians' debut at Southport in August 1971, his best season in terms of matches played was in 1972-73 when he was involved in 40 league games, netting two goals.

On leaving Exeter in March 1977, he returned to Stockport County for a second spell at the club, but his stay was a short one and he was released at the end of the season. His final league club was Rochdale, whom he signed for in August 1977.

Morrin then played for Bangor City in the Northern Premier League and in 2014 was living in Westhoughton, near Bolton.

PHILLIPSON-MASTERS Forbes, Ernest (b. Bournemouth 14th November 1955)
One of the few players to have spent two separate loan spells at Exeter City, the first in 1976-77 and the second in 1985.

He originally signed for Southampton as an apprentice goalkeeper in August 1972, but was given a free transfer two years later.

He was persuaded to return as a centre-half by Saints, which proved to be successful, going on to make nine league appearances.

Phillipson-Masters signed for Exeter City on loan in September 1976 and after making his debut against Scunthorpe United, went on to feature in the next five matches before returning to The Dell.

He also had loan spells with AFC Bournemouth (7 league appearances, 2 goals) and Luton Town (10 league matches) before being transferred to Plymouth Argyle for £50,000 in 1979. He enjoyed a good spell at Home Park making 119 league appearances.

The defender then signed for Bristol City in November 1982 where he added a further 94 league matches and four goals.

However, he was back at St James' Park in March 1985, again on loan, as he appeared in a further seven league matches for Exeter City, scoring one goal against Halifax Town.

He played one season (1985-86) for Yeovil Town, then moving into management in non-league football in the Dorset area, combined with working as a painter and decorator. In 2014, he was living in Verwood, Dorset.

RANDELL Colin, William (b. Swansea 12th December 1952)
A former Welsh Schools and Under-23 international, Randell joined Coventry City as an apprentice, signing a full contract in May 1970.

He never made a league appearance though and moved to Plymouth Argyle in September 1973.

He played in the Argyle sides that reached the semi-final of the Football League Cup in 1973-74 and won promotion in 1974-75, making a total of 139 league outings, scoring nine goals.

Randell followed his Argyle team mate Bobby Saxton, who was manager at Exeter City in September 1977 for a fee of £10,000. Saxton had tried to sign the player in the summer, but was unsuccessful.

Making his debut at Peterborough United, Randell went on to feature in 40 league matches, scoring one goal (against Lincoln City) in his first season at St. James' Park.

He was just as consistent the following season, but with Saxton having become manager of Plymouth Argyle, the midfielder returned to Home Park in July 1979 for a fee of £60,000, where he added another 110 league appearances and eight goals.

Randell again followed Saxton, who had become manager of Blackburn Rovers, signing for the Ewood Park club in August 1982 for £40,000. 73 appearances and seven goals later, he moved to Newport County in March 1984.

His stay at County (15 appearances) only lasted until July 1985 though, for he joined his home town club of Swansea City, his final Football League club featuring in 22 league matches, netting one goal.

Randell was appointed player-manager of Barry Town, and then became player-manager at Briton Ferry Athletic. He later became head of PE with South Wales Police.

ROBERTS Lee, John (b. Market Drayton 23rd March 1957)
An apprentice with Shrewsbury Town, Roberts signed his first full professional contract for them in January 1975, but was to feature in only 15 league games, scoring one goal.

He moved to Exeter City on loan in March 1977, and thus played his part in the Grecians' promotion winning team. His debut was against Crewe Alexandra at Gresty Road and he went on to make 7 league appearances.

Exeter were keen to keep the player, but he did return to Shrewsbury. However, a fee of £8,000 persuaded the Shrews to sell him to Exeter in September 1977, despite having played against them the previous week!

Roberts went on to become a regular first team player at City and will be remembered for scoring a goal at Newcastle United in the 5th round of the FA Cup in February 1981 that earned the Grecians a repay, which they subsequently won 4-0.

Released at the end of the 1982-83 season, Roberts was forced to retire due an injury.

He returned to live in his home town of Market Drayton where he later became a postman.

Roberts was appointed manager of Market Drayton Town in 2003 and was in charge for two years.

He had a second spell as manager there in October 2009, but resigned after just two weeks following a disagreement.

ROBERTSON Archibald, Lamond (b. Paisley 27th September 1947)
Burnley signed Robertson as a 19-year-old from Glasgow Benburb in September 1966, but he had to wait for his league debut until moving to Bury in June 1968 when he played five times for the Gigg Lane club.

His next move to Halifax Town in February 1969 was to prove to be a successful one as he won a regular place in the side and scored 20 goals in 150 league games.

He was transferred to Brighton and Hove Albion in December 1972 and featured in 46 league games, scoring nine goals. His move to Exeter City in June 1974 was part of a transfer and player exchange deal that took Fred Binney to the south coast club and Robertson and John Templeman to St James' Park.

Robertson, regarded as one of the finest ball and creative players to have worn the City shirt, also had his fair share of run-ins with the referee! This led him to being sent off on more than one occasion.

Nonetheless, he still played in 133 league matches for the Grecians and scored 25 goals.

It wasn't long before other clubs started to notice this undoubted talent and he eventually left Exeter for £8,000, signing for Leicester City in September 1977.

Robertson only played seven league matches for Leicester and in October 1978 moved on to Peterborough United.

His stay was again a short one though for after just 15 league appearances and one goal he signed for Bradford City in January 1979.

This was to be his last League club, playing until the end of the 1980-81 season and adding 43 league games and three goals to his career tally.

Robertson was appointed player-manager at Northwich Victoria in July 1981.

After his playing career finished he became an independent financial advisor and scout for Sheffield United. In 2010 Robertson was living in Goostrey, Cheshire and in March of that year was appointed caretaker at the Goostrey Village Hall.

TEMPLEMAN John, Henry (b. Yapton 21st September 1947)
A versatile defender who played both wing-half and full-back, Templeman joined Brighton from Arundel Town in July 1966 as a teenager and spent eight years on the south coast, playing in 226 league matches and scoring 16 goals.

He moved to Exeter City in May 1974 as part of an exchange deal that saw Grecians' striker move to Brighton for £25,000 and Templeman and Lammie Robertson joining the Devon club,

Templeman made his debut against Barnsley at Oakwell on the opening day of the 1974

-75 season. He was a member of the squad that won promotion in 1976-77.

Joining Swindon Town on a free transfer in July 1979, he had one season with them playing in 21 league matches, before moving back to Pagham, near Bognor Regis, where he became a district agent for the Prudential Building Society.

Templeman had a spell as manager of Sussex County League side, Arundel, but was sacked in November 1988. He was a taxi driver in Brighton and living in Bognor Regis in 2014.

WEEKS Graham (b. Exeter 3rd March 1958)
The locally born midfielder signed for the club as an apprentice and then as a full time professional in March 1976.

He was only 19 when Exeter won promotion, having made his debut in a 3-1 defeat at Colchester United in September 1976.

He was with the club for two seasons, before a short spell at AFC Bournemouth, signing for them in May 1978 and featuring in 3 league matches.

Signing for Bideford and then Exmouth Town, he enjoyed great success at the latter club who were a strong Western League team in the early 1980s.

A knee injury while wicket keeping in a cricket match ended his career. He then worked as a technician for BT in Exeter. Weeks was living in Exeter in 2014.

1976/77 Grecians Statistics Section

STATISTICS 1976/77

EXETER CITY FIRST TEAM FIXTURES, RESULTS, ATTENDANCES, GOALSCORERS

Aug 14	Plymouth Argyle (FLC1)	A	1-0	8,688	Kellow
Aug 18	Plymouth Argyle (FLC1)	H	1-0	8,859	Jordan
Aug 21	Hartlepool	A	2-2	1,602	Kellow 2
Aug 28	Cambridge United	H	1-1	3,606	Kellow
Aug 31	Norwich City (FLC2)	H	1-3	9,449	Kellow
Sep 4	Colchester United	A	1-3	2,516	Smith (og)
Sep 11	Rochdale	H	2-1	2,829	Beer, Kellow
Sep 18	Halifax Town	A	2-1	1,424	Kellow, Beer
Sep 25	Watford	A	1-4	5,079	Beer
Sep 29	Scunthorpe United	H	2-0	2,934	Beer 2
Oct 2	Crewe Alexandra	H	3-0	3,337	Beer 2, Hatch
Oct 9	AFC Bournemouth	A	0-2	4,621	
Oct 16	Workington	H	0-0	2,958	
Oct 23	Southend United	A	0-2	4,605	
Oct 30	Southport	H	3-1	2,835	Robertson 3 (2 pens)
Nov 3	Brentford	H	3-2	2,779	Kellow 2, Robertson
Nov 6	Swansea City	A	0-0	3,856	
Nov 12	Huddersfield Town	H	2-0	3,657	Kellow, Robertson
Nov 20	Southend United FAC1	H	1-1	4,434	Hatch
Nov 22	Southend United (FAC1R)	A	1-2*	6,604	Kellow
Nov 27	Darlington	A	1-2	2,997	Kellow
Dec 4	Doncaster Rovers	H	0-2	2,891	
Dec 27	Torquay United	H	3-0	6,446	Saxton, Kellow, Jennings
Jan 1	Swansea City	H	2-0	3,596	Kellow 2
Jan 3	Southport	A	1-1	1,840	Jennings
Jan 8	Barnsley	H	1-0	3,784	Kellow
Jan 22	Hartlepool	H	3-1	3,285	Hodge, Kellow, Robertson (pen)
Jan 29	Bradford City	A	1-1	4,979	Hodge
Feb 5	Cambridge United	A	1-1	4,428	Beer
Feb 12	Colchester United	H	1-0	6,132	Hodge
Feb 19	Rochdale	A	2-1	1,523	Weeks, Beer
Feb 26	Halifax Town	H	1-0	5,995	Beer
Mar 2	Aldershot	A	2-2	3,789	Kellow, Templeman
Mar 5	Watford	H	2-2	5,867	Beer, Kellow
Mar 11	Crewe Alexandra	A	0-2	2,500	
Mar 15	Scunthorpe United	A	1-4	2,147	Jennings
Mar 19	AFC Bournemouth	H	1-1	4,065	Robertson
Mar 26	Workington	A	3-1	1,365	Beer, Jennings 2
Apr 2	Southend United	H	3-1	4,156	Kellow, Beer, Saxton
Apr 8	Torquay United	A	1-0	7,900	Beer
Apr 9	Newport County	H	1-0	5,243	Hodge
Apr 12	Brentford	A	0-1	7,640	
Apr 16	Stockport County	H	2-1	4,474	Robertson (pen), Hodge
Apr 20	Bradford City	H	0-0	7,827	
Apr 23	Huddersfield Town	A	1-0	4,717	Hatch
Apr 26	Newport County	A	3-0	3,550	Jennings, Beer, Hodge
Apr 30	Darlington	H	1-0	6,722	Beer
May 3	Barnsley	A	4-3	5,141	Beer 2, Kellow, Robertson (pen)
May 7	Doncaster Rovers	A	3-0	3,447	Beer 2, Kellow
May 14	Aldershot	H	3-0	10,751	Hodge, Beer, Jennings

* After extra time.

FIRST TEAM LEAGUE APPEARANCES
Hore 46; Kellow 44; Hatch 43; Jennings 43; Robertson 43; Beer 38; Weeks 37(3); Hodge 35; Templeman 35; Key 31; Saxton 28; Baugh 15; Morrin 15; Hooker 13; Clapham 7(2); Holman 7; Phillipson-Masters 6; Jordan 5(2); Roberts 5(2); Gay 5(1); Darke 5; Green 0(1).

FIRST TEAM LEAGUE GOALSCORERS
Beer 21; Kellow 19; Robertson 9; Hodge 7; Jennings 7; Hatch 2; Saxton 2; Templeman 1; Weeks 1; Own goals 1.

FIRST TEAM F.A. CUP APPEARANCES
Hatch 2; Holman 2; Hooker 2; Hore 2; Jennings 2; Kellow 2; Key 2; Morrin 2; Robertson 2; Saxton 2; Weeks 2; Hodge 0(1).

FIRST TEAM F.A. CUP GOALSCORERS
Hatch 1; Kellow 1.

FIRST TEAM FOOTBALL LEAGUE CUP APEPARANCES
Beer 3; Hatch 3; Hodge 3; Hooker 3; Hore 3; Kellow 3; Key 3; Saxton 3; Templeman 3; Jordan 2; Morrin 2; Jennings 1; Clapham 1(1).

FIRST TEAM FOOTBALL LEAGUE CUP GOALSCORERS
Kellow 2; Jordan 1.

LEAGUE ATTENDANCES
Highest at St. James' Park: 10,751 v Aldershot, 14th May 1977
Lowest at St. James' Park: 2,779 v Brentford, 3rd Nov 1976.

Highest away attendance: 7,900 v Torquay United, 8th April 1977
Lowest away attendance: 1,365 v Workington, 26th Mar 1977

Average League attendance for the season at St. James' Park: 4,624

FINAL LEAGUE TABLE

	P	W	D	L	F	A	Pts
Cambridge United	46	23	13	7	87	40	65
EXETER CITY	46	25	12	9	70	46	62
Colchester United	46	25	9	12	77	43	59
Bradford City	46	23	13	10	78	51	59
Swansea City	46	25	8	13	92	68	58
Barnsley	46	23	9	14	62	39	55
Watford	46	18	15	13	67	50	51
Doncaster Rovers	46	21	9	16	71	65	51
Huddersfield Town	46	19	12	15	60	49	50
Southend United	46	15	19	12	52	45	49
Darlington	46	18	13	15	59	64	49
Crewe Alexandra	46	19	11	16	47	60	49
AFC Bournemouth	46	15	18	13	54	44	48
Stockport County	46	13	19	14	53	57	45
Brentford	46	18	7	21	77	76	43
Torquay United	46	17	9	20	59	67	43
Aldershot	46	16	11	19	49	59	43
Rochdale	46	13	12	21	50	59	38
Newport County	46	14	10	22	42	58	38
Scunthorpe United	46	13	11	22	49	73	37
Halifax Town	46	11	14	21	47	58	36
Hartlepool	46	10	12	24	47	73	32
Southport	46	3	19	24	33	77	25
Workington	46	4	11	31	41	102	19

1977/78 Grecians Statistics Section

EXETER CITY FIRST TEAM FIXTURES, RESULTS, ATTENDANCES, GOALSCORERS

Aug 13	Plymouth Argyle (FLC1)	H	2-2	6,712	Robertson (2 pens)
Aug 16	Plymouth Argyle (FLC1)	A	0-0*	7,639	
Aug 20	Walsall	A	3-1	5,174	Beer 2, Kellow
Aug 23	Plymouth Argyle (FLC1R)	A	1-0	8,776	Beer
Aug 27	Bury	H	2-2	5,236	Hodge, Kellow
Aug 31	Aston Villa (FLC2)	H	1-3	13,768	Robertson
Sep 3	Shrewsbury Town	A	2-0	3,302	Atkins (og), Kellow
Sep 10	Port Vale	H	4-1	5,026	Robertson 2 (2 pens), Hodge, Holman
Sep 13	Rotherham United	A	0-1	4,889	
Sep 17	Peterborough United	A	1-1	5,016	Kellow
Sep 24	Portsmouth	H	0-1	5,875	
Sep 26	Carlisle United	H	0-1	5,106	
Oct 1	Chesterfield	A	0-0	3,771	
Oct 3	Tranmere Rovers	A	1-2	3,807	Roberts
Oct 8	Wrexham	H	0-1	4,722	
Oct 12	Sheffield Wednesday	H	2-1	4,564	Jennings, Holman
Oct 15	Lincoln City	A	2-1	4,704	Randell, Kellow
Oct 22	Preston North End	H	2-0	5,444	Jennings, Kellow
Oct 29	Swindon Town	A	0-4	7,021	
Nov 5	Oxford United	H	2-1	4,830	Hodge (pen), Bowker
Nov 12	Gillingham	A	0-1	5,714	
Nov 19	Bradford City	H	1-0	4,747	Hodge (pen)
Nov 26	Newport County (FAC1)	A	1-1	6,227	Bowker
Nov 30	Newport County (FAC1R)	H	4-2	5,713	Roberts, Hatch, Kellow, Templeman
Dec 3	Cambridge United	H	2-4	4,932	Kellow 2 (2 pens)
Dec 9	Colchester United	A	1-3	3,267	Holman
Dec 17	Minehead (FAC2)	A	3-0	3,200	Randell (2), Kellow
Dec 26	Plymouth Argyle	A	2-2	12,349	Roberts, Kellow
Dec 27	Hereford United	H	1-0	6,722	Bowker
Dec 31	Oxfod United	A	0-0	4,688	
Jan 2	Chester	H	1-1	6,193	Ingham
Jan 7	Wolves (FAC3)	H	2-2	14,377	Roberts, Holman
Jan 10	Wolves (FAC3R)	A	1-3	20,000	Kellow
Jan 14	Walsall	H	1-1	5,3149	Kellow
Jan 17	Sheffield Wednesday	A	1-2	9,596	Bowker
Jan 21	Bury	A	0-5	3,730	
Jan 28	Shrewsbury Town	H	1-1	3,906	Kellow
Feb 8	Port Vale	A	0-4	3,333	
Feb 11	Peterbrough United	H	1-0	4,017	Holman
Feb 28	Portsmouth	A	1-1	10,260	Cahill (og)
Mar 4	Wrexham	A	1-2	15,317	Bowker
Mar 8	Rotherham United	H	1-0	4,016	Kellow
Mar11	Lincoln City	H	3-0	4,280	Bowker, Holman (2)
Mar 18	Preston North End	A	0-0	9,189	
Mar 22	Swindon Town	H	0-0	4,449	
Mar 25	Hereford United	A	0-4	4,436	
Mar 28	Plymouth Argyle	H	0-0	8,334	
Apr 1	Chester	A	1-2	1,996	Holman
Apr 3	Carlisle United	A	0-2	3,693	
Apr 8	Gillingham	H	2-1	3,982	Bowker, Kellow
Apr 15	Bradford City	A	2-1	4,924	Holman, Kellow
Apr 18	Chesterfield	H	0-0	3,200	
Apr 22	Colchester United	H	0-0	3,853	
Apr 26	Tranmere Rovers	H	4-2	3,156	Bowker (2), Delve, Hatch
Apr 29	Cambridge United	A	1-2	8,741	Bowker

* - After extra time.

FIRST TEAM LEAGUE APPEARANCES
Bowker 46, Hore 46, Kellow 46, Templeman 44, Key 41, Randell 40, Hatch 38(1), Holman 36(1), Hodge 31(1), Saxton 25, Roberts 24(2), Jennings 23(5), Giles 23, Weeks 12(1), Delve 11, Baugh 5, Ingham 4(2), Heale 3(1), Robertson 3(1), Beer 3, Forbes 2.

FIRST TEAM LEAGUE GOALSCORERS
Kellow 14, Bowker 9, Holman 8, Hodge 4, Beer 2, Jennings 2, Roberts 2, Robertson 2, Delve 1, Hatch 1, Ingham 1, Randell 1, Own goals 2.

FIRST TEAM F.A. CUP APPEARANCES
Bowker 5, Hatch 5, Hore 5, Kellow 5, Key 5, Randell 5, Saxton 5, Templeman 5, Holman 4, Roberts 4, Jennings 3, Giles 2, Hodge 1, Weeks 1.

FIRST TEAM F.A. CUP GOALSCORERS
Kellow 3, Randell 2, Roberts 2, Bowker 1, Hatch 1, Holman 1, Templeman 1.

FIRST TEAM FOOTBALL LEAGUE CUP APPEARANCES
Baugh 4, Beer 4, Hatch 4, Hodge 4, Hore 4, Jennings 4, Kellow 4, Saxton 4, Templeman 4, Weeks 4, Bowker 3, Robertson 1(1).

FIRST TEAM FOOTBALL LEAGUE CUP GOALSCORERS
Robertson 3, Beer 1.

LEAGUE ATTENDANCES
Highest at St. James' Park: 8,334 v Plymouth Argyle, 28th Mar 1978
Lowest at St. James' Park: 3,156 v Tranmere Rovers, 26th Apr 1978

Highest away attendance: 15,317 v Wrexham, 4th Mar 1978
Lowest away attendance: 1,996 v Chester, 1st Apr 1978

Average League attendance for the season at St. James' Park: 4,887

FINAL LEAGUE TABLE

	P	W	D	L	F	A	Pts
Wrexham	46	23	15	8	78	45	61
Cambridge United	46	23	12	11	72	51	58
Preston North End	46	20	16	10	63	38	56
Peterborough United	46	20	16	10	47	33	56
Chester	46	16	22	8	59	56	54
Walsall	46	18	17	11	61	50	53
Gillingham	46	15	20	11	67	60	50
Colchester United	46	15	18	13	55	44	48
Chesterfield	46	17	14	15	58	49	48
Swindon Town	46	16	16	14	67	60	48
Shrewsbury Town	46	16	15	15	63	57	47
Tranmere Rovers	46	16	15	15	57	52	47
Carlisle United	46	14	19	13	59	59	47
Sheffield Wednesday	46	15	16	15	50	52	46
Bury	46	13	19	14	62	56	45
Lincoln City	46	15	15	16	53	61	45
EXETER CITY	46	15	14	17	49	59	44
Oxford United	46	13	14	19	64	67	40
Plymouth Argyle	46	11	17	18	61	68	39
Rotherham United	46	13	13	20	51	68	39
Port Vale	46	8	20	18	46	67	36
Bradford City	46	12	10	24	56	86	34
Hereford United	46	9	14	23	34	60	52
Portsmouth	46	7	17	22	41	75	31

1976/77 Other Statistics Section

FA CUP 1976/7

Round	Home	Away		
1	Aldershot	Portsmouth	1	1
1	Barnsley	Boston United	3	1
1	Barrow	Goole Town	0	2
1	AFC Bournemouth	Newport County	0	0
1	Brentford	Chesham United	2	0
1	Brighton	Crystal Palace	2	2
1	Bury	Workington	6	0
1	Cambridge United	Colchester United	1	1
1	Chester	Hartlepool United	1	0
1	Crewe Alexandra	Preston North End	1	1
1	Crook Town	Nuneaton Borough	1	4
1	Doncaster Rovers	Shrewsbury Town	2	2
1	Droylsden	Grimsby Town	0	0
1	Dudley Town	York City	1	1
1	Enfield	Harwich & Parkeston	0	0
1	Exeter City	Southend United	1	1
1	Gillingham	Watford	0	1
1	Huddersfield Town	Mansfield Town	0	0
1	Kettering Town	Oxford United	1	1
1	Leatherhead	Northampton Town	2	0
1	Lincoln City	Morecambe	1	0
1	Matlock Town	Wigan Athletic	1	0
1	Reading	Wealdstone	1	0
1	Rochdale	Northwich Victoria	1	1
1	Rotherham United	Altrincham	5	0
1	Scarborough	Darlington	0	0
1	Scunthorpe United	Chesterfield	1	2
1	Sheffield Wednesday	Stockport County	2	0
1	Southport	Port Vale	1	2
1	Stafford Rangers	Halifax Town	0	0
1	Swansea City	Minehead	0	1
1	Swindon Town	Bromley	7	0
1	Tooting & Mitcham United	Dartford	4	2
1	Torquay United	Hillingdon Borough	1	2
1	Tranmere Rovers	Peterborough United	0	4
1	Walsall	Bradford City	0	0
1	Waterlooville	Wycombe Wanderers	1	2
1	Weymouth	Hitchin Town	1	1
1	Wimbledon	Wokingham Town	1	0
1	Wrexham	Gateshead	6	0
1R	Darlington	Scarborough	4	1
1R	Mansfield Town	Huddersfield Town	2	1
1R	Northwich Victoria	Rochdale	0	0
1R	Southend United	Exeter City	2	1
1R	Crystal Palace	Brighton	1	1
1R	Grimsby Town	Droylsden	5	3
1R	Shrewsbury Town	Doncaster Rovers	4	3
1R	Halifax Town	Stafford Rangers	1	0
1R	Harwich and Parkeston	Enfield	0	3
1R	Hitchin Town	Weymouth	2	2
1R	Newport County	AFC Bournemouth	3	0
1R	Oxford United	Kettering Town	0	1
1R	Portsmouth	Aldershot	2	1
1R	Preston North End	Crewe Alexandra	2	2
1R	York City	Dudley Town	4	1
1R	Bradford City	Walsall	0	2
1R	Colchester United	Cambridge United	2	0
1R2	Crewe Alexandra	Preston North End	0	3
1R2	Northwich Victoria	Rochdale	2	1
1R2	Weymouth	Hitchin Town	3	3
1R3	Weymouth	Hitchin Town	1	3
2	Enfield	Crystal Palace	0	4
2	Grimsby Town	Chesterfield	0	1
2	Hillingdon Borough	Watford	2	3
2	Hitchin Town	Swindon Town	1	1
2	Kettering Town	Tooting & Mitcham United	1	0
2	Lincoln City	Nuneaton Borough	6	0
2	Northwich Victoria	Peterborough United	0	1
2	Portsmouth	Minehead	2	1
2	Port Vale	Barnsley	3	0
2	Rotherham United	York City	0	0
2	Southend United	Newport County	3	0
2	Wrexham	Goole Town	1	1
2	Wycombe Wanderers	Reading	1	2
2	Bury	Shrewsbury Town	0	0
2	Halifax Town	Preston North End	1	0
2	Leatherhead	Wimbledon	1	3
2	Darlington	Sheffield Wednesday	1	0
2	Mansfield Town	Matlock Town	2	5
2	Colchester United	Brentford	2	1
2	Northwich Victoria	Peterborough United	4	0
2R	Goole Town	Wrexham	0	1
2R	Swindon Town	Hitchin Town	1	0
2R	Walsall	Chesterfield	0	0
2R	York City	Rotherham United	1	1
2R	Shrewsbury Town	Bury	2	1
2R	Swindon Town	Hitchin Town	3	1
2R2	Chesterfield	Walsall	0	1
2R2	Rotherham United	York City	2	1
3	Birmingham City	Portsmouth	1	0
3	Blackpool	Derby County	0	0
3	Burnley	Lincoln City	2	2
3	Cardiff City	Tottenham Hotspur	1	0
3	Carlisle United	Matlock Town	5	1
3	Charlton Athletic	Blackburn Rovers	1	1
3	Coventry City	Millwall	1	0
3	Darlington	Orient	2	2
3	Everton	Stoke City	2	0
3	Fulham	Swindon Town	3	3
3	Halifax Town	Luton Town	0	1
3	Hereford United	Reading	1	0
3	Hull City	Port Vale	1	1
3	Ipswich Town	Bristol City	4	1
3	Kettering Town	Colchester United	2	3
3	Leeds United	Norwich City	5	2
3	Leicester City	Aston Villa	0	1
3	Liverpool	Crystal Palace	0	0
3	Manchester City	West Bromwich Albion	1	1
3	Manchester United	Walsall	1	0
3	Northwich Victoria	Watford	3	2
3	Nottingham Forest	Bristol Rovers	1	1
3	Notts County	Arsenal	0	1
3	Oldham Athletic	Plymouth Argyle	3	0
3	QPR	Shrewsbury Town	2	1
3	Sheffield United	Newcastle United	0	0
3	Southampton	Chelsea	1	1
3	Southend United	Chester	0	4
3	Sunderland	Wrexham	2	2
3	West Ham United	Bolton Wandeers	2	1
3	Wimbledon	Middlesbrough	0	0
3	Wolves	Rotherham United	3	2
3R	Port Vale	Hull City	3	1
3R	Bristol Rovers	Nottingham Forest	1	1
3R	Crystal Palace	Liverpool	2	3

3R	Swindon Town	Fulham	5	0
3R	West Bromwich Albion	Manchester City	0	1
3R	Blackburn Athletic	Charlton Athletic	2	0
3R	Chelsea	Southampton	0	3
3R	Lincoln City	Bumley	0	1
3R	Wrexham	Sunderland	1	0
3R	Derby County	Blackpool	3	2
3R	Newcastle United	Sheffield United	3	1
3R2	Orient	Darlington	3	0
3R2	Nottingham Forest	Bristol Rovers	6	0
4	Arsenal	Coventry City	3	1
4	Aston Villa	West Ham United	3	0
4	Birmingham City	Leeds United	1	2
4	Blackburn Rovers	Orient	3	0
4	Cardiff City	Wrexham	3	2
4	Chester	Luton Town	1	0
4	Colchester United	Derby County	1	1
4	Ipswich Town	Wolves	2	2
4	Liverpool	Carlisle United	3	0
4	Manchester City	QPR	1	0
4	Middlesbrough	Hereford United	4	0
4	Newcastle United	Manchester City	1	3
4	Nottingham Forest	Southampton	3	3
4	Northwich Victoria	Oldham Athletic	1	3
4	Port Vale	Bumley	2	1
4	Swindon Town	Everton	2	2
4R	Everton	Swindon Town	2	1
4R	Southampton	Nottingham Forest	2	1
4R	Derby County	Colchester United	1	0
4R	Wolves	Ipswich Town	1	0
5	Aston Villa	Port Vale	3	0
5	Cardiff City	Everton	1	2
5	Derby County	Blackburn Rovers	3	1
5	Leeds United	Manchester City	1	0
5	Liverpool	Oldham Athletic	3	1
5	Middlesbrough	Arsenal	4	1
5	Southampton	Manchester United	2	2
5	Wolves	Chester	1	0
5R	Manchester United	Southampton	2	1
6	Everton	Derby County	2	0
6	Liverpool	Middlesbrough	2	0
6	Manchester United	Aston Villa	2	1
6	Wolves	Leeds United	0	1
SF	Leeds United	Manchester United	1	2
SF	Everton	Liverpool	2	2
SFR	Liverpool	Everton	3	0
F	Manchester United	Liverpool	2	1

LEAGUE CUP 1976/77

Round								
1	Aldershot	Gillingham	1	1	0	2		
1	AFC Bournemouth	Torquay United	0	0	0	1		
1	Bradford City	Oldham Athletic	1	1	3	1		
1	Bury	Preston North End	2	1	1	1		
1	Cardiff City	Bristol Rovers	2	1	4	4		
1	Chester	Hereford United	2	0	3	4		
1	Chesterfield	Rotherham United	3	1	0	3		
1	Crewe Alexandra	Tranmere Rovers	2	1	1	3		
1	Crystal Palace`	Portsmouth	2	2	1	0		
1	Doncaster Rovers	Lincoln City	1	1	1	1	2	2 AET
1	Grimsby Town	Sheffield Wednesday	0	3	0	0		
1	Halifax Town	Darlington	0	0	1	1	1	2
1	Huddersfield Town	Hartlepool United	2	0	2	1		
1	Mansfield Town	Scunthorpe United	2	0	0	2	1	2
1	Millwall	Colchester United	2	1	1	2	2	4
1	Oxford United	Cambridge United	1	0	0	2		
1	Plymouth Argyle	Exeter City	0	1	0	1		
1	Port Vale	Wrexham	1	1	0	1		
1	Reading	Peterborough United	2	3	1	0	1	3
1	Rochdale	Blackburn Rovers	0	1	1	4		
1	Southend United	Brighton	1	1	1	2		
1	Southport	Carlisle United	1	2	1	0	2	3
1	Swansea City	Newport County	4	1	0	1		
1	Swindon Town	Northampton Town	3	2	0	2		
1	Watford	Brentford	1	1	2	0		
1	Workington	Stockport County	0	0	0	0	0	2
1	York City	Barnsley	0	0	0	0	1	2
1	Shrewsbury Town	Walsall	0	1	0	1		
2	Everton	Cambridge United	3	0				
2	Arsenal	Carlisle United	3	2				
2	Blackpool	Birmingham City	2	1				
2	Bristol City	Coventry City	0	1				
2	Chester	Swansea City	2	3				
2	Crystal Palace`	Watford	1	3				
2	Doncaster Rovers	Derby County	1	2				
2	Exeter City	Norwich City	1	3				
2	Fulham	Peterborough United	1	1				
2	Ipswich Town	Brighton	0	0				
2	Liverpool`	West Bromwich Albion	1	1				
2	Middlesbrough	Tottenham Hotspur	1	2				
2	Northampton Town	Huddersfield Town	0	1				
2	Orient	Hull City	1	0				
2	Scunthorpe United	Notts County	0	2				
2	Southampton	Charlton Athletic	1	1				
2	Walsall	Nottingham Forest	2	4				
2	Wolves	Sheffield Wednesday	1	2				
2	Aston Villa	Manchester City	3	0				
2	Blackburn Rovers	Stockport County	1	3				
2	Bradford City	Bolton Wanderers	1	2				
2	Bury	Darlington	2	1				
2	Cardiff City	QPR	1	3				
2	Chelsea	Sheffield United	3	1				
2	Gillingham	Newcastle United	1	2				
2	Manchester United	Tranmere Rovers	5	0				
2	Rotherham United	Millwall	1	2				
2	Stoke City	Leeds United	2	1				
2	Torquay United	Burnley	1	0				
2	West Ham United	Barnsley	3	0				
2	Wrexham	Leicester City	1	0				
2	West Bromwich Albion	Liverpool	1	0				
2R	Brighton	Ipswich Town	2	1				

3	Chelsea	Huddersfield Town	2	1	
3	Stockport County	Everton	0	1	
3	Aston Villa	Norwich City	2	1	
3	Blackpool	Arsenal	1	1	
3	Charlton Athletic	West Ham United	0	1	
3	Millwall	Orient	0	0	
3	Nottingham Forest	Coventry City	0	3	
3	QPR	Bury	2	1	
3	Sheffield Wednesday	Watford	3	1	
3	Derby County	Notts County	1	1	
3	Fulham	Bolton Wanderers	2	2	
3	Manchester United	Sunderland	2	2	
3	Newcastle United	Stoke City	3	0	
3	Tottenham Hotspur	Reading	2	3	
3	Torquay United	Swansea City	1	2	
3	West Bromwich Albion	Brighton	0	2	
R	Arsenal	Blackpool	0	0	
R	Notts County	Derby County	1	2	
R	Sunderland	Manchester United	2	2	
R	Bolton Wanderers	Fulham	2	2	
R	Orient	Millwall	0	0	
R2	Arsenal	Blackpool	2	0	
R2	Manchester United	Sunderland	1	0	
R2	Bolton Wanderers	Fulham	2	1	at Birmingham
R2	Millwall	Orient	3	0	at Arsenal
4	Arsenal	Chelsea	2	1	
4	Brighton	Derby County	1	1	
4	Everton	Coventry City	3	0	
4	Swansea City	Bolton Wanderers	1	1	
4	Aston Villa	Wrexham	5	1	
4	Manchester United	Newcastle United	7	2	
4	Millwall	Sheffield Wednesday	3	0	
4	West Ham United	QPR	0	2	
R	Bolton Wanderers	Swansea City	5	1	
R	Derby County	Brighton	2	1	
5	Aston Villa	Millwall	2	0	
5	Derby County	Bolton Wanderers	1	2	
5	Manchester United	Everton	0	3	
5	QPR	Arsenal	2	1	
:	Everton	Bolton Wanderers	1	1	1 0
'	QPR	Aston Villa	0	0	2 2 0 3
	Aston Villa	Everton	0	0	at Wembley
R	Aston Villa	Everton	1	1	at Hillsborough
R2	Aston Villa	Everton	3	2	at Old Trafford

1976/77 Club Appearances Division 4

AFC BOURNEMOUTH

		A	S	G
Baker	Kieron	41		
Butler	Goff	45		
Miller	Keith	46		1
Benson	John	28		
Morgan	Stuart	28	1	
Barton	Frank	42		12
Riley	Hugh	41	1	5
Johnston	Peter	41		6
Paterson	Tom	28	4	9
Reeves	Kevin	19	1	6
Buttle	Steve	24		1
Impey	John	38	2	1
Rudge	John	11	3	2
Cunningham	Ian	19	2	
McAlinden	Robert	1		
Gritt	Steve	4	2	3
Chalk	Stephen	5		
Howarth	Jack	24		6
Cave	Mickey	16		2
Stuckey	Bruce	5		

ALDERSHOT

		A	S	G
Johnston	Glen	44		
Whittle		5		
Wallace	Jim	22		
Butler	Joe	19	7	
Earls	Michael	27	3	
Richardson	John	1		
Walton	Ronnie	28	1	
Morrissey	Pat	41		9
Howarth	Jack	17		4
Bell	Terry	31	1	13
Warnock	Neil	6		1
Crosby	Malcolm	41	1	3
Howitt	David	40	1	
Wallace	R	6	3	
Wooler	Alan	42	1	1
Brodie	Murray	29	2	10
Mancini	Terry	21		
Jopling	Joe	24	3	
McGregor	Alex	34		5
Hibbs	Gary	4	2	
Hilton	Pat	12	1	
Needham	Andy	8		2
Bambridge	Steve		2	
Rockett	Trevor	2		
Youlden	Tommy	2		
Own Goal				1

BARNSLEY

		A	S	G
Springett	Peter	46		
Murphy	Barrie	46		
Gorry	Martin	12		1
Otulakowski	Anton	10		
Burke	Peter	8		
Pickering	Mike	45		1
Felton	Graham	24		3
Peachey	John	39	2	12
Joicey	Brian	46		25
Brown	Kenny	46		3
Millar	Alistair	45		3
Price	Peter	4	4	1
Harris	Leslie	2	6	1
Saunders	John	40		3
Warnock	Neil	21	2	3
Pugh	Graham	25	1	2
Mallender	Gary		1	
Yates	David	4		
Chambers	Philip	9		1
Collins	John	25		
Lathan	John	6	1	
Wigg	Ron	3	3	
Own Goals				3

BRADFORD CITY

		A	S	G
Downsborough	Peter	45		
Hardcastle	Peter	36		1
Cooper	Ian	5		
Johnston	Rodney	40		3
Middleton	John	41		2
Fretwell	David	46		2
Watson	Garry	33	3	7
Rayner	Warren	1	2	
McFadzean	Clive	1		
Hall	David	15	2	1
Hutchins	Don	44		14
Napier	John		1	
McGinley	Billy	17	6	2
Cooke	Joseph	40		17
Dolan	Terry	43	1	12
Podd	Cec	43		
Ingram	Gerry	15	2	9
Ratcliffe	David	3		
Spark	Alex	7	1	
Punton	Bill	1		
Wright	Bernie	20		3
Nicholls	Philip	10	1	2
Own Goals				3

BRENTFORD

		A	S	G
Priddy	Paul	37		
Fraser	John	39		2
Pritchett	Keith	11		1
Bence	Paul	10	1	
Goldthorpe	Bob	19		2
Smith	Nigel	32	2	
Allan	Mike	40		1
Scales	Terry	12		
Cross	Roger	21		9
McCulloch	Andy	18	2	10
Graham	Jackie	42		4
French	Mickey	15	4	4
Salman	Danis	16	2	1
Johnson	Terry	24	3	8
Aylott	Steve	5		
Sharp	Tom	2	2	
Redknapp	Harry	1		
Walker	Paul	1	1	
Glover	Allan	6		
Riddick	Gordon	15		
Sweetzer	Gordon	25	2	23
Carlton	David	31	1	
Rolph	Gary	6	1	
Scrivens	Steve	5		
Cox	Graham	3		
Burns	Tony	6		
Smillie	Neil	3		

CAMBRIDGE UNITED

		A	S	G
Webster	Malcolm	46		
Tuddenham	Tony	7	1	
Baldry	William	22		
Batson	Brendan	43		
Fallon	Steve	43		4
Howard	Trevor	36		4
Horsfall	Tommy	22	1	6
Spriggs	Stephen	41		9
Biley	Alan	46		19
Bowker	Keith	12	5	1
Watson	Graham	30		6
Lyon	David	1	1	
Finney	Tommy	40	1	16
Stringer	David	38		1
Seddon	Ian	20	3	1
Eades	Terry	8		
Hall	Jim	24		15
O'Neill	Tom	1	4	1
Streete	Floyd	1	2	1
Murray	Jim		1	
Harper	Colin	15		
Own Goals				3

COLCHESTER UNITED

		A	S	G
Walker	Mick	44		
Dyer	Paul	29	5	
Williams	John	43		
Bunkell	Ray	16	2	2
Smith	Lindsay	45		6
Packer	Mike	35	4	5
Garwood	Colin	40	2	16
Gough	Bobby	43		17
Allinson	Ian	31	8	7
Leslie	Steve	40	1	2
Cook	Michael	46		3
Dowman	Steve	33	3	12
Froggatt	John	43		6
Bright	Stewart	5		
Foley	Stephen	10		
Dominey	Barry	1	2	
Ellis	Glenn	2		
Own Goal				1

CREWE ALEXANDRA

		A	S	G
Crudgington	Geoff	32		
Lowry	Tommy	45		
Evans	Micky	21		[illegible]
Lugg	Ray	40		[illegible]
Bowles	Paul	29	4	[illegible]
Bevan	Paul	31		[illegible]
Davies	David	24	1	
Humphreys	Gerry	20		
Abbott	Peter	27	4	[illegible]
Nicholls	Terry	18		
Purdie	Bernard	40	1	
Cheetham	Hughie	12	3	
Mayman	Paul	38	1	
Davies	Wyn	36	1	
Rimmer	Warwick	18	9	
Tully	Kevin	33	1	
Roberts	Ian	28		
Brand	Andrew	14		
Spence	Colin		1	
Own Goals				

DARLINGTON

		A	S	G
Ogley	Alan	34		
Nattress	Clive	46		4
Cochrane	Jimmy	42	1	
Craig	Derek	44		4
Noble	Bobby	19		3
Crosson	David	39		
Lyons	Barry	39		4
Sinclair	Colin	7		2
Ferguson	Ronnie	29	7	6
Rowles	Eddie	46		13
Stone	John	40		3
Walker	Len	8		
Wann	Dennis	30		4
Young	Eric	20	5	3
Holbrook	Steve	15	4	3
Lees	Norman		2	
Seal	Jimmy	31		5
Owers	Phil	12		
Maitland	Lloyd	5		1
Own Goals				4

DONCASTER ROVERS

		A	S	G
Peacock	Dennis	46		
Brookes	Stanley	42	1	2
Creamer	Peter	5	1	
Robinson	Fred	37	2	2
Reed	Stephen	30	1	
Taylor	Brian	46		9
Miller	Ian	46		5
Wignall	David	17	5	
O'Callaghan	Brendan	46		15
Kitchen	Peter	43		23
Laidlaw	Joe	44	1	7
Ternent	Ray	2	1	
Murray	Alan	36	1	3
Uzelac	Steve	21	1	1
Wignall	Steve	11		
Binch	David	1	1	
Woodcock	Tony	6		2
Jones	Mark	3	1	
Bailey	Ian	9		
Walker	Paul	4		
Snodin	Glyn	1	3	
Olney	Kevin	7	1	
McConville	Ian	1	1	
Bowden	Peter	1		
Boden	Ken	1		
Own Goals				2

HALIFAX TOWN

		A	S	G
Gennoe	Terry	26		
Flavell	Bobby	33		3
Kent	Paul	12		
McHale	Ray	4		2
Trainer	Jack	45	1	1
Phelan	Albert	39		
Jones	Alan	5		
Johnston	John	37	3	6
Bullock	Micky	40	2	9
Jones	George	8	1	1
Lawson	Jimmy	43		5
Bell	Derek	20	6	2
Rylands	David	5		
McGill	Jimmy	20	1	
Carroll	Joe	35	2	5
Bradley	Lee	20	5	1
McCann	Jimmy	2		1
Harris	Geoff		1	
Hoy	Bobby	30		7
Loska	Tony	31		
Dunleavy	Chris	29		4
Leonard	Mick	19		
Ferguson	Mike	2		
Chmilowski	Roman	1		

HARTLEPOOL UNITED

		A	S	G
Richardson	Graham	10		
Goad	Alan	30	7	1
Maggiore	Tony	14		
Veitch	Tommy	10		
Scott	Robert	37		
O'Donnell	John	30	1	1
Elliot	Kevin	20	3	1
Spelman	Mike	9		
Endean	Barry	13	1	2
Scaife	Robert	38	1	6
Bielby	Paul	31	8	6
Potter	George		1	
Edgar	Edward	36		
Luckett	Paul	8		
Johnson	Kevin	4		
Rowlands	John	14		4
Harley	John	4		1
Prudham	Eddie	3		
Reed	Hugh	6		1
Wiggett	Dave	36		1
Creamer	Peter	34		3
McMaster	Chris	2	1	
Davies	Geoff	5		1
Poskett	Malcolm	29	1	10
Spraggon	Frank	1		
Simpkin	Chris	28		
McMordie	Eric	23		1
Goldthorpe	Wayne	6	1	1
Turnbull	Terry	13		3
Cunningham	Dave	10	2	1
Smith	Trevor	2		
Own Goals				3

HUDDERSFIELD TOWN

		A	S	G
Poole	Terry	24		
Cooper	Paul	2		
Oliver	Peter	41		1
Smith	Steve	44		3
Baines	Stephen	43	1	5
Hague	Neil	25		2
Firth	Franny	8		2
Fowler	Martin	36	3	1
Goldthorpe	Wayne	5	2	2
Butler	Mick	23	3	3
Maitland	Lloyd	10	2	
Sidebottom	Arnold	18	5	2
Newton	Bob	15	2	2
Hart	Peter	44		1
Jones	Chris	9	5	2
Johnson	Kevin	38		13
Gilligan	John		1	
Gray	Terry	17	1	6
Walker	Paul	1		
Campbell	Bobby	19	1	8
Howey	Peter	3		1
Taylor	Richard	9		
Eccles	Terry	17		3
McCaffrey	Jim	14	1	
Sweeney	Alan	21		

NEWPORT COUNTY

		A	S	G
Plumley	Gary	46		
Morgan	Peter	13	1	
Bell	Gary	45		2
Emanuel	John	46		1
Walker	Ronnie	39	1	1
Derrett	Steve	44		
Villars	Tony	23	6	1
Clark	Brian	39	2	8
Woods	Edward	41	2	12
Parsons	John	9	1	3
White	Andy	16	3	1
Jones	Roderick	28	6	1
Williams	Mark	23	5	1
Hooper	Wayne	3	1	
Egan	Chris	5	2	
Murray	Don	16	2	
Aizlewood	Mark	4	1	
Vaughan	Nigel	1		
Relish	John	26		4
Bruton	Dave	6		1
Preece	Paul	17	1	5
Byrne	Tony	16		
Own Goals				1

ROCHDALE

		A	S	G
Poole	Mike	44		
Hallows	Paul	46		
Lacey	Tony	42		
Hanvey	Keith	19		4
Summerscales	Bill	44		2
O'Loughlin	Nigel	42	2	3
Melledew	Steve	42	1	6
Mountford	Bob	33	1	12
Whelan	Tony	34		4
Mullington	Phil	34	7	4
Tarbuck	Alan	22		1
Helliwell	David	20	11	3
Mulvaney	Dick	4	1	
Cooper	Gary	17	5	5
Boslem	Bill	13		
Bannon	Ian	23		
Mason	Stuart	2		
Hamstead	George	3	1	
Dungworth	John	14		3
Mullen	Jimmy	6	2	1
Shyne	Chris	2		
Own Goals				2

SCUNTHORPE UNITED

		A	S	G
Letheran	Glan	27		
Czucman	Mike	30	1	1
Peacock	John	40	1	1
Oates	Robert	42	2	1
Wiggington	Clive	46		5
Money	Richard	38		
Wadsworth	Mike	19	9	3
Collier	Graham	28	3	
Keeley	Nolan	46		12
Green	Rick	27		4
Pilling	Styart	32	1	3
Davidson	Angus	35	6	3
O'Connor	Doug	10		4
Markham	Peter	19		
O'Meara	Alan	13		
Bridges	Bernard	1		
Dale	Alan		2	
Lee	Robert	14	2	
Kilmore	Kevin	16	3	3
Lumby	Jim	16		8
Walton	Ian	1		
Bernard	Geoff	6		
Own Goal				1

SOUTHEND UNITED

		A	S	G
Freeman	Neil	36		
Moody	Alan	45		7
Townsend	Neil	27	1	1
Hadley	Anthony	28	3	4
Ford	Andrew	46		
Nicholl	Terry	10		
Clark	Paul	21	4	
Little	Alan	33	1	5
Cunningham	David	13	1	1
Parker	Stuart	19	1	13
Pountney	Ron	21	2	
Goodwin	Steve	40	2	5
Denny	Paul	8	1	2
Young	David	34	1	
Laverick	Mickey	34		4
Dyer	Steve		1	
Price	Ken	1		
Banks	Frank	28		
Silvester	Peter	1		
Polycarpou	Andy	7	3	1
Morris	Colin	23		3
Rafter	Sean	10		
Parker	Derrick	21		6

SOUTHPORT

		A	S	G
Coates	John	16		
Sibbald	Bobby	26		1
Blair	Kenny	17		
O'Neill	Tom	43		4
Higham	John	46		
Rhodes	Tony	7	2	
Hughes	David	22		1
Wilson	Alan	46		6
Galley	Keith	26	9	2
Taylor	Paul	30		2
Snookes	Eric	32	4	
Ryan	David	9		
O'Riley	Paul	1	2	
Dewsnip	George	42	1	5
Marshall	Cliff	11	2	
Lyon	David	11	2	1
O'Brien	Tony	11	1	1
Wilkinson	Billy	10		
Jones	George	19		5
Harrison	Tony	21		
Brookes	Steve	21		1
Smith	John	17	1	2
Brookfield	Tony		2	
Brown	Keith	4		
Birchall	Paul	3		
Fisher	Hugh	15		
Own Goals				2

STOCKPORT COUNTY

		A	S	G
Holbrook	Ian	37		
Loadwick	Derek	42		
McNeill	Alan	36	1	
Lennard	Dave	39		4
Thompson	Alan	43		6
Fogarty	Ken	30		3
McBeth	George	37	1	3
Fletcher	Peter	28	3	9
Daniels	Barney	43	2	17
Massey	Steve	19	3	2
Rutter	John	46		1
Hardman	Colin		1	
Park	Terry	2	1	
Pimblett	Frank		1	
Buckley	Ian	19	9	2
Johnson	Jeff	6	2	
Sutcliffe	Peter	10	6	1
Smith	Graham	18	2	
Baxter	Stuart	4		
Feely	Peter	2		
Edwards	Paul	2		
Jackson	Phil	10	1	1
Darling	Malcolm	11		2
Morrin	Tony	13		1
Hopkinson	Paul	9		
Own Goal				1

SWANSEA CITY

		A	S	G
Potter	Steve	41		
Evans	Wyndham	43		
Bartley	Dany	45		1
Smith	George	35	2	8
May	Eddie	46		6
Bruton	David	26	2	
Conway	Michael	23	2	8
Curtis	Alan	46		14
James	Robbie	46		14
Bray	Geoff	3		1
Lally	Pat	46		
Charles	Jeremy	36	5	23
Moore	Gary	16	4	6
Schroeder	Nico	1		
Reece	Gil		2	
Chappell	Les	39	1	5
Harris	Paul	4	2	1
Griffiths	Jeff		4	
Brown	Graham	4		
Stead	Micky	5		1
Harvey	Leighton	1		
Own Goals				4

TORQUAY UNITED

		A	S	G
Lee	Terry	27		
Lynch	Barry	28	2	
Sandercock	Phil	35		2
Twitchin	Ian	31	3	1
Stocks	David	4		
Dunne	Jimmy	40		1
Provan	Andy	19	1	3
Rudge	David	32	4	2
Boulton	Clinton	32		3
Kennedy	David	37	1	3
Brown	Billy	44		18
Kruse	Pat	23		1
Hickman	Mike	3		1
Lane	Kevin	2	5	2
Ayre	Colin	2		
Morrall	Steve	33	3	2
Chatterley	Lew	13		4
Forbes	Duncan	7		
Foster	George	6		3
Bray	Geoff	7		2
Bence	Paul	5		
Robbins	Robbie	19		
Lee	Colin	23		10
Williamson	Charlie	5		
Vassallo	Barrie	15		1
Green	Mike	13		
Tomlin	David	1		

WATFORD

		A	S	G
Rankin	Andy	37		
Howe	Trevor	16		
Walsh	Jimmy	15	2	
Bond	Dennis	44		5
Walley	Tom	12	1	
Garner	Alan	46		2
McCarthy	Kevin	6	1	
Joslyn	Roger	37		3
Mercer	Keith	46		22
Jenkins	Ross	22	13	10
Downes	Bobby	35		2
Geidmintis	Tony	32	1	
Coffill	Peter	23	4	2
Mayes	Alan	40	3	14
Horsfield	Arthur	37		4
Gibbs	Peter	1		
Poole	Richard	3	4	1
Blissett	Luther	1	3	
Craker	Lawrence	9		1
Eades	Terry	4		
Pritchett	Keith	32		
Bristow	Guy		1	
Sherwood	Steve	8		
Own Goals				1

WORKINGTON

		A	S	G
Rogan	Mike	40		
Kisby	Chris	38		2
Ellison	Ray	20		1
Dawes	Malcolm	20	2	
Brown	Bobby	34		
Kavanagh	Eamon	37		5
Honour	John	29	1	
Leng	Michael	43		2
Harris	Martin	36	3	5
Lowrey	Patrick	15		3
Ashworth	Philip	38	1	7
Monkhouse	Graham	4		
Moore	Malcolm	22		2
Donaghy	Barry	13	4	
Higgins	Mike	11	4	1
Goodwin	Dave	7		
Williamson	Colin	11	4	2
Johnston	Ian	17		
Blant	Colin	21		
Owen	Bobby	8		2
Prudham	Eddie	15		6
Coleman	Ted	10	2	1
McDonald	Neil	5	1	
Wallace	Ken	5	1	
Scholes	Martin	3	1	
Marshall	Davod	2		
Laisby	John	2		
Own Goals				2

1977/78 Other Statistics Section

FA CUP 1977/8

Round				
1	AP Leamington	Enderby Town	6	0
1	Arnold	Port Vale	0	0
1	Barnet	Peterborough United	1	2
1	Barnsley	Huddersfield Town	1	0
1	Bath City	Plymouth Argyle	0	0
1	Blyth Spartans	Burscough	1	0
1	Boreham Wood	Swindon Town	0	0
1	Bradford City	Crewe Alexandra	0	1
1	Brentford	Folkestone	2	0
1	Carlisle United	Stafford Rangers	2	0
1	Chester	Darlington	4	1
1	Chesterfield	Halifax Town	1	0
1	Colchester United	AFC Bournemouth	1	1
1	Doncaster Rovers	Shrewsbury Town	0	1
1	Enfield	Wimbledon	3	0
1	Gillingham	Weymouth	1	1
1	Leatherhead	Swansea City	0	0
1	Lowestoft Town	Cambridge United	0	2
1	Minehead	Wycombe Wanderers	2	0
1	Newport County	Exeter City	1	1
1	Nuneaton Borough	Oxford United	2	0
1	Portsmouth	Bideford	3	1
1	Preston North End	Lincoln City	3	2
1	Reading	Aldershot	3	1
1	Rotherham United	Mossley	3	0
1	Scarborough	Rochdale	4	3
1	Sheffield Wednesday	Bury	1	0
1	Southport	Runcirn	2	2
1	Spennymoor United	GooleTown	3	1
1	Stockport County	Scunthorpe United	3	0
1	Tilbury	Kettering Town	0	1
1	Tilbury	Kettering Town	2	2
1	Tooting & Mitcham United	Northampton Town	1	2
1	Torquay United	Southend United	1	2
1	Tranmere Rovers	Hartlepool United	1	1
1	Walsall	Dagenham	1	0
1	Watford	Hendon	2	0
1	Wealdstone	Hereford United	0	0
1	Wigan Athletic	York City	1	0
1	Workington	Grimsby Town	0	2
1	Wrexham	Burton Albion	2	0
1R	Port Vale	Arnold	5	2
1R	Runcon	Southport	1	0
1R	AFC Bournemouth	Colchester United	0	0ae
1R	Hartlepool United	Tranmere Rovers	3	1
1R	Plymouth Argule	Bath City	2	0
1R	Swansea City	Leatherhead	2	1
1R	Swindon Town	Boreham Wood	2	0
1R	Exeter City	Newport County	4	2
1R	Hereford United	Wealdstone	2	3
1R	Weymouth	Gillingham	0	1
1R	Kettering Town	Tilbury	2	3
1R2	AFC Bournemouth	Colchester United	1	4
2	AP Leamington	Southend United	0	0
2	Blyth Spartans	Chesterfield	1	0
2	Carlisle United	Chester	3	1
2	Crewe Alexandra	Scarborough	0	0
2	Gillingham	Peterborough United	1	1
2	Grimsby Town	Barnsley	2	0
2	Hartlepool United	Runcorn	4	2
2	Minehead	Exeter City	0	3
2	Portsmouth	Swansea City	2	2
2	Preston North End	Wrexham	0	2
2	Rotherham United	Spennymoor United	6	0
2	Shrewsbury Town	Stockport County	1	1
2	Swindon Town	Brentford	2	1
2	Walsall	Port Vale	1	1
2	Watford	Colchester United	2	0
2	Wealdstone	Reading	2	1
2	Wigan Athletic	Sheffield Wednesday	1	0
2R	Port Vale	Walsall	1	3
2R	Southend United	AP Leamington	4	0
2R	Stockport County	Shrewsbury Town	1	2
2R	Peterborough United	Gillingham	2	0
2R	Swansea City	Portsmouth	2	1
2R	Scarborough	Crewe Alexandra	2	0
3	Orient	Norwich City	1	1
3	Birmingham City	Wigan Athletic	4	0
3	Blackburn Rovers	Shrewsbury Town	2	1
3	Blyth Spartans	Enfield	1	0
3	Brighton	Scarborough	3	0
3	Bristol City	Wrexham	4	4
3	Burnley	Fulham	1	0
3	Cardiff City	Ipswich Town	0	2
3	Carlisle United	Manchester United	1	1
3	Charlton Athletic	Notts County	0	2
3	Chelsea	Liverpool	4	2
3	Derby County	Southend United	3	2
3	Everton	Aston Villa	4	1
3	Exeter City	Wolves	2	2
3	Grimsby Town	Southampton	0	0
3	Hartlepool United	Crystal Palace	2	1
3	Hull City	Leicester City	0	1
3	Leeds United	Manchester City	1	2
3	Luton Town	Oldham Athletic	1	1
3	Mansfield Town	Plymouth Argyle	1	0
3	Middlesbrough	Coventry City	3	0
3	Nottingham Forest	Swindon Town	4	0
3	Peterborough United	Newcastle United	1	1
3	QPR	Wealdstone	4	0
3	Rotherham United	Millwall	1	1
3	Sheffield United	Arsenal	0	5
3	Stoke City	Tilbury	4	0
3	Sunderland	Bristol Rovers	0	1
3	Tottenham Hotspur	Bolton Wanderers	2	2
3	Walsall	Swansea City	4	1
3	West Bromwich Albion	Blackpool	4	1
3	West Ham United	Watford	1	0
3R	Wrexham	Bristol City	3	0
3R	Bolton Wanderers	Tottenham Hotspur	2	1ae
3R	Millwall	Rotherham United	2	0
3R	Oldham Athletic	Luton Town	1	2
3R	Southampton	Grimsby Town	0	0
3R	Wolves	Exeter City	3	1
3R	Manchester United	Carlisle United	4	2
3R	Newcastle United	Peterborough United	2	0
3R	Norwich City	Orien	0	1
3R2	Grimsby Town	Southampton	1	4
4	Arsenal	Wolves	2	1
4	Bristol Rovers	Southampton	2	0
4	Ipswich Town	Hartlepool United	4	1
4	Manchester United	West Bromwich Albion	1	1
4	Middlesbrough	Everton	3	2
4	Newcastle United	Wrexham	2	2

4	West Ham United	QPR	1	1
4	Brighton	Notts County	1	2
4	Chelsea	Burnley	6	2
4	Millwall	Luton Town	4	0
4	Nottingham Forest	Manchester City	2	1
4	Derby County	Birmingham City	2	1
4	Bolton Wanderers	Mansfield Town	1	0
4	Stoke City	Blyth Spartans	2	3
4R	QPR	West Ham United	6	1
4R	West Bromwich Albion	Manchester United	3	2
4R	Wrexham	Newcastle United	4	1
5	Arsenal	Walsall	4	1
5	Bristol Rovers	Ipswich Town	2	2
5	Millwall	Notts County	2	1
5	Orient	Chelsea	0	0
5	QPR	Nottingham Forest	1	1
5	Wrexham	Blyth Spartans	1	1
5	Derby County	West Bromwich Albion	2	3
5	Middlesbrough	Bolton Wanderers	2	0
5R	Blyth Spartans	Wrexham	1	2
5R	Chelsea	Orient	1	2
5R	Nottingham Forest	QPR	1	1
5R	Ipswich Town	Bristol Rovers	3	0
5R2	Nottingham Forest	QPR	3	1
6	Middlesbrough	Orient	0	0
6	Millwall	Ipswich Town	1	6
6	West Bromwich Albion	Nottingham Forest	2	0
6	Wrexham	Arsenal	2	3
6R	Orient	Middlesbrough	2	1
SF	Ipswich Town	West Bromwich Albion	3	1
SF	Orient	Arsenal	0	3
F	Arsenal	Ipswich Town	0	1

LEAGUE CUP 1977/8

Round									
1	Aldershot	Colchester United	1	1	1	4			
1	Brentford	Crystal Palace	2	1	1	5			
1	Bristol Rovers	Walsall	1	2	0	1			
1	Burnley	Chester	2	0	0	1			
1	Bury	Crewe Alexandra	3	0	1	1			
1	Cambridge United	Brighton	0	0	0	0	0	3	
1	Chesterfield	Barnsley	4	1	0	3	2	0	
1	Darlington	Scunthorpe United	0	0	1	3			
1	Exeter City	Plymouth Argyle	2	2	0	0	1	0	
1	Gillingham	Wimbledon	1	1	1	3			
1	Grimsby Town	Hartlepool United	3	0	2	1			
1	Hereford United	AFC Bournemouth	2	0	2	4	1	2	
1	Huddersfield Town	Carlisle United	1	1	2	2	2	1	
1	Mansfield Town	Lincoln City	0	1	0	0			
1	Fulham	Orient	0	2	2	1			
1	Oxford United	Shrewsbury Town	3	0	2	2			
1	Peterborough United	Bradford City	4	1	1	1			
1	Portsmouth	Newport County	3	1	2	3			
1	Port Vale	Preston North End	2	1	1	2	1	2	
1	Rochdale	Halifax Town	1	1	2	1			
1	Rotherham United	York City	3	0	0	3	1	1	RU op
1	Sheffield Wednesday	Doncaster Rovers	5	2	3	0			
1	Southend United	Northampton Town	2	3	1	2			
1	Swansea City	Swindon Town	1	3	1	2			
1	Torquay United	Cardiff City	1	0	2	3	1	2	
1	Tranmere Rovers	Southport	0	1	2	2			
1	Watford	Reading	2	1	0	1	5	0	
1	Wrexham	Stockport County	1	0	1	1			
2	Bristol City	Stoke City	1	0					
2	Arsenal	Manchester United	3	2					
2	Birmingham City	Notts County	0	2					
2	Blackpool	Sheffield Wednesday	2	2					
2	Bolton Wanderers	Lincoln City	1	0					
2	Brighton	Oldham Athletic	0	0					
2	Burnley	Norwich City	3	1					
2	Charlton Athletic	Wrexham	1	2					
2	Crystal Palace	Southampton	0	0					
2	Grimsby Town	Watford	1	2					
2	Huddersfield Town	Coventry City	0	2					
2	Ipswich Town	Northampton Town	5	0					
2	Liverpool	Chelsea	2	0					
2	Nottingham Forest	West Ham United	5	0					
2	Peterborough United	Scunthorpe United	1	1					
2	Portsmouth	Leicester City	2	0					
2	Sheffield United	Everton	0	3					
2	Sunderland	Middlesbrough	2	2					
2	Swindon Town	Cardiff City	5	1					
2	Walsall	Preston North End	0	0					
2	Wolves	Luton Town	1	3					
2	Blackburn Rovers	Colchester United	1	1					
2	Chesterfield	Manchester City	0	1					
2	Derby County	Orient	3	1					
2	Exeter City	Aston Villa	1	3					
2	Newcastle United	Millwall	0	2					
2	Oxford United	Bury	1	1					
2	QPR	AFC Bournemouth	2	0					
2	Rochdale	Leeds United	0	3					
2	Southport	Hull City	2	2					
2	Tottenham Hotspur	Wimbledon	4	0					
2	West Bromwich Albion	Rotherham United	4	0					
2R	Sheffield Wednesday	Blackpool	3	1					

2R	Colchester United	Blackburn Rovers	4	0			
2R	Middlesbrough	Sunderland	1	0			
2R	Oldham Athletic	Brighton	2	2			
2R	Southampton	Crystal Palace	2	1			
2R	Hull City	Southport	1	0			
2R2	Brighton	Oldham Athletic	1	2			at Leicester
3	Arsenal	Southampton	2	0			
3	Bolton Wanderers	Peterborough United	3	1			
3	Burnley	Ipswich Town	1	2			
3	Everton	Middlesbrough	2	2			
3	Hull City	Oldham Athletic	2	0			
3	Luton Town	Manchester City	1	1			
3	Millwall	Bury	1	1			
3	Nottingham Forest	Notts County	4	0			
3	Portsmouth	Swindon Town	1	1			
3	Sheffield United	Walsall	2	1			
3	West Bromwich Albion	Watford	1	0			
3	Aston Villa	QPR	1	0			
3	Leeds United	Colchester United	4	0			
3	Liverpool	Derby County	2	0			
3	Tottenham Hotspur	Coventry City	2	3			
3	Wrexham	Bristol City	1	0			
3R	Middlesbrough	Everton	1	2			
3R	Bury	Millwall	2	0			
3R	Manchester City	Luton Town	0	0			
3R	Swindon Town	Portsmouth	4	3			
3R2	Luton Town	Manchester City	2	3			at Man Utd
4	Arsenal	Hull City	5	1			
4	Bury	West Bromwich Albion	1	0			
4	Ipswich Town	Manchester City	1	2			
4	Liverpool	Coventry City	2	2			
4	Nottingham Forest	Aston Villa	4	2			
4	Sheffield Wednesday	Everton	1	3			
4	Bolton Wanderers	Leeds United	1	3			
4	Wrexham	Swindon Town	2	0			
4R	Coventry City	Liverpool	0	2			
5	Bury	Nottingham Forest	0	3			
5	Wrexham	Liverpool	1	3			
5	Leeds United	Everton	4	1			
5	Manchester City	Arsenal	0	0			
5R	Arsenal	Manchester City	1	0			
SF	Liverpool	Arsenal	2	1	0	0	
SF	Leeds United	Nottingham Forest	1	3	2	4	
F	Nottingham Forest	Liverpool	0	0	0	1	

1976/77 Club Appearances Division 3

BRADFORD CITY

		A	S	G
Downsborough	Peter	46		
Podd	Cec	34	3	
Spark	Alex	25	1	
Martinez	Eugene	12	5	
Nicholls	Philip	9	1	
Fretwell	David	35	1	1
Watson	Gary	32		6
Dolan	Terry	45		8
Cooke	Joe	28	10	8
Wright	Bernie	45	1	10
Hutchins	Don	45		9
Middleton	John	39	1	1
Ratcliffe	David	8	5	1
Hardcastle	Peter	26		
Smith	Brian	8		
Jones	Graham		3	
Grimes	Vince	7		
Johnson	Rodney	20		3
Wood	Mick	12		
McNiven	David	18		5
Gallagher	Barry	2		
Baines	Stephen	10	1	1
Own Goals				2

BURY

		A	S	G
Forrest	John	46		
Keenan	Gary	37		2
Kennedy	Keith	45		1
Thomson	John	34	4	3
Tucker	Billy	33		5
Hatton	Dave	39		
Woolfall	Alan	10		3
Mcllwraith	Jim	32	3	7
Rowland	Andy	41		14
Entwistle	Wayne	10	1	2
Robins	Ian	45		4
Bailey	Tony	24	1	
Stanton	Brian	35	7	10
Suddick	Alan	30	4	2
Curran	Terry	2		
Hamstead	George	8		1
Wilson	Daniel	9	3	1
Johnson	Steve	9	2	1
Whitehead	Alan	6		1
Murty	Joe		1	
Madden	Craig	1	3	
Darling	Malcolm	1	1	
Farrell	Peter	9		4
Own Goal				1

CAMBRIDGE UNITED

		A	S	G
Webster	Malcolm	35		
Batson	Brendan	28		
Streete	Floyd	17	4	3
Stringer	David	46		
Fallon	Steve	46		8
Howard	Trevor	44		1
Watson	Graham	35		6
Spriggs	Steve	37	1	5
Silveseter	Peter	2	2	1
Finney	Tom	44		13
Biley	Alan	44		21
Morgan	Sammy	34	3	4
Baldry	William	1		
Murray	Jim	12	8	1
Owen	Terry	1		
Smith	Lindsay	27		1
Hansbury	Roger	11		
Buckley	Ian	17	3	
Avery	Roger		1	
Cozens	John	16	5	2
Sweetzer	Gordon	8		3
Adams	Steve	1	1	
Own Goals				3

CARLISLE UNITED

		A	S	G
Swinburne	Trevor	31		
Carr	Peter	35	1	
McCartney	Mike	46		6
Bonnyman	Phil	32	1	8
McDonald	Ian	34		2
Parker	Bobby	44		2
McVitie	George	45		5
Ludlam	Steve	16		
Lathan	John	28	2	3
Rafferty	Bill	30		11
Martin	Dennis	6	1	
Tait	Mick	39	4	10
Hoolickin	Stve	9		
Mutrie	Les	4	1	
Ross	Alan	15		
Hamilton	Jimmy	34	1	4
Clarke	Frank	8	1	
Collins	Andy	27		
Fell	Geoff		2	
Kemp	David	13		4
Sawyers	Keith	5	2	
McLean	David	3	3	
Lumby	Jimmy	2		1
Own Goals				3

CHESTER

		A	S	G
Millington	Grenville	10		
Raynor	Paul	34		
Walker	Jim	32		
Delgado	Bob	41		3
Storton	Trevor	41		4
Oakes	Alan	44		5
Mason	Stuart	6	1	1
Edwards	Ian	33		6
Kearney	Mike	22	1	4
Jeffries	Derek	23	2	1
Burns	David	5	1	
Jones	Bryn	15	5	2
Howat	Ian	10	2	4
Crossley	Paul	31		9
Phillips	Ron	42		7
Lloyd	Brian	36		
Livermore	Doug	32		5
Edwards	Nigel	13		
Nickeas	Mark	18		1
Mellor	Ian	17		5
Clutton	Nigel	1		
Own Goals				2

CHESTERFIELD

		A	S	G
Ogrizovic	Steve	16		
Tartt	Colin	46		1
Burton	Ken	46		1
Kowalski	Andrew	39		1
Cottam	John	46		3
O'Neill	Sean	40		
Jones	Alan	11		2
Dearden	Bill	17	5	2
Green	Ricky	27	3	9
Parker	Stuart	19	2	6
Cammack	Steve	44		9
Pollard	Gary	16	3	
Heppolette	Ricky	18		2
Hunter	Leslie	12	5	2
Fern	Rod	37	1	14
Badger	Len	6		
Tingay	Phil	7		
Simpson	Gary	12	1	3
Letheran	Glan	23		
Chamberlain	Glyn	14	1	
Walker	Phil	10		2
Own Goal				1

COLCHESTER UNITED

		A	S	G
Walker	Mick	46		
Cook	Michael	44		1
Williams	John	28	1	1
Leslie	Steve	41		3
Packer	Mike	44		2
Dowman	Steve	43		5
Garwood	Colin	28	2	7
Gough	Bobby	42		13
Froggatt	John	25		2
Foley	Stephen	29	3	7
Allinson	Ian	45		6
Bunkell	Ray	22		1
Dyer	Paul	21	9	
Wignall	Steve	32	2	2
Rowles	Eddie	9		3
Evans	Tony	5	2	
Wright	Steve	1		
Cotton	Russell	1	1	
Own Goals				2

GILLINGHAM

		A	S	G
Hillyard	Ron	44		
Williams	Nigel	24		
Armstrong	Gary	27	1	1
Overton	John	44		2
Shipperley	Dave	24		2
Knight	Graham	41		1
Nicoll	Terry	44		4
Weatherley	Mark	16	8	2
Price	Ken	42	1	20
Westwood	Danny	45		17
Richardson	Damien	43		11
Hughes	Billy	20	7	1
Hunt	Peter	23		
Crabbe	John	41		4
Burrows	Phil	5		
Walker	Pat	5	5	1
Buttress	Mike	5	1	
Young	Charles	11		1
Wheatley	Steve	2		

HEREFORD UNITED

		A	S	G
Charlton	Kevin	1		
Emery	Steve	39		2
Burrows	Phil	26		
Layton	John	42		1
Marshall	Julian	40	1	3
Ritchie	Steve	24		1
Briley	Les	27		1
Spiring	Peter	30	4	2
Davey	Steve	31		5
McNeil	Dixie	7		3
Carter	Roy	12	1	1
Sheedy	Kevin	33	1	3
Hughes	Tommy	13		
Jefferson	Derek	13		
Sinclair	Colin	13		2
Proudlove	Andy	6	5	
Holmes	Kevin	4		
Crompton	Steve	23	2	5
Mellor	Peter	32		
Fear	Keith	6		
Stephens	Ken	26		1
Price	Chris	13		
Barton	Frank	18		2
Cornes	Stuart	13		
Redrobe	Eric		1	
Bouston	Brian	4	2	
Phillips	Stuart	1		
Holmes	Billy	9	6	2

LINCOLN CITY

		A	S	G
Grotier	Peter	44		
Guest	Brendan	31	1	
Crombie	Dean	20		
Booth	Dennis	13		1
Smith	Mick	3	2	1
Cooper	Terry	31	2	2
Fleming	John	24	2	3
Ward	John	5		3
Hubbard	Phil	44	1	2
Graham	Peter	40	1	9
Harding	Alan	35		5
Eden	Alan	4	2	
Leigh	Dennis	37	1	1
Cockerill	Glen	10	3	1
Branfoot	Ian	1		
Neale	Phil	40		3
Cox	Mark	3	1	
Wiggington	Clive	41		4
Cork	Alan	5		
Jones	Alan	23		4
Gordon	Jimmy	2		
Harford	Mick	25	2	9
Hoult	Alan	2	2	1
Laybourne	Keith	1		
Hobson	Gordon	5		2
Hughes	David	2		
Smith	Dave	15	5	
Own Goals				2

OXFORD UNITED

		A	S	G
Burton	Roy	38		
Fogg	David	46		2
Drysdale	Brian	15		
Bodel	Andy	37		3
Clarke	Colin	29		
Jeffrey	Billt	44		3
McGrogan	Hugh	27	5	2
Duncan	Colin	45		3
Foley	Peter	43		19
Seacole	jasn	33	5	9
Taylor	Les	46		6
Berry	Paul	7	2	1
Curran	Hugh	29	4	11
Briggs	Max	2		
Kingston	Andy	26		
Milkins	John	8		
Doyle	John	3		
Stott	Ian	6		2
White	Archie	2	7	
Briggs	Gary	20		2
Own Goal				1

PETERBOROUGH UNITED

		A	S	G
Waugh	Keith	26		
Hindley	Peter	40		
Lee	Jeff	26		
Doyle	Bobby	46		2
Turner	Chris	46		5
Ross	Ian	46		
Slough	Alan	45		6
Camp	Steve	6	1	1
Sargent	Gary	18	5	3
Robson	Tommy	31	6	14
Rogers	Andrew	2		
Carmichael	Jack	27	3	
Oakes	Keith	4	6	
Hughes	Lyndon	23		1
Butlin	Barry	34		7
Cozens	John	7	1	1
Barron	Jim	20		
Cliss	Tony	3		1
Earle	Steve	1		
McEwan	Billy	29		1
Anderson	Trevor	26		5

PLYMOUTH ARGYLE

		A	S	G
Barron	Paul	41		
Smart	Kevin	23		
Uzzell	John	44		1
Horswill	Mick	29	3	1
Foster	George	46		3
Craven	John	30		2
Johnson	Brian	20	2	6
Delve	John	19	1	
Austin	Terry	29		11
Trusson	Mike	12	3	2
Rogers	Alan	28	1	2
Hall	Brian	13	1	6
Peddelty	John	1	3	
Harrison	Chris	29	2	1
Bason	Brian	22	1	
Binney	Fred	18		9
Taylor	Brian	26	1	5
Megson	Gary	24		2
Graves	Mark	1		
Banton	Geoff	6		
Sutton	Dave		1	
Fear	Keith	17		6
Perrin	Steve	11		3

PORT VALE

		A	S	G
Connaughton	John	38		
McGifford	Graham	20		
Griffiths	Neil	32	1	4
Ridley	John	40		
Alcock	Terry	3		
Bentley	Bill	31	1	
Lamb	Alan	40		3
Beech	Ken	26		1
Beamish	Ken	41	1	13
Brownbill	Derek	19	2	3
Hemmerman	Jeff	13	2	5
Bailey	Terry	36	3	3
Harper	Colin	4		
Cullerton	Mike	8	9	2
Harris	Dave	41		1
Dance	Trevor	8		
Bithell	Brian	2		
Sutcliffe	Peter	26	4	4
Dulson	Gary	19	1	
Chamberlain	Neville	9	1	2
Kennerley	Kevin		1	
Hawkins	Graham	15	1	1
Froggatt	John	11	1	3

PORTSMOUTH

		A	S	G
Middleton	Steve	26		
Roberts	Phil	33		
Wilson	Billy	36		1
Ellis	Peter	29	1	
Foster	Steve	30	1	3
Cahill	Paul	14	1	1
Gilchrist	Paul	22	1	2
Kemp	David	33		16
Green	Clive	8	1	
Mellows	Micky	42	1	
Pollock	Matt	11	3	4
Stokes	Bobby	23	1	2
Denyer	Peter	41		3
Piper	Norman	23	3	2
Barnard	Leigh	8	3	
Pullar	David	22	2	1
Viney	Keith	2	2	
Figgins	Phil	19		
Hand	Eoin	12		1
Ruggeiro	John	6		1
Taylor	Tony	17		
Piper	Steve	13	2	
McCaffrey	Jimmy	11		1

PRESTON NORTH END

		A	S	G
Tunks	Roy	46		
McMahon	John	30		1
Wilson	Harry	18		
Doyle	Stephen	25	7	1
Baxter	Michael	45		5
Cross	Graham	40		1
Coleman	Gordon	45		4
Brown	Jimmy	2		
Thomson	Ricky	25	1	7
Elwiss	Mike	46		11
Bruce	Alex	45		27
Burns	Francis	36	2	
Cameron	Danny	40		
Smith	John	14	1	3
Robinson	Michael	8	2	2
Haslegrave	Sean	38		
Uzelac	Steve	2		
Spavin	Alan	1	4	
Own Goal				1

ROTHERHAM UNITED

		A	S	G
McAllister	Tom	46		
Forrest	Gerald	44		
Breckin	John	45		1
Rhodes	Mark	32	1	3
Green	John	40	1	1
Spencer	Tommy	11		1
Finney	Richard	44		13
Phillips	Trevor	41		8
Young	Tommy	3	4	
Goodfellow	Jimmy	45		2
Crawford	Alan	28		7
Habbin	Dick	1	1	
Stancliffe	Paul	32		3
Womble	Trevor	12	6	2
Gwyther	David	39		8
Matthews	Paul	8		
Smith	Ian	3	1	
Dawson	Richard	7		1
Nix	Peter	15		1
Pugh	David	10	1	

SHEFFIELD WEDNESDAY

		A	S	G
Turner	Chris	23		
Walden	Richard	46		
Rushbury	David	45		4
Cusack	David	29	2	1
Dowd	Hugh	26	1	
Leman	Denis	23	10	2
Johnson	Jeff	39		1
Prendergast	Mike	13	1	3
Tynan	Tommy	43	1	16
Porterfield	Ian	38		
Bradshaw	Paul	25	2	2
Wylde	Roger	36		9
McKeown	Lindsay		2	
Hope	Bobby	5	3	
Darling	Malcolm	1	1	
Mullen	James	41		4
Nimmo	Ian	2	1	
Gregson	Colin	1	1	
Hinch	Jimmy		1	
Grant	David	24		1
Bolder	Bob	23		
Owen	Gordon	2		
Hedley	Graeme	6		1
Hornsby	Brian	13		3
Smith	Mark	2		
Own Goals				3

SHREWSBURY TOWN

		A	S	G
Mulhearn	Ken	43		
Hayes	Steve	19		
Roberts	Lee	3		
Turner	Graham	29		2
Griffin	Colin	29	2	
Atkins	Ian	40	1	10
Nixon	Jon	21	2	3
Hornsby	Brian	29		7
Bates	Chic	26		8
Lindsay	Jimmy	35		
Maguire	Paul	37	4	8
Leonard	Carleton	37		
Irvine	Sammy	43	1	10
Loughnane	Peter	18	5	3
Cross	Steve	1		
Keay	John	20	1	1
Durban	Alan	17		2
King	John	36	1	
Wardle	Bob	3		
Biggins	Steve	9		7
Moore	Kevin	5		
Bowers	Danny	6		
Own Goals				1

SWINDON TOWN

		A	S	G
Allan	Jimmy	45		
McLaughlin	John	45		
Trollope	John	40		1
Stroud	Ken	36	1	3
Aizlewood	Steve	29		3
Prophett	Colin	46		1
Moss	David	45		16
Kamara	Chris	37	3	10
French	Mikey	2	1	
McHale	Ray	43	2	10
Anderson	Trevor	18	1	4
Ford	Andrew	28	6	
Guthrie	Chris	38	1	12
Cunningham	David	17	4	3
Gilligan	Augustine	3	1	
Roberts	Kevin	1		
Lewis	Russell	1	1	
Carter	Roy	20	4	2
Bates	Chic	12	2	1
Own Goals				1

TRANMERE ROVERS

		A	S	G
Johnson	Dickie	45		
Mathias	Ray	46		
Flood	Eddie	43		1
Parry	Leslie	45		
Philpotts	David	44	1	1
Evans	Clive	46		2
Peplow	Steve	41	1	7
Palios	Mark	41		8
Moore	Ronnie	43		17
Tynan	Bobby	45		6
Allen	Russell	43		13
James	John	5	14	1
Cliff	Eddie	8	3	1
Bramhall	John	7	3	
West	Gordon	1		
Craven	Steve	3		

WALSALL

		A	S	G
Kearns	Mike	42		
Taylor	Brian	12		1
Caswell	Brian	36		3
Newton	Henry	16		
Hynd	Roger	20		
Serella	Dave	44		3
Shelton	Gary	7	5	
Bates	Mick	43		3
Evans	Alun	35	4	4
Buckley	Alan	46		24
Birch	Alan	30	1	4
Clarke	Kelvin		2	
Wood	Alf	26	3	2
Dennehy	Miah	36	3	8
Robertson	Jimmy	16		
Harrison	Colin	32		
Green	Ronald	1		
Moseley	Graeme	3		
Macken	Tony	30		
King	Jeff	16		1
Austin	Terry	11	3	6
Paul	Ian	4		
Penn	Donald		1	
Own Goals				2

WREXHAM

		A	S	G
Lloyd	David	1		
Hill	Alan	26	4	
Dwyer	Alan	45		
Davis	Gareth	46		2
Roberts	John	41		4
Thomas	Mickey	41	2	7
Shinton	Bobby	46		16
Sutton	Mel	46		2
Ashcroft	Billy	3		1
Lee	Stuart	5	1	
Griffiths	Arfon	15	5	1
Lyons	John	14	7	6
Niedzwiecki	Eddie	15		
Evans	Mickey	24		1
Cartwright	Les	41		4
Cegielski	Wayne	5	4	
Whittle	Graham	37		18
Davies	Dai	30		
McNeil	Dixie	23		13
Kenworthy	Steve	1		
Williams	Michael	1		
Buxton	Steve		1	
Own Goals				3

OTHER GRECIANS PUBLICATIONS FROM REL8 MEDIA

Exeter City Down the Years

Every game, every player . . . From the formation of the club up until 2012. A comprehensive record of Exeter City Football Club.

ISBN 978-0-9555307-9-1 £9.99 (+ £2 postage / packing to UK)

Grecians Going Up - A Journal of Exeter City, 1963/4

A detailed account of City's first-ever promotion season.

ISBN 978-0-9574645-1-3 £11.99 (+ £2 postage / packing o UK)

Order on-line at **www.rel8mediapublishing.weebly.com**

Order by post from:

Rel8 Media, Unit 7, Woodend Business Centre, Cowdenbeath, Fife, KY4 8HG.